THE NEW QUEER GOTHIC

SERIES PREFACE

Gothic Literary Studies is dedicated to publishing groundbreaking scholarship on Gothic in literature and film. The Gothic, which has been subjected to a variety of critical and theoretical approaches, is a form which plays an important role in our understanding of literary, intellectual and cultural histories. The series seeks to promote challenging and innovative approaches to Gothic which question any aspect of the Gothic tradition or perceived critical orthodoxy. Volumes in the series explore how issues such as gender, religion, nation and sexuality have shaped our view of the Gothic tradition. Both academically rigorous and informed by the latest developments in critical theory, the series provides an important focus for scholarly developments in Gothic studies, literary studies, cultural studies and critical theory. The series will be of interest to students of all levels and to scholars and teachers of the Gothic and literary and cultural histories.

SERIES EDITORS

Andrew Smith, University of Sheffield
Benjamin F. Fisher, University of Mississippi

EDITORIAL BOARD

Kent Ljungquist, Worcester Polytechnic Institute Massachusetts
Richard Fusco, St Joseph's University, Philadelphia
David Punter, University of Bristol
Chris Baldick, University of London
Angela Wright, University of Sheffield
Jerrold E. Hogle, University of Arizona

For all titles in the Gothic Literary Studies series
visit *www.uwp.co.uk*

The New Queer Gothic
Reading Queer Girls and Women in Contemporary Fiction and Film

Robyn Ollett

UNIVERSITY OF WALES PRESS
2024

© Robyn Ollett, 2024

All rights reserved. No part of this book may be reproduced in any material form (including photocopying or storing it in any medium by electronic means and whether or not transiently or incidentally to some other use of this publication) without the written permission of the copyright owner except in accordance with the provisions of the Copyright, Designs and Patents Act. Applications for the copyright owner's written permission to reproduce any part of this publication should be addressed to the University of Wales Press, University Registry, King Edward VII Avenue, Cardiff CF10 3NS.

www.uwp.co.uk

British Library Cataloguing-in-Publication Data
A catalogue record for this book is available from the British Library.

ISBN 978-1-83772-138-2
eISBN 978-1-83772-139-9

The right of Robyn Ollett to be identified as author of this work has been asserted in accordance with sections 77 and 79 of the Copyright, Designs and Patents Act 1988.

Typeset by Marie Doherty
Printed by CPI Antony Rowe, Melksham, United Kingdom

Contents

Acknowledgements   vii

Introduction: The New Queer Gothic   1

Part I

1 'She herself is a haunted house': The Origins of the New Queer Gothic in the Work of Twentieth-Century Women Writers   45

2 Miles away from Screwing? The Queer Gothic Child in *Florence and Giles*   87

Part II

3 'What happened to my sweet girl?': Conventions of the New Queer Gothic and Queer Subjectivity in *Black Swan* and *Jack & Diane*   119

4 'The Saviour who came to tear my life apart': The Queer Postcolonial Gothic of *The Handmaiden*   143

Part III

5 Queering the Cannibal in *Raw*   171

6 'She would never fall, because her friend was flying with her': Gothic Hybridity, Queer Girls and Exceptional States in *The Icarus Girl* and *The Girl with all the Gifts*   198

| Conclusion: Queering Gender and Queers of Colour in the New Queer Gothic | 225 |

Notes	235
Bibliography	255
Index	277

Acknowledgements

This book is the product of my doctoral research and PhD thesis of the same name. The writing of my thesis saw deaths, relationship breakdowns, mental breakdowns, pet loss, threat of homelessness and, finally, a global pandemic. And so, I am genuinely proud to have this in print, it is certainly my biggest achievement to date and it took quite a lot to get here. There are a few people that I would like to thank for their support during my PhD journey, without whom I could not have secured a contract for this book. First, thanks go to the fabulous Dr Rachel Carroll, my supervisor and dear friend, and to Dr Darren Elliott, my examiner, mentor and champion. Thanks go to my family: my partner Patrick Reed for being the best caretaker, muse, literary interlocuter and muscle relaxant; my Mam, Susan Ollett, for reading every book before me since I was an undergrad, so that I always had someone to talk to about them; my Dad, Stewart, for his horrendous (and grounding) sense of humour; my late Nanna, Beryl Madden, for teaching me about strong women; and my late Grandad, Tommy Clough, who passed away in my third year of study, thanks for being proud of me.

To my academic soulmate, work wife and brilliant friend, Dr Louise Logan Smith, thank you for letting me sew myself to you for those four or five years. To my bestie, neighbour and all-round amazing heritage scholar, Dr Rosemary Stubbs, thank you for taking me for walks when I was hyperventilating over any one of the national crises to hit us in the past few years. To Dr Helen Davies, the most selfless academic and tireless mentor that I have ever met, thanks for being so real, honest and wonderful. Thanks to my non-academic soulmates, Jack Iverson and Chris Liggitt, my emotional support humans and chosen family. Thanks to Dr Sarah Ilott, who made academia look really cool, and thanks to Lewi

Mondal for maintaining that illusion. Thanks to Dr Louise Powell, a fantastic playwright and gorgeous friend. Thanks to my late first-born, Zeus, for all the love and for making sure I look after my books, and thanks to my living son, Frankie, a real boy and not a dog – the purest and 'goodest' of all boys. Thank you to all the staff and students at Teesside University, particularly Dr Rob Hawkes, Dr Leanne Bibby and Dr Jane Ford, as well as the English studies class of 2020, my first and most cherished cohort. Thanks as well to Stirling University's gender studies master's students, among which are some incredibly inspiring New Queer Gothic and Queer Horror scholars. Sincere and heartfelt thanks to the wonderful individuals who have supported the preparation of this publication, Dr Ardel Haefele-Thomas, and University of Wales Press's Sarah Lewis and copy editor Sarah Meaney.

Finally, I'd like to thank every person who has made me feel welcome in higher education and academia, as a student and now as a lecturer. There is a specific kind of imposter syndrome plaguing working-class academics that is a direct result of the hideous structural inequality imposed on us by a morally bankrupt Tory government.

Cheers. It takes a village, people!

Introduction
The New Queer Gothic

༄

This book examines a body of work that exists across international fiction and film published or produced in the past fifteen to twenty years that crucially articulates the relationship between Queer narratives, issues and subjectivities, and the themes relevant to their context within the Gothic mode. I name this body of work the New Queer Gothic; the texts within are identifiable from their shared contemporaneity, as well as their critical engagement with queerness and Gothicity on axes of political, cultural and representational value. I propose the 'New Queer Gothic' as a term that can be used to describe a new means of critiquing relevant contemporary fiction and cinema contingent on, yet divergent from, the tangents and modes of Queer and Gothic literary and film criticism that came before it. It is the overarching concern of *The New Queer Gothic* that I address the deficit in current scholarship close to the topic of exploration into the representation and signification of female subjectivity. I will make the case that there is a recognisable privileging of white, male, homosexual issues in current scholarship within the fields of Queer cinema, the female Gothic and queer Gothic studies. Much of this scholarship, I will argue, is limited by essentialist gender politics, which also works to exclude and marginalise queer women, whether those queer girls and women be lesbians, bisexuals, pansexuals, questioning people, transpeople or nonbinary people who may not even identify with 'girl' and 'woman' descriptors. It is, therefore, crucial that this study proclaim a call to arms and focus its attention on the representation of queer girls and women, first by exploring and canonising the kinds of text within which these figures can be found, and, second, by offering new perspectives on methods of reading their textual and visual presence.

By way of offering a rationale for a focus on female subjectivity and issues pertaining specifically to queer girls and women within the New Queer Gothic, this Introduction offers an analysis of the constituent parts of this new mode. The first part of the Introduction that follows asks what aspects of existing critical theory require further investigation, evaluating the three main contextual frameworks important to this study: the queer Gothic; new queer cinema; Gothic film; and finally, feminism and the Gothic. The second part of this Introduction will discuss my focus on female subjectivity. Drawing on selected examples of scholarship that engage with fields of study such as the female Gothic will allow me to curate a genealogy of the ways in which female subjectivity has been engaged with in the literary Gothic in previous centuries. The second part of this Introduction will describe and evaluate the book's use of feminism and Queer theory, particularly the relationship between these two disciplines and the antisocial thesis of Queer theory, before offering an outline of the chapters to follow.

The Queer Gothic

The Gothic has been a popular mode of fiction since at least the publication of Horace Walpole's *The Castle of Otranto* in 1764, while queer theory only entered academic thought and cultural imagination within the past thirty years. In those years, the common critical practice of many critics has been to 'queer' texts from the eighteenth and nineteenth centuries. These queer readings of classic texts often use contemporary theory (e.g., poststructuralism) to highlight hidden narratives of queerness, whether that be same-sex desire in the subtext, or metaphors of gendered transgression.

Importantly, this work offers opportunities for alternative narratives to challenge metanarratives and works to assert marginalised gendered and sexual identities as existing in the nuances and subtexts of literary history. Analyses of contemporary texts owe much to these earlier queer readings of Gothic texts, but changes in sociopolitical attitudes, as well as shifting discursive understanding and activist energy, mean that queerness is no longer relegated to the shadows or to subtexts preoccupied with depravity, perversion or shame. As this book will attest, there exists an abundance of contemporary fiction and film that can be considered New Queer Gothic, a category that identifies a genre as well as a means of reading texts with common themes. The canon of New Queer Gothic, as I propose it, can include any contemporary piece of fiction or cinema representative of queer issues and narratives and situated in a Gothic context. Queer issues are identifiable predominantly via characterisation and expressions of same-sex desire, though they can also include other indications in narrative and characterisation that suggest antipathy to heteronormative systems. The conventions of the Gothic are widely accepted and well-engaged with; from recognisable tropes in setting – haunted houses, crumbling mansions, claustrophobic public and private spaces – to familiar motifs in characterisation and narrative – where such figures as the Gothic child, the Gothic heroine or the ingénue come into play. In *The Coherence of Gothic Convention* (1980), Eve Kosofsky Sedgwick argues that the Gothic's major conventions 'are coherent in terms that do not depend on that psychological model, although they can sometimes be deepened by it'.[1] Here Sedgwick touches on the irrevocable interrelation of these tropes to the theoretical framework with which they are most often engaged: while this group of conventions 'has been the centre of critical attempts to value the Gothic for its portrayal of "depth," a shift of focus shows that even here the strongest energies inhere in the surfaces' (p. 12). Catherine Spooner has more recently contended that 'it is not sufficient simply to reverse this model and privilege surface but rather consistently foreground it in order to interrogate the surface-depth relationship'.[2] Approaches to reading the Gothic via psychoanalytical models become all the more important when it comes to analysing sexuality and subjectivity within the Gothic; arguably the two most considered aspects of current queer Gothic scholarship. It is *The New Queer Gothic*'s argument that although the relationship between the Queer and the Gothic is an ongoing discourse that must continue to be critiqued and negotiated, the sites where these two worlds meet prove precarious places for representation, owing to the history of criticism that they share. For this reason, one of the central preoccupations of this book is finding the most effective methods of critiquing these representations through synthesising the knowledge and theories available to us. Contemporary queer Gothic texts, belonging to the category of the New Queer Gothic, sometimes offer new ways of thinking about sexual subjectivity, sometimes they re-present outdated stereotypes and sometimes they manage a curious mix of both. The crucial influences and formative terms that have acted as catalysts for the development of the New Queer Gothic relate largely to recapitulations within Gothic studies with varying specialist focuses; its theoretical origins, however, should first be understood in the context of three key frameworks, beginning with the queer Gothic.

In what can be appreciated as a ground-breaking critical text of the field, George Haggerty's *Queer Gothic* (2006) interrogates the relationship between Gothic fiction and the emergence of representative queer sexualities. Haggerty offers a persuasive argument that not only are the two interrelated, but that much of the emerging research and knowledge of sexology popularised in the nineteenth century is informed by eighteenth-century Gothic fiction. Haggerty attributes the beginning of a cultural dialogue about sexuality and queerness to these texts that predated the advent of sexual and gendered identity becoming codified in modern society. Specifically, Gothic plays such as Matthew Lewis's *The Castle Spectre* (1797), Joanna Baillie's De Montfort, *A Tragedy* (1798) and Percy Bysshe Shelley's *Censi* (1819) significantly contributed to the history of sexology in the nineteenth century. These plays offer a level of preparatory work that anticipates Freud and offer an intriguing background to his paradigm-shifting insights. Indeed, had we known these plays, we might talk of a 'Baillie syndrome' or the 'Walpolonian displacement'. Instead, we are left to make this claim for ourselves.[3] Haggerty's focus in this work is limited to eighteenth, nineteenth and some twentieth-century

Introduction

Gothic fiction and drama. However, his readings of Walpole's *The Castle of Otranto*, Mary Shelley's *Frankenstein* (1818) and Robert Louis Stevenson's *Strange Case of Dr Jekyll and Mr Hyde* (1886) are invaluable to any study of contemporary texts that continue to propel queer themes and tropes into contemporary Gothic fictions. There is some attempt to include same-sex female desire and subjectivity in Haggerty's canon; for example, Haggerty suggests Shirley Jackson's *Haunting of Hill House* (1959) as one such text that effectively 'revises the earlier plight of the Gothic heroine' (p. 4). However, the theories of female subjectivity and same-sex desire between women included throughout Haggerty's analysis are heavily indebted to the traditions of the female Gothic, a context to which I shall return . Simply put, the female Gothic's (over)investment in mother-daughter relationships and, more specifically, the essentialist preoccupation with reproductive sexuality is at odds with how this thesis understands queerness. Another related point of departure is that Haggerty's work on the queer Gothic draws exclusively on psychoanalytic interpretations of sexuality and subjectivity. The representations that this book considers differ because my arguments do not rely on one theoretical framework to expose historical Gothic fiction's role in anticipating sexology. Rather, this book takes an updated, multivalent approach to deciphering the representations of female subjectivity as they exist in contemporary, twenty-first-century queer Gothic works of fiction. I make no claim that the texts included here are especially worthy of queer critique on the grounds of queer authorship (out of all the authors and filmmakers that this study encounters, only Sarah Waters is an out queer individual); however, they all navigate representations of sexuality after the advent of queer theory, and queer feminist thinking has had time to permeate beyond academia to affect the narratives and politics of literary and popular culture in a more knowing way than ever before. William Hughes and Andrew Smith's book *Queering the Gothic* (2009) is another obvious site of inspiration and a further important point of departure for me in writing this *The New Queer Gothic*. This edited collection encompasses chapters structured chronologically, which tackle classic Gothic texts such as Shelley's *Frankenstein* through to modernist texts such as E. M. Forster's *A Passage to India* (1924) and various twentieth and twenty-first-century texts, like the music videos of Michael Jackson and Will Self's *Dorian* (2002). Hughes and Smith have argued that the 'Gothic has, in a sense, always been "queer"', noting that this special genre has 'until comparatively recently . . . been characteristically perceived in criticism as being poised astride the uneasy cultural boundary that separates the acceptable and familiar from the troubling and different'.[4] Hughes and Smith's working understanding of queerness in the Gothic is not wholly contingent on sexual subjectivities; rather, it 'is predicated on something more pervasive, and at times, more elusive than sexual identity. It is more, even, than the campness with which the Gothic is so frequently – and so glibly associated in criticism.' Ironically, their next testament is rather glib: 'To be queer, when taken outside of the sexual connotation of that term', they qualify, 'is to be different' (p. 3). This is something that this book recognises with caution – I would argue that 'different' is far too facile a term with which to approach readings of subjectivities and issues that are non-detachable from the real lives and the people they represent. While the critical collections offered by Haggerty and Hughes and Smith have a lasting impact on the queer Gothic genre, crucially starting conversations and debates around what it means to queer the Gothic, their applications of queer theory are often very anachronistic. The readings comprised in this book use primary texts written or produced after the 1990s. The engagement with cultural production shaped by queer politics and contexts is a critical practice shown in the wide historical canon that Hughes and Smith, in particular, draw on. The two critical works discussed above show a transition in the interface between Gothic criticism and queer theory in suggesting a distance from over-investment in identity politics and speculation into authorial or auteur identity and intention. The engagements made by this book aim to make this leap from identity to representation more overtly.

While reading sexual identities into the Gothic canon and beyond is an important task, this book is more interested in looking towards new means, methods and modes of observing, categorising and reading New Queer Gothic fiction. One of the initial steps of this undertaking is to imagine 'queerness' in its poststructuralist definition, as a rejection of identity. Starting with the notable ways in

Introduction

which the Gothic continues to be a site at which the conditions for this rejection are possible, Misha Kavka explains:

> The distinction between homo- and heterosexuality is shown in the Gothic to be a site of paranoid defence, with the same blurred boundaries as those between feminine and masculine. We have thus come to understand the Gothic as a spectacle of the mutual interpretations of categories that social and ideological institutions have long striven to keep separate.[5]

The Gothic, for most critics, has always been queer, particularly considering queerness has been generally understood as a means of describing fiction that is 'different' in its approaches to gendered and sexual identity. Dale Townshend goes so far as to say, 'if contemporary popular culture is anything to go by, the Gothic is more in need of a straightening out than a queering up'.[6] Townshend states that the 'task of queering the Gothic has already been achieved. Either that, or it was never necessary in the first place' (p. 12). Discussing the Gothic renaissance staples of the Victorian *fin de siècle*, such as Oscar Wilde's *The Picture of Dorian Gray* (1891) and Stevenson's *Strange Case of Dr Jekyll and Mr Hyde*, these 'queer' characters are irrevocably tied to the 'selfconscious sense of what constitutes a particularly homosexual way of being', closely related as they are, in terms of chronology, 'to the discursive birth of the homosexual' (p. 32). Townshend claims that the eighteenth-century forebears of these nineteenth-century gay anti-heroes were at least more deserving of the queer moniker because they were not limited to singular sexual attachments without fluidity or ease of movement: it is no coincidence then, that, in place of the sexual versatility of subjects such as Ambrosio (Matthew Gregory Lewis's *The Monk*, 1796) and Vathek (William Beckford's *Vathek*, 1786), Dorian and Dr Jekyll are forced to make recourse to their Gothic doubles, substituting for the permissive terrains of eighteenth-century queer desiring the restricted structures of the homosexual doppelgänger and its public heterosexual other. Queer becomes homosexual, as perversion becomes nineteenth-century inversion: imprisonment in the Gothic dungeons of the eighteenth-century Gothic romance has been transformed into the numerous forms of increased subjection attendant upon the structures of modern sexual paradigms. Within this situation, horrific doubling or a fragmented self, in fiction as in life, seems the only option, and this recourse to doubling is maintained as a significant motif of the New Queer Gothic. However, desire for multiple gendered and sexual objects is, happily, also a feature of contemporary texts. The queer double will always feature in the queer Gothic genre, if not to lament sociopolitical attitudes of public and private identity, then certainly as an intertext with one of the most influential pieces of queer Gothic literature. Shelley's *Frankenstein* has been credited by Mair Rigby as a text that 'reminds us that modern sexual discourse has constructed queerness as forbidden knowledge, as something that must be recognised, but which is dangerous because, once recognised, it is imagined to infect and overwhelm the subject'.[7] Rigby appreciates Frankenstein as engaging with 'queerness' not only through the use of doubling but also via its themes of social ostracism and a nuanced relationship with death:

> The fact that all of the above assumptions about what it means to be 'Queer' continue to inform ideas about sexual nonconformity into the twenty-first century suggests again that we encounter not the repression of sexual meaning in Gothic textuality but its ongoing production and proliferation. (p. 51)

Here, Rigby suggests twenty-first-century attitudes on sexual nonconformity reflect those of the nineteenth century, which would read as problematic if it were not evidenced by the endurance of *Frankenstein* as one of the most popular intertexts for contemporary queer Gothic fictions, especially those that unpick dualities of queer (particularly homosexual) subjectivity and the connections between queerness and death that feed into ideas about futurity and reproduction.

In its twenty-first century adaptations across Anglo-American popular culture, both Gothic media and its reception corroborate Robin Wood's famous contention that the genre, at least in its decidedly horrific modes, represents a 'return of the repressed'.[8] Andrew Owens suggests that what Wood argued was true of 1980s horror cinema is still pertinent today; what returns to wreak havoc

Introduction

across our collective screens and cultural fantasies in the guise of the Gothic monster is sexuality itself.[9] Indeed, if queer sexualities have been historically repressed in the West, then the Gothic does prove a more than suitable home, as the turn to the subject of the genre is the 'struggle for recognition of all that our civilisation represses or oppresses, its re-emergence dramatized, as in our nightmares, as an object of horror, a matter of terror'.[10] But is this true of all the interventions that the Gothic makes into queer culture. My contention is most offerings currently available in the field of the queer Gothic recognise the need to move past this issue of representing repression, yet frustratingly fall short of exploring further alternatives. Owens concludes his chapter, a descriptive glossary on the queer Gothic's key voices, mentioning Eve Kosofsky Sedgwick's oeuvre, Haggerty (2006), Hughes and Smith (2009) and Haefele Thomas (2012), with the recognition that the supernatural themes that continue to pervade the Gothic are 'no longer drawn exclusively as tragic representations of repressed sexuality'.[11] This suggests a recognition of the need to look past dated methods of reading but without any proposals for alternative or innovative methodologies in current queer Gothic scholarship. This pattern, or recognition without action, further provokes the necessity to reinvigorate Queer criticism's key aims through adapting the apertures through which we observe shifts in our culture and our cultural production.

New Queer Cinema and Gothic Film

The New Queer Cinema movement of the 1990s brought queer identities and issues to the forefront of art-house representation, which paved the way for better visibility in mainstream cinema. As well as proving representationally progressive, this movement also introduced and encouraged Queer authorship and Queer filmmaking techniques. Born out of AIDS-activism films in the late 1980s, New Queer Cinema entered the world at a time when sexuality, gender and race were among the most hotly debated categories of identity politics in both academic and popular culture. While its influence spreads far beyond a few key terms and figures, it came to be defined by a group of significant filmmakers and the work they produced. Tom Kalin, Todd Haynes, Gus Van Sant, Jennie Livingstone and Cheryl Dunye are among the most well-known of New Queer Cinema directors. Kalin had a career in AIDS-activism cinema before coming to direct one of the foundational New Queer films of the 1990s, his debut feature film, *Swoon* (1991). This film courted controversy in presenting a homicidal homosexual couple, a plotline we might now recognise as falling into the 'Killer-Queer' stereotype established by films such as Alfred Hitchcock's *Psycho* (1960). However, Kalin, as a queer auteur, justified the film's pathologising of its gay characters as queers who happened to kill rather than killers who killed because they were queer. The film worked to critique the equation popular belief made between queerness and villainy, and Kalin makes a metaphor out of this: during their trial the men are shown to be perceived as more monstrous for their 'perverse' sexual identities than for the crime for which they stand accused.

Perhaps the most significant New Queer Cinema director, Haynes straddles the two worlds of art-house and mainstream cinema with work ranging from avant-garde biopic animations such as *Superstar: The Karen Carpenter Story* (1988), to popular films like *Carol* (2016), depicting the struggles of lesbian identity and motherhood in 1950s America. Haynes's film *Poison* (1991) was a defining film of New Queer Cinema. In three parts 'Homo', 'Horror' and 'Hero', it follows a narrative about homosexuality in a prison setting. The film offered controversially violent and sometimes disturbing depictions and so was not well received by many gay audiences. However, Haynes's efforts of queered filmmaking, structuring and style were appreciated by more academic viewers. Gus Van Sant is the most well-known of the New Queer directors; his 1992 film *My Own Private Idaho* is now widely considered a queer classic. Having a foot planted firmly in both the queer world of art-house cinema and Hollywood's mainstream, Van Sant gained popularity with films such as *Good Will Hunting* (1997) and the shot-for-shot remake of *Psycho* (1998) and was able to finance the smaller (and queerer) projects more accepted in an independent art-house context. The decision to remake Psycho, perhaps the most historically queer-phobic film of all time, was obviously divisive, although Van Sant hoped to re-appropriate the text, offering a Warhol-esque picture of postmodern questioned authorship.[12] B. Ruby Rich, who coined the term 'New Queer Cinema' in 1992, describes the films of the movement as characterised by their 'homo-pomo' style: 'there are traces in all of them of appropriation and pastiche, irony, as well as a reworking of history with social constructionism very much in mind'.[13] These identifiers remain, for this study at least, mainstays of New Queer Gothic films. Rich, along with other commentators of the movement, observes a gender gap and an institutional privileging of gay male experience:

> What will happen to the lesbian and gay film-makers who have been making independent films, often in avant-garde traditions, for decades already? Surprise, all the new movies being snatched up by distributors, shown in mainstream festivals, booked into theatres, are by the boys. Surprise, the amazing new lesbian videos that are redefining the whole dyke relationship to popular culture remain hard to find. (p. 17)

It remains true that many New Queer Cinema films did represent white gay male identities, and few represented lesbians, queer women or queers of colour, at least two of the movement's most famous films, Jennie Livingstone's *Paris is Burning* (1990) and Cheryl Dunye's *The Watermelon Woman* (1997) appeared to offer some balance. Critics such as Elizabeth Guzik believe the overall gender imbalance kept titles concerning women niche. She notes that while New Queer Cinema grew, 'the women's list of such films is still short enough to assure that those films on the list are often seen repeatedly if only because there are not many of them, creating yet another specialised fan community'.[14] Connecting representation to the demand of queer audience and fandom, Guzik goes on to write about 1990s films that presented queer women through the lesbian killer and killer queer stereotypes that this book will later elaborate on.[15] While many gay white men were making films about other gay white men, female director Jennie Livingston brought the drag scene of New York City to art-house cinemas along with better representation for the trans and queer of colour community. Daniel T. Contreras notes that in *Paris is Burning*, 'race becomes a signifier of utopian longings',[16] importantly using a drag community to metonymically represent discourses that form utopic ideals, not only of gender but of also of racial identity. That race is being denaturalised at the same time as gender, signals, for Contreras, 'its importance not only to New Queer Cinema, but also to debates and activism of the early 1990s around queer politics' (p. 124). This book works to continue this investigation into the intersections of sexual, gendered and racial politics that are accessed through texts of note to queer representation. The New Queer Gothic texts explored will be analysed with the critical context and reception of New Queer Cinema in mind. The cultural visibility that films such as *Paris is Burning* and Dunye's *Watermelon Women* acquired not only facilitated future visibility and representation for queer women and queers of colour, but provoked some incredibly important questions about the conditions and parameters of identity politics and representation. In Dunye's film, the main character (played by Dunye) is a working-class Black lesbian filmmaker researching an uncredited Black actress in one of her favourite old films. She discovers, to her delight, that she was right to choose this elusive figure as a sapphic hero when learning about her true queer identity and off-screen romantic relationship with the white woman who directed the film. These discoveries parallel the development of the protagonist's own relationship with a white woman, and this offers some provocative questions about the power dynamics and the cultural history of interracial lesbian relationships, which in turn speaks to the implications of racial inequality in contemporary queer feminism. Indeed, these are discussions that my work will continue, with the refocusing of how these issues and politics are explored in a contemporary Gothic context. The debates provoked by drag as a queer art form and an essential mode of queer community formation in the 1990s have informed the arguments at the crux of this study; predominantly concerning the relationship between queer theory and identity politics at the intersection between race, sex and gender. Judith Butler's commentary of drag, communicated through her analysis of *Paris is Burning* in *Gender Trouble* (1990), never commits to qualifying drag as always subversive. Butler writes that drag can be 'used in the service of both the denaturalization and reidealization of hyperbolic hetero-sexual gender norms'. For Butler, drag seems, at best, a site of ambivalence, 'one which reflects the more general situation of being implicated in the regimes of power by which one is constituted and, hence, of being implicated in the very regimes of power that one opposes'.[17] In the male-dominated world of the New Queer Cinema, Christine Vachon has proved to be a pivotal figure. Vachon produced Todd Haynes's *Poison* (1991), Tom Kalin's *Swoon* (1992) and Rose Troche's *Go Fish* (1994). Beyond the New Queer Cinema movement of the 1990s, Vachon continued to produce films important to queer audiences, with Kimberley Pierce's *Boys Don't Cry* (1999) and further work with Todd Haynes on *Far from Heaven* (2002) and *Carol* (2016). In a recent interview, Vachon voiced that she 'takes exception, to some degree, with the label "Queer Cinema", reasoning that many people find it difficult to say what marks a film as queer. She described it as a 'kind of limiting category that feels old fashioned',[18] whereas when the movement began it was clear that these films were made by and for queer and LGBT communities because there was previously very little access for queer audiences to find films that represented them. The question of queer spectatorship is important here because, as Vachon notes, the parameters of queer identity are arguably more ambiguous in today's society compared to the area in the late 1980s and early 1990s when the activist communities were particularly vociferous in the midst of the AIDS epidemic.

Anneke Smelik, in an acknowledgement of the gender gap that New Queer Cinema presented in the 1990s, reasons that 'New Queer Cinema is AIDS cinema: not only because the films ... emerge out of a time of and the preoccupations with AIDS, but because their narratives and also their formal discontinuities and disruptions, are all AIDS-related.' Smelik thus suggests that the gender imbalance was an unavoidable consequence when those chiefly affected by the crisis were gay men. She does, however, remark on a parallel 'small wave of art films in the mid-1990s featuring young lesbian couples who seal their affections for each other in blood'. Among those included are *Sister My Sister, La Ceremonie, Heavenly Creatures, Fun* and *Butterfly Kiss*.[19] Like New Queer Cinema's films, these worked to understand queer characters' 'complex psychic lives rather than reject or despise them'. Smelik uses Lacanian psychoanalysis to read these films as working 'against rather than with the stereotype of the dangerous lesbian'. For this reason, Smelik concludes that they are 'certainly closer to the work of lesbian and gay filmmakers within New Queer Cinema than to the lesbian chic of Hollywood movies' (p. 69). She uses term 'lesbian chic' to reference 1920s cinema that presented female characters who would cross-dress and/or freely engage in same-sex displays of affection. These films were produced before the censorship of the Hays Code banned the overt representation of queer characters and issues. Pre-Code cinema boasted queer female icons such as Marlene Dietrich's androgynous cabaret singer in *Morocco* (1930) or Greta Garbo as *Queen Christina* (1933). Conversely, films produced under the restrictions of the Hays Code, such as Hitchcock's *Rebecca* (1940), worked to establish the dangerous or killer lesbian stereotypes with characters like the housekeeper Mrs Danvers, who keeps her dead mistress's possessions in perfect condition, caressing her underwear and furs lasciviously (and menacingly) as she gives her new mistress a tour of the Gothic house. How Queer and Gothic films are considered in contemporary criticism is highly contingent on those Hollywood films produced before and after the Hays Code in the early 1930s. As Vito Russo's *The Celluloid Closet* (1981) attests, along with the subsequent 1995 documentary of the same name, under the censorship of the Code, queer narratives and characterisations were either omitted from Hollywood films or changed completely. What the Code achieved involved casting queer characterisation into either the comic, the camp, the pitiable or the weak, with 'invert' characters tending to die by the end of any narrative. To my study, the most relevant effect that Code censorship had on queer representation was to relegate any trace of non-heteronormative presentation to the sinister, villainous characters whose queerness presented as pathological and usually malevolent. This trend in representation shared significant overlaps with the 'killer-queer' trope. As I will divulge in the coming chapters, however, queer villainy and even monstrosity hold more representational and political value than one might think. One aspect of the Gothic and queerly coded cinema of the late 1930s through to the 1960s is that it comes from source texts authored by closeted queer women,[20] and, although internalised homophobia or transphobia may be less prevalent in our present time and culture, these introspective conflicts paved the way for queer, closeted or questioning audiences to engage with those feelings and challenge the systemic inequalities that oppress, marginalise and threaten their identities.

While the films that this book considers as New Queer Gothic cannot be considered as existing within the same genealogy of those belonging to the New Queer Cinema movement, they can be appreciated as facilitating a certain culture of politically charged, activist-driven filmmaking that essentially paved the way for more effective cinematic representation of queer people.

This book appreciates queer Gothic film as a progression of New Queer Cinema and of contemporary queer Gothic fiction in its translation into visual and affective media. However, I also recognise queer Gothic film as a separate mode inclusive of literary adaptations, genre films and art-house films. Films that carry the Gothic aesthetic in their *mise en scène*, setting, narrative and characterisations, and that explore queerness either via plot or characterisation can be described as queer Gothic films. While this specific genre is under-researched, much critical attention has been paid to films described as lesbian and gay horror, or Queer Horror. The British Film Institute website currently lists the ten most popular lesbian and gay horror films, including James Whale's *The Old Dark House* (1932) and *Bride of Frankenstein* (1935), Lambert Hillyer's *Dracula's Daughter* (1936), Mark Robson's *The Seventh Victim* (1943), Robert Wise's *The Haunting* (1963), Roy Ward Baker's *The Vampire Lovers* (1970), Harry Kümel's *Daughters of Darkness* (1970), Curt McDowell's *Thundercrack!* (1975) and Jack Sholder's *A Nightmare on Elm Street 2: Freddy's Revenge* (1985).[21] Many of these films are discussed by critics interchangeably as horror films and as Gothic films, which either suggests that many films belong to both traditions, or that theorisation between these two terms remains unresolved in current scholarship. Some examples that this book identifies as watershed moments in the genealogy of queer Gothic cinema include Robert Wiene's *The Cabinet of Dr Caligari* (1920), F. W. Murnau's *Nosferatu* (1922), Tod Browning's *Dracula* (1931), James Whale's *Frankenstein* (1931), *Rebecca* (1940), Roman Polanski's *Rosemary's Baby* (1968), Dario Argento's *Suspiria* (1977) and Guillermo del Toro's *Crimson Peak* (2015). Each of these films crucially feature sexual narratives in Gothic contexts, and each are expressive of queer themes. *Crimson*

Peak, perhaps more explicitly, presents a narrative where an incestuous sexual relationship lies at the centre of the anti-futurist Gothic plot. Other texts that have had a significant impact on the New Queer Gothic genre include Jonathan Demme's *The Silence of the Lambs* (1991) and Paul Verhoeven's *Basic Instinct* (1992), both of which depict progressive feminist themes while also representing queerphobic, transphobic and misogynistic attitudes. While *The Silence of the Lambs* was more transparent in its Frankensteinian allusions – with Gumb's 'workshop of filthy creation'[22] – *Basic Instinct* only nods to some Gothic tropes. These films are important milestones in that they paralleled the New Queer Cinema movement: received with outrage from queer communities, films like these, which so explicitly drew on out-dated stereotyping, justified the political aims of the movement. The 'killer queer' is one of the most recognisable and enduring of such offensive tropes and has been identified by many critics as demonstrative of a sea-change in thinking about queer politics begun in the 1980s, peaking around the time that queer people were persecuted by a paranoid public who demonised homosexuals at the height of the AIDS epidemic. Films such as *Cruising* (1980) starring Al Pacino, highlighted explicit parallels between gay subculture, clubbing and homicidal violence, and the detrimental impact that this representation had on spiking hate crime against queer people contributed to the apologist disclaimer included in later screenings by director William Friedkin. The AIDS epidemic influenced many of the activist films coming out of the New Queer Film movement – including Bill Sherwood's *Parting Glances* (1986) Todd Verow's *Frisk* (1995), Todd Haynes's *Poison* (1991), Tom Kalin's *Swoon* (1992), Gregg Araki's *The Living End* (1992), Cheryl Dunye's *The Watermelon Woman* (1996) Jennie Livingston's *Paris Is Burning* (1990) and Rose Troche's *Go Fish* (1994) – but it was also a crucial theme of specifically queer Gothic films such as Tony Scott's *The Hunger* (1983). *The Hunger* made overt connections between blood, death, queer sexualities, relationships and lifestyles, specifically equating sexual involvement with the bisexual vampire character, Miriam Blaylock (Catherine Deneuve), with the deterioration of the body, shown in the accelerated ageing of David Bowie's character. Although released before the AIDS epidemic, the film's presentation of living dead emaciated ex-lovers vengefully attacking Miriam speaks to the very Gothic discourse that came to surround representations of AIDS in mainstream as well as art-house cinema of the 1980s and 1990s. Some of the texts that this book focuses on can be appreciated to straddle the genres of queer Gothic and horror, especially those that offer specific spectacles of the corporeal or body horror. In discussing the Gothic on screen, Misha Kavka notes that 'there is no established genre called Gothic cinema or Gothic film', instead, she argues that there are visual codes that have contributed to the cultural legacy of the Gothic throughout the twentieth century. These codes, Kavak explains, invariably draw on the literary Gothic but are contingent on the use of space: when the conventional themes of the literary Gothic are cast on screen, their discomfiting representation invariably draws its effect from the plasticity of space. Paradoxically, when the literary Gothic is transferred to a two-dimensional screen, the effect of fear is produced through transformations, extensions and misalignments of size and distance that are possible only in three-dimensional space. Gothic film thus reveals and reconstructs an underlying link between fear and the manipulation of space around the human body.[23] The visual codes that construct the Gothic in film, then, are inherently connected to the body in relation to space and to ideas of liminality. The cinematic medium exploits uses of framing and compositions of visible and malleable space: 'film can thus be turned toward representing something that needs to retain a degree of the unrepresentable in order to be affective'. Kavka distinguishes between Gothic film and horror film in discussing 'the world of difference between not being able to see something that remains shadowed or off-screen (the Gothic), on the one hand, and being able to see something terrifying . . . but from which we want to avert our gaze (horror), on the other' (pp. 226–7). In his book *Horror: A Literary History*, Xavier Aldana Reyes offers a much more elegant definition, affirming that the distinction between the Gothic and horror lies in the understanding of the Gothic as mode and of horror as an affective marker.

Aldana Reyes's work on body horror relates to both horror film and Gothic cinema and offers alternative ways of reading to the oversubscribed psychoanalytic frameworks.[24] Using affect theory, Aldana Reyes discusses the process of becoming a 'body without organs' on screen. He builds on Deleuze and Guattari, who, he writes, 'see this process as one of organic progression rather than one of transmutation, a moment of passage deeply invested in sensation as intrinsically related to the effect of art in the human'.[25] Aldana Reyes explains that 'in the case of corporeal horror, affect works by establishing a moment of', what he terms, 'becoming meat', where a character or on-screen body is not set on 'a direct transmogrification into meat. Instead, it starts a process of passage for audiences, who are both aware of their human nature as spectators whilst sensorially compelled to rejoice in the organic side of their bodies, or the non-subjective.' He then notes that affect is a state situated as paradox in its incurring a responsive feeling while also maintaining a lack of emotion. This desubjectivation impulse towards affect is important to consider along with my aims to come away from frameworks and discourses with which queer theory has long been associated; psychoanalysis being the key example. The notions of 'becoming meat' and a 'body without organs' work to provoke audiences to think about the biological as well as the socially constructed self, and these ideas are explored in an explicitly queer context by Darren Elliott-Smith in his book *Queer Horror Film and Television* (2016). Here, the dematerialisation of zombie bodies in the Bruce La Bruce films, *Otto Or Up with Dead People* (2008) and *LA Zombie* (2010), offers a way for the respective protagonists to either 'orally assimilate and assume machismo' or become engorged by it and exist as 'a grotesquely unsatisfied hypermasculine "ideal" in the form of the zombie phallus'.[26] It is clear from these readings alone that Elliott-Smith's book is very much focused on male or masculine-gendered identity. Considering the lion's share of its chapters focus on male homosexuality, I would question the prominence of the term 'queer' in the book's title; however, Elliott-Smith recognises this: 'Admittedly, the central focus on gay men in this book is more identarian that the term queer might suggest' (p. 4). Elliott-Smith introduces his book with the premise that 'homosexuality either bleeds in to the film extra-textually via the authorial expressivity of their gay and lesbian directors, writers or producers (such as F.W. Murnau, James Whale, Joel Schumacher or Stephanie Rothman) or it is read into the film via subversive, ironic reading strategies or a camp appreciation of the films themselves' (p. 2). He continues

Introduction

by qualifying his working definition of 'Queer Horror' as horror that is crafted by male directors and producers who self-identify as gay, bi, queer or transgendered and whose works features homoerotic or explicitly homosexual narratives with 'out' gay characters. One of the central questions attending Elliott-Smith study is: 'when monstrousness as a metaphor for the threat homosexuality poses to heteronormativity ceases to be coded and instead becomes open, then what does it mean?' *The New Queer Gothic* will make some marked incursions into the project of deciphering the relationship between queer identities and Gothic contexts and themes, and part of uncovering new ways of reading queer Gothic characters and narratives involves widening the scope of the canon available for analysis. Elliott-Smith's book is specific to analyses of 'out' gay, mostly white, men, whose subjectivity within queer horror 'is often fashioned by dis-identification with both female and male subjectivity'. While this proves an interesting insight into gay male subcultures, the contemporary anxieties of which are turned and projected onto themselves in queer horror, it also relies on identarian politics and seems to give credence to Jeffreys's claims that 'queer' will first and foremost always recall male homosexuality. Focusing more frequently on the 'antisocial' theories of Bersani and Edelman, Elliott-Smith suggests that other queer modalities are often reduced to projects of assimilation that recall Lisa Duggan's discussion of homonormativity. While gay and lesbian studies look to restore visibility of a gay and lesbian social group to culture and is inclusive and reparative in its intent, queer theory takes an alternative path. Focusing instead on the stigmatisation (including, but not exclusive to, same-sex desire), queer theory views the project of their integration and inclusion into the mainstream as a process of cultural normalisation or assimilation (pp. 3–4). As this book will show, there are queer methods of reading reparatively that reap various results not limited to these processes of normalisation and assimilationist mechanisms.

Feminism and the Gothic

The first and most thoroughly engaged branch of feminist criticism within the study of the Gothic is widely appreciated as the

'Female Gothic', a term first coined by Ellen Moers in 1976 in *Literary Women*. What began with Moers's definition – 'the work that women writers have done in the literary mode that, since the eighteenth century, we have called Gothic' pertaining to such authors as Sophia Lee (1750–1824), Ann Radcliffe (1764–1832) and Mary Shelley (1797–1851) – has come to encompass female-focused Gothic texts of any authorship. When Moers coined this term, Gothic texts authored by women were appreciated as valuable and insightful to questions of female subjectivity. Moers's best-remembered feminist intervention in Gothic criticism concerned reading Shelley's *Frankenstein* as a birth myth, with its 'horror' pertaining to the abandonment of the new-born monster, a crux Moers found 'most interesting, most powerful, and most feminine'.[27] The Female Gothic has, since its inception, been bound to ideas of female subjectivity in relation to reproductive sexuality: it would be very unlikely to find an edited collection on Shelley or feminist criticism of Gothic literature that does not include Moers's essay on the Female Gothic. Having proven to be incredibly influential, her important contribution certainly set a tone of essentialist, binary-based thinking about sex and gender. Susanne Becker is one such author who has since developed the Female Gothic's scope, stating her definitions to encompass the idea of Gothic texture, which she describes as shaped by an opposition to the tradition of structuring feminine Gothic horror around implications of the 'unfeminine', a structure based on binaries in which one privileged identity in a Gothic narrative is given subject status and devalues any Others to an object position.[28] Becker splits this observation into two considerations. On the syntactic level, the heroine – her body, her money and so on – presents as an object of value for the villain's desire and quest for power. On the semantic level, the heroine personifies values that contrast with the villain's moral corruption. Accordingly, on the pragmatic level, the gothic heroine represents, in perfect incorporation, the 'ideal feminine' of her cultural-historical context (p. 46). Becker uses Charlotte Brontë's *Jane Eyre* (1847) as a key example of a trend in feminist Gothic literature that operates within this structure but, importantly, that illustrates female desire and liberates women from being narratively constructed in relation to men (p. 53). Indeed, this is an aspect of the Female Gothic that is

Introduction

formative to thinking queerly about female subjectivity and the representation of women in contemporary Gothic fictions. Works of traditional Female Gothic that construct women in relation to the narrative's men, is a motif that Claire Kahane attributes to 'the latent configuration of the Gothic paradigm' to that of a helpless daughter confronting the erotic power of a father or brother, 'with the mother noticeably absent'. Kahane's argument, however, laments a gender bias in the critical landscape at the time of her writing, in the 1980s, when she claims that male critics typically privilege Gothic texts authored by men that concern male protagonists. Justifying her impulse to focus on women's writing and subjectivity, Kahane argues that this gender bias occurs in order to elaborate on 'the oedipal dynamics of a Gothic text, and effectively restrict if not exclude female desire even from texts written by women'.[29] Kahane has, however, related the notion of female annihilation in narrative to a female-authored text laden with oedipal dynamics, citing Shirley Jackson's *The Haunting of Hill House* (1959) as a novel representative of Eleanor's failure to fulfil feminine expectation, leading her to be punished further for expressing agency and desire outside normative gender convention.

In *Femicidal Fears: Narratives of the Female Gothic Experience*, Helene Meyers argues that much contemporary Female Gothic narrative is comprised of plots with a trajectory towards the actual and/or symbolic annihilation of women.[30] Sue Chaplin has related these to earlier examples of Female Gothic fiction, noting that these plots 'turn upon fraught questions concerning female agency and the female body that do not seem capable of resolution through the intervention of the law'.[31] According to Marie Mulvey Roberts, the driving forces of patrimony, power and possession are ultimate sites of trauma and suffering for the women of Gothic narrative: 'the female body has been stigmatised by patriarchal controls, both systematically and institutionally, as in the Freudian Law of the Father and institution of marriage. Driving forces have been power, possession and patrimony.'[32] Chaplin develops this insight in her discussion of popular contemporary texts such as Stephenie Meyer's *Twilight* saga (2005–8),[33] stating that these paradigms do not merely evaporate over time; their conservatism, she argues, does not reaffirm patriarchal power systems 'but rather invest in a nostalgic fantasy of paternal law as constructing a safe place for women in a culture increasingly unable to sustain the cultural and juridical law of the father'.[34] While Chaplin's argument is persuasive, her sample source suggests an interesting compromise within contemporary Female Gothic: in the *Twilight* saga, there is ample representation of female desire (which the film adaptations imply is capable of mitigating any suffering or threat of annihilation in the plot). However, the fantasy sold to millions of young readers worldwide is one of heteronormativity and fulfilment of ideal femininity via reproduction, much of which centres on the possession and violent destruction of the central girl's body.[35] Lucie Armitt surveys other representations of Gothic girlhood, concluding that the texts are problematic because of their investment in the biological essentialism of representing the female where there needs to be less reductive explorations into the subjectivity of women and girls:

> Though magnetic attraction sometimes defines the bonds between girls in these narratives, such bonds are constantly fraught with danger, betrayal, or loss. Repeatedly, the Gothic girl child must undergo trauma on her journey toward womanhood and blood, that fluid especially associated with the female adolescent, plays a particularly horrific role in narratives such as *Carrie*, if Moers is right and the Gothic especially offers its heroines adventures they cannot find elsewhere, the price it seems they must pay for having them is learning to go it alone.[36]

Armitt describes the ideological and political problems that the girl has typically faced in Gothic fiction, the reason I proposed the mode and method of the New Queer Gothic is not to proactively transform how we read these figures, but rather than lament the position of the girl and woman, we can look for reasons to celebrate her that embrace a broader understanding of subjectivity not limited by essentialist paradigms.

Three key frameworks are essential to the foundational thinking behind the New Queer Gothic as a newly identified genre and mode of reading contemporary queer Gothic fictions. First, the current field of study, termed the 'queer Gothic', is an obvious point of departure that this book finds lacking in theoretical and analytical rigour. Second, the New Queer Cinema movement of the 1990s was a pioneering period of representational and political significance to which any project concerning incursions into queer representation owes a debt of gratitude; the debates provoked here also feed into the crux of this book's rationale for a focus on female subjectivity. Third, the relationship between feminist politics and Gothic studies revealed by the genealogy of the Female Gothic has further supplemented such a rationale. I will now develop the import of some wider issues in the literary Gothic and offer a comprehensive account of the relationship between feminism and queer theory by way of introducing the novel methodology that this book adopts; namely, an observation and demonstration of the mode's conventions followed by proposed methods of analysis, to critique the New Queer Gothic, queerly of course, and in tandem with its necessarily feminist standpoint.

Feminism and Queer Theory

Queer theory with a feminist agenda is the critical means via which *The New Queer Gothic* proposes a new perspective, capable of highlighting repressive means of representation, as well as analysing and celebrating a canon that current criticism neglects. The central crux of this book lies in the tension between queer theory and identity politics. Queerness, by definition, refuses identity and queer subjectivity largely disregards categorisation: if this book's main contention is that too many previous and current relevant areas of study and critical interlocutors focus on men and homosexuality, how can a focus on women and female queerness effect any change to understanding queerness as all-encompassing, as different from lesbian and gay studies, and challenging social and political constructs of identity and power? The reasoning behind this decision – seemingly to fight fire with fire – begins with Annamarie Jagose's comprehensive analysis of the complex relationship that queer theory maintains with feminism. Considering thinkers such as Judith Butler and Teresa de Lauretis that engaged with queer theory as a means of thinking about lesbian and gay sexualities 'beyond the narrow rubrics of either deviance or preference',[37] Jagose ponders the 'curious dialectic between the openendedness of queer, its resistance to any definitional specificity, and the spectre of its own diminishing critical and political value'. Jagose also discusses the important feminist work of the 1980s that prefigured some queer thinking – this was organised around the 'radical antifoundationalist interrogation of the category of women'.[38] Iris Marion Young is cited by Jagose to qualify her own rationale for focusing on women's perspectives in queer thinking. In 1994, Young defined women as 'a serial collective defined neither by her a common identity nor by a common set of attributes that all the individuals in the series share, but rather it names a set of cultural constraints and relations to the practico-inert objects that condition action and its meaning'.[39] This strategy of defining women, appreciative of the systemic practices of oppression women continue to face, enabled Jagose in 2009, and enables us a decade later, to continue the maintenance of a workable notion of women as collective. Jagose relates such a strategy to the work of Linda May Alcoff who 'similarly advocates a positional definition in which what "women" can mean is a consequence of the interrelationship between historically available but shifting contexts'.[40] However, the assimilationist gestures of queer theory appearing in the 1990s continue to be a hotly contested and problematised set of notions. This book will provide analyses in the coming chapters conducive to an argument that acknowledgement of identity does not undermine an exploration of queer subjectivity. It is not the aim of this book to argue that the New Queer Gothic is a genre representative exclusively of women, however, but it does recognise an urgency to focus its analyses on female subjectivity within the New Queer Gothic because, for too long, similar topics of study have privileged the white homosexual experience: this is a noticeable issue across all current scholarship professing to encumber queerness. There is some balance offered by Paulina Palmer's body of work, particularly *Lesbian Gothic: Transgressive Fictions* (1999) and *The Queer Uncanny: New Perspective on the Gothic* (2012), which investigate the relationship between lesbian subjectivity and Gothic fiction with a focus on how queerness relates to the uncanny in the Gothic and characters with queer sexual and gendered identities. Palmer's work is important as an overview but rarely develops the scope and wider impact of the queer Gothic.

Introduction

The queerness explored in Palmer's work functions similarly to that of Darren Elliott-Smith's in focusing on the representation of a specific identity within LGBTQI codification. The focus of this monograph acknowledges texts that are representative of same-sex desire; however, none of the characters discussed identify fully as belonging to any one specific sexual identity category. Terms like 'homosexual men' and 'lesbian women' function only to describe the same-sex desire of those groups, 'queerness', on the other hand, involves challenging heteronormative frameworks and it would be reductive to use this term to only describe a subject's sexual preferences. Works that take as their focus homosexual men's and lesbian women's issues and subjectivities are incredibly valuable to understanding some aspects of how queer identity has historically related and continues to relate to the Gothic. However, to date, there exists no comprehensive investigation into the relationship between the representation of queer girls and women in the context of the Gothic mode in which we find their representation. Again, I propose this new genre of fiction and film at the same time as offering new ways to read these texts, methods that encourage an intersectional approach, reading queerly with a feminist standpoint and making enquiries that engage with wider questions to do with reconciling some feminist and queer thinking.

As the Gothic is understood as a mode of fiction with permeable borders, it follows that what constitutes the contemporary Gothic proves equally malleable. From sensational tales of false face, of Othered lovers and clandestine desire in the eighteenth and nineteenth century, the twentieth and twenty-first centuries are seen by most critics as doing similar things with narrative based on anxiety over selfhood, identity and belonging, be that in a gendered, sexual or colonial context. Relationships and kinship have always featured in Gothic fiction. For Steven Bruhm, however, these things are irrevocably altered with the advent of psychoanalysis.

What is revealed by contemporary Gothic fiction, he writes, is 'a world after Freud and the degree to which that domestic scene is predicated on loss'. Bruhm discusses domestic materiality as one defining feature indicative of the Gothic's relationship to its contemporaneity, arguing that where once outside influences of the economy, religion and patriarchal cultures and 'incestuous privation' in the eighteenth century, now 'the contemporary Gothic registers the (Freudian) impossibility of familial harmony'.[41] Because the family, and particularly the queer family, proves to be such an enduring motif in contemporary Gothic film and fiction, this book will argue that the queer family dynamic is characteristic of contemporary Gothic and a cornerstone of queer characterisation. As well as domestic spheres, Bruhm is intrigued by contemporary Gothic's relationship to time. He writes that 'the Gothic's basic investment in ravaging history and fragmenting the past meshes with our own investments now as we attempt to reinvent history as a way of healing the perpetual loss of modern existence'.[42] While this thinking corresponds with the general notions of ennui in postmodern criticism of the Gothic, moreover, it recalls ideas around queer temporalities that are underlined by Elizabeth Freeman in the introduction to her article 'Queer Temporalities'. Freeman draws on the works of Jack Halberstam, whose book *In a Queer Time and Place* (2005) argues that subcultures and punk offer the potential of regression as a method of dissent and means of rejecting normative regimes of temporality. Freeman's work draws on Lee Edelman whose polemic *No Future: Queer Theory and the Death Drive* (2004) calls for a rejection of normative systems of futurism, and on the notion of queer temporality that intermingles with Kathryn Bond Stockton's theories of lateral temporality as a means of describing and understanding growing up queer. Historically, queer people have been treated by homophobic societies as outcasts, and the idea of familial belonging is a fraught one. Freeman notes that 'since sexual identity emerged as a concept, gays and lesbians have been figured as having no past: no childhood, no origin or precedent in nature, no family traditions or legends, and, crucially, no history as a distinct people'.[43] Queer historiographers, Freeman writes, have since worked to create archives and 'structures of feeling' that work to write non-heteronormative people back into history. Freeman concedes, however, that there is much contention over identity politics and questions of privilege in queer temporality, and this is a crux in many considerations of queer ethics, evidenced by its refrain throughout this book. Developing the connections that Freeman makes to explain queer temporality, I will focus on questions of queer subjectivity to argue that the most powerful dialectic between sex and temporality can only be explored properly when new reading methods become possible, when new modes of writing emerge and older modes become suddenly, dazzlingly accessible to us.[44] The methodology that I adopted in the writing of this book allows me to proffer the New Queer Gothic as a body of texts and a mode of reading that responds to the call of contemporary scholars to continue reading queerly.

New modes and methods of reading must contend with new trends in production in the late capitalist culture and economy in which we live. The enduring appeal of the Gothic for contemporary audiences has, for Catherine Spooner, much to do with its commercialisation. While it should not be forgotten that this is no new trend in the Gothic, it being one of the original causes for its rejection in the eighteenth century, its contemporary commercialisation stretches beyond the generations of (Spooner states, mostly white, middle-class) teens living in the United Kingdom and the United States whose enduring fascination with Gothic subcultures offers an alternative to mainstream music, media, aesthetic and styling. Spooner further notes a rise in critical attention afforded to the genre, reasoning that its popularity among academics is owed to its investment in the 'thrill of the forbidden, which in this context is not entirely different from the thrill of the low-brow'.[45] Spooner describes the Gothic as suddenly especially sympathetic to liberal-left ideologies of contemporary society: 'championed by feminists and queer theorists for its level of attention to women and non-heteronormative sexualities; the reading material of the masses; the spaces in which colonial guilt could be explored and exorcised'. However, she tempers this view by suggesting that the Gothic can by packaged for any and all political agendas: 'It is a perfect product, readily available and simply adapted to the needs and purposes of a wide variety of consumers.'[46] This sobering summation is hard to contest when thinking of the recent popularity of contemporary Gothic television and film franchises that represent overtly conservative values, particularly franchises such as the *Twilight* saga. The queer Gothic might be assumed to have an inherent resistance to such conservative values, but, as will be made clear in this book's analyses, the precarity of political and identarian representation within the genre must be closely scrutinised. What most scholarly studies of contemporary Gothic have in common is a discussion of the marketability of the Gothic, which comes with its transition from the margins to the mainstream and its relationship to popular culture and different audiences. One valuable text to these discussions is Chloé Germaine Buckley's *Twenty-First-Century Children's Gothic* (2019). As this book will explore the figure of the Gothic child, not necessarily as a reader but as a representation within fiction, Buckley's study of the relationship between the real child and the fiction written with them in mind is noteworthy. Drawing on Rosi Braidotti's work on nomadic subjectivity, Buckley's contention is that the nomadism of the Gothic child in twenty-first century children's Gothic 'offers an affirmative account of subjectivity that undoes the othering often initiated by a discourse that reads Gothic monstrosity through the lens of social and cultural anxiety'.[47] Buckley observes the perpetuation of the idea that the Gothic genre of the post-9/11 period is saturated in representations of the 'Other' as a Gothic and monstrous creature, which adds texture to her theorising of how the twenty-first century child reader is figured in critical scholarship as passive. Furthermore, Buckley relates the perception of the passive child to the ways in which children's Gothic is appreciated as a 'paradoxical pedagogy', and how twenty-first century childhood might already be constructed and considered Gothic; as 'a site of trauma, but also the privileged space of imaginative engagement with the liberating energies of the Gothic'.[48] Buckley argues that the figure of the zombie as a transgressive symbol of nomadic subjectivity is rejective of co-option into the dominant discourse of genres like children's literature and Gothic studies. Buckley's thesis is interesting because she reads the identity figuration of the girl protagonist is Darren Shan's *Zom-B* (2012) as antithetical to normative binaries (active/passive, subject/object) of 'pedagogical formulations extant in Gothic studies' (p. 69). Buckley also uses her study of children's Gothic to provide a challenge to the discourses (e.g., Botting, 2014) within Gothic studies that exclude certain types of text from canons of criticism. Reconfiguring canons of criticism, especially in relation to fictions categorised as for young-adult audiences, is work that this book aims to continue, with the argument that New Queer Gothic texts encompass a fusion of mainstream and high literature and culture.

Introduction

The New Queer Gothic draws on the politics and ethics of other modes of Gothic studies besides the queer Gothic. This book's final chapter, with its focus on states of exception and hybrid identity in two novels featuring girl protagonists, will argue that reading the New Queer Gothic can 'help us understand and transform reality'.[49] This quotation is from Michael Löwy and describes the value of non-realist fiction with regard to the real effects that it has on understanding real-world problems and power structures. Postcolonial Gothic studies is as much a genre as the queer Gothic. As a mode of reading Gothic fiction, the postcolonial Gothic is like the queer Gothic, in that its concerns are specific to the politics of identity and representation while also drawing on interdisciplinary theory. Sarah Ilott describes the frequency with which postcolonial authors have adopted the Gothic mode, owing to its ability to register the horrors of colonial violence while critiquing colonial discourse. Ilott explains that the suitable language supplied by the Gothic works effectively to 'write back to a body of imperial Gothic literature that supported the colonial project through the othering of colonised peoples; and it recognises the "boomerang effect" that renders the Frankensteinian monstermakers themselves monstrous'.[50] In this way, parallels between the emancipatory or reparative effect of some queer readings of Gothic can be appreciated to draw on ideas of the Gothic continuum expressing a spectrum of regressive and progressive political standpoints, reflexively attendant as both a critical reading practice and a writing mode.[51] Ilott describes the postcolonial Gothic as able to expose the mechanisms of violence and racism still at work in the wake of European colonialism by making visible the 'profoundly unequal' access that people around the world have to economic and social opportunity, power and wealth, calling attention to the 'newly materialist focus' used by Gothic authors of the twenty-first century to foreground these systems of inequality as well as new gestures of racism and colonial violence. While some might argue that using the Gothic mode as a vehicle to express, discuss and try to deal with these very real, ongoing human issues, and the lived experience of violence, trauma and violence for populations around the world is escapist, Ilott, importantly makes the case that 'the Gothic is not a means of escape, but a means of re-engagement with the lived realities of twenty-first-century postcolonial societies in the face of systemic violence and the structural exclusion of minority voices' (p. 22). In contesting the Lukácsian idea that society should be critiqued only via realism, Ilott draws on the Warwick Research Collective (WReC). The WReC are proponents of works of fantasy belonging to the Gothic genre and irrealist writing:

> The simultaneity of material and immaterial regimes of production – of spilled blood and evanescent credit, to put it sloganistically – which is a pervasive and conspicuous feature of peripheral social formations, especially, does not readily lend itself to representation through the relative facticity of realist forms of the 'ideal-type'. The inmixing of the imaginary and the factual that characterises 'irrealist' writing is arguably more sensitive to this simultaneity, to the seemingly incongruous conjunction of 'abstract' and 'scarring' modes of capitalisation. Irrealist aesthetics might then be presented as corresponding not to any depreciation of realism, but to a refinement of it, under the specific circumstances of combined and uneven development.[52]

This quotation from the WReC works to support the representational and political value of the postcolonial Gothic and complements the argument of Michael Löwy who makes a case for the term 'critical irrealism'. Arguing that contemporary social reality should look beyond realism as the only acceptable art form, Löwy proffers that there are many 'nonrealist works of art which are valuable and contain a powerful critique of the social order'.[53] These notions regarding the wider political and ontological applications and values of Gothic genres of fiction can translate onto the ways in which the New Queer Gothic provokes readings that draw on topics such as hybridity and biopolitics. As one of the key critical frameworks applied throughout this book, 'queer theory' exists as a large umbrella term encompassing various tangents and gestures. My working understanding appreciates the field's Foucauldian and Butlerian roots as a poststructuralist way of thinking about sexuality and an anti-essentialist way of thinking about gender, while also recognising queer theory's genesis in the fields of feminism and lesbian and gay studies. Crudely, there exists two main arteries at the heart of queer theory that are significant to this book. One follows

Sedgwickian thinking and calls for redemptive assimilated queerness that, to some degree, encompasses a desire for equality that sometimes risks straying into the realm of 'homonormativity'. This term was coined by Lisa Duggan in 2003 to describe the presentations of queerness that heteronormative society can and will tolerate: palatable queerness, of the kind that mimics heterosexual, normative dynamics of behaviour, relationships and parenting. The other follows the more polemic thinking of Leo Bersani and Lee Edelman, who call for a more radical anti-normative queerness – this is sometimes referred to as 'antisocial' queer theory, it relishes difference, failure and alterity, and laments assimilated queerness as a de-fanged, domesticated, disingenuous form of 'queer'. This book will examine blood flow in both directions. Part II of the book engages heavily with a Sedgwickian framework of queer theory, primarily hinging its readings of New Queer Gothic film on the theorising extant in her last book, *Touching Feeling*, which explores the notion of paranoid and reparative reading. Eve Kosofsky Sedgwick's work in *Epistemology of the Closet* (1990) informs some of the thinking in Parts I and III, particularly regarding how homosocial desire, or the triangulation of desire, can be used to theorise relationships within same-sex and heterosexual relationships represented in works of nineteenth-century fiction to expose patriarchal systems of power. These ideas will be discussed in Chapter 1, which discusses Anne Rice's *Interview with the Vampire* as a foundational text of the New Queer Gothic genre in the representation of queer kinship that it offers. Sedgwick's 1992 book, *Between Men*, lays out some important ideas on how feminism has historically related to sexuality and how it continues to relate to sexuality at the juncture when queer theory was in its infancy but gaining traction through the work of Sedgwick and others. In *Between Men*, Sedgwick plotted a theoretical spectrum of feminism, situating Marxist feminism and radical feminism at opposing ends and explaining that radical feminism only occupies the farther 'left' position because it appreciates gender and 'gender alone, to be the most radical diversion of human experience, and a relatively unchanged one'.[54] Sedgwick describes the success with which second-wave feminists have sought to place sexuality at a site of prominent interrogation, using as her example what she calls an 'exceedingly heterogenous group of texts' – Sandra Gilbert and

Susan Gubar's 'Madwoman in the Attic' (1979), Kathleen Barry's *Female Sexual Slavery* (1979), Susan Griffin's *Pornography and Silence* (1981), Andrea Dworkin's *Pornography: Men Possessing Women* (1981) and Jane Gallop's *The Daughter's Seduction* (1982) – which share the view that sexuality is the central problem in the formation of woman's experience. Sedgwick focuses on their commonality in essentialism, and their impulsive privileging of sexuality where the subject and object of female heterosexuality is, by default, male. Radical feminism,[55] according to Sedgwick, balks at the idea that the meaning of sexuality and gender have ever changed or at the likelihood of them ever changing: 'In addition, history even in the residual, synchronic form of class or radical difference and conflict becomes invisible or excessively coarsened and dichotomized in the universalising structuralist view.'[56] These assessments made by Sedgwick and developed in the later works of queer feminist thinkers, are foundational to the research undertaken to form the following six chapters. Of course, Sedgwick's work is not only essential in the ways it described the relationship queer theory that has had with feminism; equally important is her theorising around LGBTQ subjectivities in a wide canon of cultural and literary representation analyses in *Tendencies* (1994). Sedgwick's methodological approach to *Tendencies* has been influential to the approach of this book because of the ways in which she envelopes fiction, politics and culture into her analytic essays, particularly with regard to her engagement with Freudian and Lacanian psychoanalysis – Sedgwick's critiques of reading the Law of the Father into narratives about familial relations and queer tutelage expose a need for queer theory to move away from reading gestures that are inappropriate to the acceleration of shifting ideologies within the realms of sex and gender construction. *The New Queer Gothic* will focus, more than anything else, on the important work that Sedgwick conducted in the writing of her last book, *Touching Feeling* (2003), which crucially and self-reflexively looks at extant modes of reading queerly and suggests a turn towards more effective treatment of pedagogy, criticism and ethics.

According to Sheila Jeffreys, those who had been 'most outraged by the new term [Queer] were lesbian feminists, who observed that though the term was supposed to be inclusive, it appeared to specifically exclude lesbians and lesbian feminists'.[57] Jeffreys points out that most generic terms for homosexuality have soon become monikers for gay men only: whole books have been written by gay male writers about 'homosexual history' or 'homosexual desire' in which lesbians are not mentioned (Rowse, 1977; Hocquenghem, 1978). The words 'homosexual' and 'gay' did not start out as pertaining exclusively to men but came to do so as a result of a simple material political reality, the greater social and economic power of men, the power that has allowed men to define what culture is and to make women invisible.[58] The questions of visibility and invisibility attendant to lesbian representation in fiction but more specifically in visual culture, continues to be a popular area of critical debate and defiance. Patricia White's ground-breaking 1999 book *Uninvited: Classical Hollywood Cinema and Lesbian Representability* – which offers queer readings of films subject to the limitations and censorship imposed by the Hays Code, such as *Rebecca* (1940) and *The Haunting* (1960) – asked 'when representation is forbidden, where do we look?'[59] More recently, critics of queer representation have reframed this question for the study of contemporary cinema. In 2016, Darren Elliott-Smith revisited this idea of queer characterisation accessible largely via monstrous representation in the vein of White's reading of the queerly malevolent Mrs Danvers in *Rebecca* but reframed the enquiry, wondering why this still occurs in cinema long after the Code's limitations: 'When monstrousness as a metaphor for the threat homosexuality poses to heteronormativity ceases to be coded and instead becomes open, then what does it mean?'[60] Clara Bradbury-Rance, in 2019, also consciously replicated White's words and their specific relevance to lesbian identity, asking 'when representation is granted, where do we look?'[61] This book will continue the work begun by these questions, investigating what wider visibility and accessibility to representation means in the context of New Queer Gothic texts.

The Antisocial Thesis

Resistance around identity politics is felt keenly in the critical response to writers such as Sedgwick. As a woman who did not herself identify as queer, and whose critical stance was to write about homosexual men, her own identity was questioned, particularly by Lee Edelman. Often considered a pioneering text for queer theory, Sedgwick's *Epistemology of the Closet* comes under Edelman's critical scrutiny, leading him to speculate that the book has a double imperative. Reacting to Sedgwick's inclusion of an anecdotal story of a man coming out to his long-term female friend, Edelman writes:

> If a certain nomination of his makes it something they can share, nothing, at least as the story is told, permits the naming of hers. She, the woman who knows (in this like Sedgwick, who begins the anecdote affirming that she 'know[s]' the woman and the man), is never other than 'woman' here, the subject of a gendered position whose analysis feminism provides. He, however, moves from a symmetrically gendered position as 'man' to the sexually determined position whose analysis belongs to Sedgwick's antihomophobic or gay male-oriented theory – a theory that has, she goes on to declare, like 'male gay writing and activism . . . a lot to learn from asking questions that feminist inquiry has learned to ask'.[62] As gay male theory must learn what feminist inquiry already knows, so the woman in Sedgwick's anecdote inhabits, like Sedgwick, the place of knowing and, in doing so, she knows two things: the first is the name for his sexuality . . . the other is the sexual charge that attaches to presuming to know that name: 'After all, the position of those who think they know something about one that one may not know oneself is an excited and empowered one'. (p. 8)

In an economy where the bountiful profits that accrue to homophobic knowingness line the pockets of a masculinist order run by heterosexually identifiable men, women's and gay men's relations to knowing, especially about each other, risk always, as Sedgwick knows full well, playing out in variously wounding ways the asymmetrical affordances of positioning by gender or sexuality.[63] What is presented here is Edelman's explanation of exactly how and why it is problematic, and fundamentally inappropriate, for someone of one identity to speculate on the sexual identity of another. However innocent the desire or claim to know might be, it always invites suspicion, assertion, co-opted paranoia; these are terms for describing how the queer subject is perceived, as subjects who should out themselves or risk being 'outed' one day. Edelman's disagreement with Sedgwick should not be misunderstood as a resentment of heterosexual women who are queer allies, but his contention with her standpoint is interesting because it provides an example that is expressive of how questions of gender and sexuality should, in some contexts, be considered separately.

Edelman's engagement with Sedgwick often centres on the fraught relationship that feminist theory and queer theory share. Following this, it is important to clarify that while some feminist theory catalysed the gestation of queer theory, queer discourse and feminist politics do not always completely correspond. Even in the works of theory used to understand the representational politics of fiction and film, there is disparity and an ever-evolving understanding of how crucial difference in identity are when it comes to speaking for, speaking of, or potentially exploiting queer people. My analysis of queer female subjectivity throughout the following six chapters will return frequently to the politics of closeting, coming-out and the ambiguity in the sexual identity of the queer characters. The debate between identity politics and queer theory, which began in the late 1980s, is a pertinent one. It runs through each of this book's chapters, not least since queer theory and feminism had an uneasy start to their relationship. Jagose describes the rapid emergence of 'queer' as a critical and activist term, arguing that the concomitant accelerated ascendancy of queer theory within the academy 'do[es] not attest to the waning of feminist theory's relevance'. Rather, Jagose suggests that the difficult relationship between some branches of feminism and queer thinking were produced by a specific set of pressures at the advent of queer theory in the 1990s and queer feminist thought in the twenty-first century speaks to another specific set of historic circumstances – an assortment of different pressures and influences that cannot be neatly narrated 'in terms of cause/effect relations'.[64] This difficult relationship, however, enabled a momentous shift toward anti-essentialist and anti-assimilationist modes of thinking about political recognition and the regulating structures of modern Western society (p. 172). While recognising the necessity of this critical tension, and without attempting the impossible task of neatly reconciling the anti-identarian queer and the feminist strands of thinking that this book draws on via its demonstration of the New Queer Gothic body/genre/mode and its subsequent readings, what *The New Queer Gothic* will do is work to prove the importance of encouraging an ongoing conversation. Identity politics, which drive much of the feminist theory that I will be using, is crucial to political claims of recognition and representation, with real-world impact; we navigate the world and understand the world via our identities. Queer deconstruction of binaries and paradigms can significantly challenge power structures that have a history of inflicting harm on the most Othered subjects in society. In many cases, 'Othered' and 'queer' subjects experience something of an elision, but the criticism and analysis presented in this book speaks to the strength and value of queerness rather than dwelling on its inherent precarity and vulnerability. Post-structural thinking is abstract, and this book aims to show that queer theory is more powerful a critical framework when its scope is rejuvenated to include other intersectional theory, inclusive of theory contingent on identity politics.

Sedgwick's aforementioned voluble interlocutor offers a different perspective on queer criticism that is a useful point of departure for my work. Edelman informs his work with similar psychoanalytic frameworks, drawing predominantly on Lacanian psychoanalysis, but where he and Sedgwick diverge is in Edelman's pursuit of the antisocial vectors of queer theory. Edelman's 2004 book, *No Future: Queer Theory and the Death Drive*, offers a polemic stance on anti-identarian or antisocial queerness in its railing against the heteronormative paradigms that penetrate all systems and functions of modern Western society. He claims that queerness names the death drive, that in resisting signification, queerness reinforces and informs the symbolic order.[65] While for other queer theorists, queerness may be described as attached to developing a sense of self, an identity, a subjectivity, Edelman prefers to theorise queerness as the remainder of the real within the Lacanian symbolic order. This remainder is sometimes referred to as the unnameable remainder or jouissance. Jouissance is described as evocative of the death drive and transcendent of the pleasure principle and the fantasy of self-realisation: 'a movement beyond the pleasure principle, beyond the distinctions of pleasure and pain, a violent passage beyond the bounds of identity, meaning, law' (p. 25). Taken as a void rather than a whole and stable form of identity, this definition of queerness maps onto existing modes of reading Gothic fiction as intensely negative and paranoid, and provides an excellent point of engagement and departure, particularly for this book's second and final chapters where I discuss queer Gothic girlhood. The mechanisms exposed by Edelman's work, however, are important to this research. His calls to challenge and contest 'reproductive futurity' implicates such notions as the idolised child and the sinthomosexual; these two figures are positioned in antithesis to one another in *No Future*. The sinthomosexual, Edelman argues, is the enemy of the child:

> the paradoxical object form of jouissance itself: a violently disruptive enjoyment that threatens the integrity of the object insofar as that object is nothing but a catachrestic positing intended to foreclose the primal negativity of ab-sense as the subtraction from being and meaning without which neither can arise.

The sinthomosexual is a character of ontological negation and an interesting figure for discussion. Edelman's canon of primary texts is limited, as he privileges white masculinity in his queer readings of popular culture, world literature and film, and all his examples of the sinthomosexual (at least as they appear in *No Future*) are white, middle-class, middle-aged or ageing men. Edelman's discussion of how the child is perceived, signified and represented in contemporary society, particularly in its relationship to heteronormative culture, is key to the arguments presented in this book. These ideas will be returned to and expanded on in the coming chapters; first, it is important to introduce the ways in which Edelman formulates conversations about queer theory via notions of the death drive together with the semantics of narrative.

The relationship between Edelman's sinthomosexual and the child is something that he unpacks across his oeuvre and is divergent again from Sedgwick but circulates around the similar topic of queerness as tutelage, offered as an education or a corruption via mentoring, abusive or familial relationships between adult and child characters. Child sexual abuse is theorised by Edelman in the film

Bad Education (2004) when he argues that 'those who are queered are libidinally stained with the negativity of the thing which is not' (p. 117).[66] The 'Child', which Edelman describes as the ultimate totem of the future, is threatened, its 'innocence' desublimated, and it is reduced from its privileged position from a one to a zero; from its position as the object of desire 'to the void at the core of the drive' (p. 126). A preoccupation of Edelman's is certainly the topic of the child, clear from his investigations into how this figure is used in relation to historical ontological thinking. Another of Edelman's preoccupations includes figurations of semantic techniques such as irony. Calling on Paul de Man's ideas about the loss of continuity and sense born out of thinking about the machinations of irony, 'that queerest of rhetorical devices', Edelman describes its relation to the death drive:

> How should we read this constant disruption of narrative signification, a disruption inextricable from the articulation of narrative as such, but as a version of the death drive . . . If irony can serve as one of the names that force of that unthought remainder, might not queerness serve as another?[67]

This suggests that queer theory can constitute the position to which irony's radical threat – which Edelman argues is displaced by heteronormative culture onto the figure of the queer – is turned, 'uncannily', when returned by those queers who embrace their figural identity or their 'disfiguration', as opposed to disowning or disavowing that figuration. The threads that Edelman brings together, of an antisocial queer theory totally opposed to any assimilative ends, welcomes the abstract gestures that constitute contemporary thinking about queer subjectivity. In his reading of Pedro Almodóvar's 2004 film *Bad Education*, Edelman reads the framing and cuts, more specifically the use of a man's back blacking-out the frame, referring to a similar technique used in Hitchcock's 'killer-queer' film *Rope* (1948), here the blocked frame and the cut suggests a closeting, not of the implicit sodomy or paedophilia:

> but of the jouissance of Ignacio in this moment of erotic education, the voiding of his subjectivity through his reduction to the anal

opening, the hole, that renders him unintelligible, a zero instead of a one, a site of ab-sense at odds with the Child as the promise of social meaning.[68]

This is interesting in the similarities it shares with the existing scholarship about queerness figured as tutelage, particularly with regard to Henry James's *The Turn of the Screw* (1898), which will form some of the discussion in Chapter 2. Queerness, according to Edelman, is necessarily opposed to futurism: 'Where Futurism always anticipates the image of the Imaginary past, a realization of meaning that will suture identity by closing that gap, queerness undoes the identities through which we experience ourselves as subjects'[69] by insisting on jouissance and the real. For these reasons, Edelman argues that an authentic, substantive identity cannot be constituted by queerness. The value of queerness, Edelman posits, is something that cannot be measured by any notion of social good; it 'voids every notion of general good'. He states that there can be no justification for it if that means queerness is qualified by what positive social value it encourages or conveys, 'its value, instead, resided in its challenges to values as defined by the social, and this in its radical challenge to the very value of the social itself' (p. 6). Here is where these arguments led my own research, without a focus on male homosexuality in queer representation, to an argumentative cul-de-sac. Among many feminist, lesbian, people of colour and intersectional critics also working in queer theory there is the argument about who Edelman's thesis is really for – explained here by Elizabeth Freeman, who wonders 'whether radical antifuturity and its corollary, the antisocial thesis, are the new postmodernity, that is, the conceptual privilege of white middle-class male subjects who are always already guaranteed a future and so can afford to jettison the idea of one'.[70] Moving forward, this will be another significant tract to develop, another great fissure, now not only between queer and identarian, but also between futurist and anti-futurist queer narratives.

This book is made up of three parts, each containing two chapters. Part I concerns the foundations of the New Queer Gothic, arguing in Chapter 1 that the literary ground broken by selected women authors writing in the twentieth century and into the twenty-first century was particularly influential to the formation of both the new genre that this book proposes and to ways of reading female subjectivity and themes connected to sexuality and queerness in contemporary Gothic fiction. The authors with whom I am concerned include Shirley Jackson (1916–65), Angela Carter (1940–92), Maryse Condé (1937–), Anne Rice (1941–2021), Jewelle Gomez (1948–) and Sarah Waters (1966–). Each of them has provided the literary world with pioneering fictions and established tropes that are now shown to be symptomatic of the genealogies these women instigated or maintained. Chapter 2 provides its first analysis of an example of New Queer Gothic fiction, John Harding's 2010 novel *Florence and Giles,* a contemporary re-envisioning of James's classic Gothic tale *The Turn of the Screw*, which has historically attracted significant attention from psychoanalytical and queer criticism. I offer a reading of this novel as an opportunity to explore the subversive force of the queer Gothic girl, exploring protagonist Florence's subjectivity via the use of language and the intertextual motifs present in the plot to discuss how this representation relates to other queer and Gothic children explored in fiction. Drawing on the work of Ellis Hanson, Leo Bersani, and the queer feminist ethics of Lynne Huffer, my aim in this chapter is to prove that via reading this Gothic girl queerly it is possible to knit together some of the fissures in feminist and queer theory.

I move away from literary fiction in Part II to consider some examples of New Queer Gothic cinema, looking at the ways in which queer women's subjectivities are represented and investigating methods of reading them. Chapter 3 provides a comparative analysis of Darren Aronofsky's *Black Swan* (2010) and Bradley Rust Gray's *Jack and Diane* (2012). In demonstrating how each of these productions can be considered as New Queer Gothic, I structure my analysis around the recognisable themes of space, mirroring and abjection, debating the feminist and queer significance that each employ via their presentations of these themes. After demonstrating their importance as New Queer Gothic texts, the chapter then turns its attention to possible methods of reading and introduces Eve Kosofsky Sedgwick's theories of paranoid and reparative reading. This important gesture of reading is an axis explored in further detail in Chapter 4. Chan-wook Park's film *The Handmaiden* (2016) is another transformative adaptation of a text that has previously

Introduction

attracted critical attention from queer and feminist criticism: Sarah Waters' neo-Victorian novel, *Fingersmith* (2002). Chapter 4 argues that, via a paranoid reparative approach, readings of *The Handmaiden* as a New Queer Gothic film can better access and engage with other important critical areas of theory, like queer and postcolonial subjectivity, and can encompass debates between queer feminist and lesbian representation and criticism. This idea of investigating the broader scope and impact of reading the New Queer Gothic in contemporary fictions with a focus on critiquing representation of female subjectivity continues in Part III.

Part III encompasses analyses of New Queer Gothic film and fiction, looking at Julia Ducournau's 2016 French film *Raw* in Chapter 5 and analysing two contemporary novels in Chapter 6. My argument in Chapter 5 is built around the project and effect of queering the cannibal in a film that presents a young woman protagonist navigating two burgeoning and connected aspects of her identity: the sexual and the cannibalistic. My analysis of *Raw* foregrounds the interesting connections that it makes between national feminist attitudes to gender and sexuality and situates it within multiple critical contexts to argue that it represents an ethics of ambivalence within the New Queer Gothic. Chapter 6 also works to explore multiple contexts in a comparative analysis of Helen Oyeyemi's 2005 novel *The Icarus Girl* and M. R. Carey's 2014 novel *The Girl with all the Gifts*. After demonstrating why each of these texts belongs to New Queer Gothic and demonstrating how they are important to an investigation into the representation of girlhood subjectivity within that genre. My work in Chapter 6 debates each novel's use of the themes of Gothic hybridity and exceptionality, analysing the ways in which these novels represent the trauma of wider issues connected to biopolitics. My arguments here will synthesise those explored in previous chapters to underscore the importance of this new mode of fiction, appreciating it as rich and fruitful ground for further investigation and as an essentially valuable aspect of Gothic studies, queer criticism and feminist thinking capable of significantly broadening our understanding of real-world issues. Through demonstrating, complicating and thoroughly analysing the New Queer Gothic, this book continues some important conversations and starts new ones.

Part I

1

'She herself is a haunted house': The Origins of the New Queer Gothic in the Work of Twentieth-Century Women Writers

൞

> She herself is a haunted house. She does not possess herself; her ancestors sometimes come and peer out of the windows of her eyes and that is very frightening.[1]

This quotation from Angela Carter's short story 'The Lady of the House of Love' provides a metaphor for women whose subjectivity is represented by certain genealogies. Gothic fiction has been an incredibly significant site of representation for women and this metaphor draws on woman's paradoxical situation in place and space, as object and subject, commenting on the effect of such 'frightening' precarity. The fictional women that this book observes could not exist without those who were written before them. This chapter argues that through recognising the formative literary works that paved the way for New Queer Gothic, we can better understand its parameters and the necessity to continue analysing the representations of female subjectivity in contemporary iterations of Gothic fiction. In discussing the American and British women writers of twentieth and twenty-first century fiction that introduced many of the key themes and concerns with which this book is preoccupied, this chapter will provide a foundation for this book's subsequent analytical chapters. Shirley Jackson (1916–65), Angela Carter (1940–92), Anne Rice (1941–) and Sarah Waters (1966–) are four female authors who have influenced not only the primary texts that this book takes as its examples for analysis, but also the modes of reading employed. It is the role of this first chapter to review the ways in which these authors have proved integral to the genesis of crucial themes and plot devices in their literary fiction; to describe how each author situates their work in the Gothic genre; to document how each author foregrounded female subjectivity in a Gothic context; and to illustrate the systems and mechanisms that limit or complicate female and queer representation in that context. The formative role that each of these women writers played in the genesis of the New Queer Gothic bolsters my overarching argument that female subjectivity is integral to contemporary queer Gothic texts yet continues to be under-recognised and under-researched. This chapter appreciates each of the authors as pioneers – not least because, as Anne Williams writes, 'any woman writing in the Gothic tradition already has two strikes against her',[2] but also because of their determination in encouraging such a rich cultural afterlife for their fiction.

The Gothic heroine of classic eighteenth and nineteenth-century literature was often the passive victim of horrors emanating from ancestral secrets or disruptive Others, but, more often than not, her trials and suffering centred on her position in relation to the men in her life and her situation in a domestic space. Feminist intervention in Gothic studies has worked to critique the ways in which female subjectivity and sexuality has been represented in a historically conservative mode. Michelle Massé describes how many classic Gothic tales, citing Horace Walpole's *The Castle of Ontranto* (1764) and Ann Radcliffe's *The Mysteries of Udolpho* (1794) and *The Italian* (1797), have long been read alongside the decidedly non-feminist Freudian psychoanalytic theories of the reality and pleasure principles. Massé writes that marriage and the heterosexual genitality that it accompanies 'is revealed as the reality principle before which the problematic pleasures of the female body yield . . . By light of day and end of novel, the heroine's nightmare visions disappear, cured by the *medicina libidinis* offered in the conservative and comic resolution' (Massé, 'Gothic Repetition').[3] Massé writes that readers, accustomed to 'repression-based analyses' assuage any fear with or for the heroine, because her fears are either unreal, hysteric, or simply nothing that cannot be fixed by her transition from her father's household to her husband's (p. 680). There are a number of mechanisms keeping the Gothic heroine frozen in this loop, which the twentieth and twenty-first-century authors analysed in this chapter present, either by way of communicating symptoms of these systems of oppression, or by way of acknowledging and parodying them. These mechanisms include discussing the Gothic as it relates to repressed desire, in relation to depth and surface models in psychoanalysis, and, moreover, the ways in which the Gothic is bound up with ideas of legitimate and illegitimate identity. If, as Massé argues, the Gothic plot is never an escape from the real world but a rehearsed repetition of domestic trauma in which the heroine is denied identity again and again, then how can the genre and its attendant criticism look beyond this praxis? If Gothic endings are read as always upholding the same interests as Freud and other proponents of patriarchal power by reinstating social constructions of gender and exposing the heroine as defined by what she is denied: power, identity and independence, then what potential readings and theoretical exploratory avenues are being missed? (p. 686). This is one of the central cruxes within feminist criticism of the Gothic and a starting point of this research project's investigation into highlighting queer theory as an important framework. Steven Bruhm makes a salient point when noting that the 'long and rich history of feminist criticism has opened up avenues for addressing problems of gender in the Gothic', but no one finds these analyses particularly surprising or exploratory because they presuppose the ubiquity of female oppression.[4] Queer theory, on the other hand, makes available a 'new purchase on sexuality' and invites critique of the idea of power in sexuality. Calling on Judith Butler's ideas in *Bodies that Matter*, as well as Eve Kosofsky Sedgwick's work in *Epistemology of the Closet* and *Tendencies*, Bruhm writes that 'the fascination with retrieving the prohibited is both psychoanalytic and Gothic', and accessing a queer reading via these thinkers 'offers a rubric by which those transgressions can be read as queer interventions in straight culture'.[5] Bruhm sees the intervention of queer theory in Gothic studies as a cause of some necessary discomfort:

> I bring the psychoanalytic Gothic to students precisely to resist the ubiquity of normalizing programmes like 'identity' and its bridesmaids. The queer Gothic might be discomforting, but it is perhaps the most effective and popular tool available for understanding the many repudiations that are needed to constitute normalcy. (p. 104)

The repudiations described by Bruhm are extant throughout the history of Gothic literature and film, especially when it comes to constituting women's sexuality and subjectivity, but this notion of discomfort is a key concern of my thesis, which will be developed via my engagement with alternative ways of reading queer women in Gothic fiction.

The Haunting Work of Shirley Jackson

Shirley Jackson's fiction exists in two disparate though interrelated parts; the memoirs and 'domestic writing' that she published in magazines throughout the early 1950s, and the supernatural short stories and Gothic thriller novels she produced towards the end of her short life. Jackson is best known for her short story 'The Lottery' (1943), a mainstay on most school syllabuses. Her legacy, and the significance of her literary impact as it pertains to this project, is one that encompasses the 'domestic writing' that flavoured her early work and her later works of female Gothic fiction, particularly *The Haunting of Hill House* (1959) and *We Have Always Lived in the Castle* (1962).

Critics such as Angela Hague and Darryl Hattenhauer have lamented a noticeable decline in the critical attention necessary in validating the literary value of Jackson's work since her death. For Hague, 'history has not been kind' to Jackson. Although popular, her fiction failed to garner much acclaim by way of awards, prizes or funding. Hague argues that her fiction should be 'read as a significant contribution to our understanding of the psychic disruption that has characterized post-war experience'.[6] In his book-length study, *Shirley Jackson's American Gothic* (2003), Hattenhauer argues that 'Jackson's reputation should be restored to the lofty position it occupied during her life'[7] – a time at which, he writes, her work sat comfortably on the reading lists of high-ranking universities, when she was held in high esteem among prolific authors and publishers alike, and was considered a benchmark for new writers of the 1960s (p. 2). Criticism on Jackson's work tends to recirculate biographical information, speculating on the impact of the author's psyche on her fiction, and this usually accompanies psychoanalytic readings of her Gothic fiction in particular; one such example of which comes from Michael T. Wilson, who discusses the plot of *The Haunting of Hill House* as informed by the 'strong possibility' that Jackson and her friend were molested by her uncle as children, that her mother had told her she was a 'failed abortion', and that, with an early life marked by trauma and an adult life marked still further by 'psychological disorders and addiction issues', Jackson wrote characters like Eleanor, also marked by 'psychological damage', as devices to lead away from visions of terror (Wilson, 'Absolute Reality').[8] Wilson goes on to speculate that Jackson's use of traditional Gothic tropes that situate victimhood with the heroine might also suggest her own methods of processing 'her experiences in life as a writer and woman, in a way that reflects a deep understanding that a glimpse of unmediated reality in all its unveiled power is not always survivable, or that one's own ability to survive such a glimpse may change over time' (pp. 121–2). While the psychoanalytic readings of Jackson's fiction will continue to prove valuable to the study of Gothic and feminist intersections, reducing the author to an analysand in this way is not productive. For Wilson, a study into Jackson's use of the Gothic mode is a vehicle for portraying the 'ineffable' in her personal life; for Hattenhauer, a study into her use of intertextuality, along with 'disunified characterization, discontinuous plots, absurd settings [and] illegible narrative point of view', provides evidence to suggest that her writing is underappreciated as horror writing when it should be lauded as 'proto-postmodern' Gothic.[9] Taken together, the broader issue these examples of criticism reveal are the ways in which women's writing is belittled and critiqued into near obscurity; its merit and value are obfuscated by confused reading practices.

While criticism on Jackson's work has often probed at the physical and psychological order in which she kept her 'house' – with critics like Wilson dissecting the author, in mind and body, emphasised by his creeping fascination towards her housekeeping habits – a central theme of Jackson's work, life and legacy is the house and its relation to female subjectivity. The house as metaphor is perhaps the most enduring motif of Gothic fiction and film and is the best remembered of Jackson's Gothic tropes. However, Jackson's importance to the Gothic genre was established prior to her exploration into the Gothic mansions and spectral hauntings. First published in *The New Yorker* in 1948, Jackson's short story 'The Lottery' told a Gothic tale about social ethics. Eric Savoy applies the Lacanian Real to the short story and convincingly situates it as Jackson's first foray into what he terms 'the dire potential of everyday life', reading the darkly lingering narrative as concluding 'on the very rock of the Real'.[10] Savoy calls this 'the essence of Jackson's novel intervention in the Gothic – the Real is at once that which hovers in the margins of the text, and that which throws a piece of itself at us, at the random reader, chosen as it were by lottery' (p. 838). Noting that her later Gothic novels return to some of the themes introduced in 'The Lottery', of the quiet terror in the everyday, Savoy subverts the idea of people picking over the 'corpse' and he vindicates that critical trend by arguing:

> Cumulatively in this work, we seem always just about to see the sunshine sketch of family life turn toward the monstrous. Curiously, this seemingly imminent darkening of reality toward the fantastic is not separable from, but is tightly interwoven with, Jackson's comic mode, which itself is a mode of excess and biting irony. For all of these stories and sketches involve the figure of a housewife – constructed between autobiography and fiction, between 'is' and 'as if' – who is barely keeping her house in order and her household together.

This quotation suggests the difficulty in divorcing the metatextual biographical information about the author from her fiction because of the extent to which Jackson interwove them; this makes her a troubling figure to analyse and a curious catalyst to my notion of female queerness within the New Queer Gothic. Figures like the

Queer Gothic child, which this book will discuss at length, are in their contemporary incarnations indebted to Jackson's playful depictions of child rearing. Jackson's 1950s sketches – published in women's magazines and collated in the collections *Raising Demons* (1953) and *Life Among the Savages* (1957) – participate in both reflecting and troubling post-war family life in a way that was, at the time, startlingly new: 'at once, in the era's prevailing construction of children's cuteness – the mode of "kids say the darnedest things" – and in tracing their uncanny ways of knowing and the unnerving intensity of their imaginative lives'. Savoy here describes the cumulative effect of this 'as if Miles and Flora, the children of James's *The Turn of the Screw*, have commerce with ghosts and then sit down to breakfast and say amusing things' (p. 84). The two archetypal queer Gothic children used here will be, without coincidence, returned to for further consideration. Jackson set the scene in many ways: the (de)construction of nuclear families in contemporary Gothic fiction, the figuration of precocious (and murderous) queer children, and a nuances subversion of 'domesticated' femininity in the post-war era.

I have introduced Jackson in much the same way that most critics do, by describing the two facets of her fiction. Savoy, however, argues for the dismantling of 'the comfortable notion that the domestic writing and the fully achieved Gothic represent the two faces of Shirley Jackson', stating his contention that 'all of her writing demonstrates the proximity of horror, not as an ominous presence that underlies daylight reality, but as something that is interwoven with reality's continuity with the Real: it is the spectre on the spectrum' (p. 841). I would argue that Jackson was a key instigator of using the uncanny trope in post-war Gothic fiction, blurring the boundaries between realist and supernatural styles to foreground the liminality of female subjectivity at the time.

In many of her short stories and, most significantly, in her two novels, *The Haunting of Hill House* and *We Have Always Lived in the Castle*, Jackson explores the themes of female entrapment, creating claustrophobic, uncanny settings in Gothic mansions and crumbling houses that are very much anthropomorphised to live and breathe alongside the female protagonists that inhabit them. While the value of Jackson's work might seem obviously important to feminist criticism, the critical reception that it received in the 1960s was rather hostile. Betty Friedan, author of *The Feminine Mystique* (1963), dubbed Jackson a 'Housewife Writer',[11] suggesting that she was part of a group of female authors more complacent than other female authors of the time because her writing at worst celebrated and at best tolerated the inferior position women held as literal and metaphoric domestic servants. Such a condemnation of her work as conspiring with and complicit in patriarchal order, is something Hague challenges:

> Had Friedan more carefully read Shirley Jackson's literary fiction, she would have understood that Jackson's characterisations of middle-class women are in fact portraits of the women she describes in *The Feminine Mystique*: women who, lacking any sense of self or ability to function in the world outside the home, begin to fragment and dissociate when forced to act independently.[12]

More recent criticism intervenes in Freidan's engagement with Jackson: Rebecca Munford has since claimed that the attention Friedan called to 'the indeterminate animism of the housewife' gave expression to 'a model of spectral femininity that is profoundly affiliated to the uncanny space of the home' (Munford, 'Spectral Femininity').[13] Commenting on the changing social and economic spaces that women could occupy, Hague describes Jackson's work as realist social commentary on the ways in which women in 1950s America were re-evaluating their places in the world, which blends supernatural metaphor and fantastical Gothic elements to portray the maelstrom of transformative effects post-war life induced:

> By focusing on female characters' isolation, loneliness, and fragmenting identities, their simultaneous inability to relate to the world outside themselves or to function autonomously, and their confrontation with an inner emptiness that often results in mental illness, Jackson displays in pathological terms the position of many women in the 1950s. But her unveiling of this era's dark corners is not limited to one gender, for her apocalyptic consciousness, sinister children, and scathing portraits of nuclear families and their suburban environments, her depiction of a quotidian and predictable world that can suddenly metamorphose into the terrifying and bizarre,

reveal her character's relations to a culture of repression, containment, and paranoia.[14]

In stories like 'A Visit' (published originally as 'A Lovely House' in 1950) and most overtly in *The Haunting of Hill House*, the home is an uncanny place where all feelings of welcome, comfort and security are subverted and come instead to represent prisons that terrify and threaten female characters with malevolent forces.

One of the most noteworthy examples of criticism focusing on the queerness and Gothicity of Jackson's work exists in George E. Haggerty's *Queer Gothic*, in which a whole chapter is dedicated to comparing *The Haunting of Hill House* with James's *The Turn of the Screw*. Here, Haggerty suggests that the ongoing conversation between gothic fiction, modern sexology and psychoanalysis shows intersecting themes common to Gothic novelists and thinkers like Foucault and Freud alike:

> The first two of Foucault's 'four great strategic unities' – '1. Hysterization of women's bodies' and '2. A pedogogization of children's sex' – come into vivid focus here. *The Turn of the Screw* and *The Haunting of Hill House* both reveal the relation between the first and second 'unities' Foucault describes and the degree to which hysteria and gender emerge naturally from gothic works like these. Gothic fiction, in other words, participates in the formation of 'specific mechanisms of knowledge and power'. Or perhaps it is more correct to say that gothic fiction sees through these mechanisms and invokes them for affective force at the same time that it exposes their limitations.[15]

Haggerty reads *The Turn of the Screw* and *The Haunting of Hill House* as evidence that Gothic novelists were 'at least as adept as Freud at exposing the workings of hysterical response', suggesting that these authors conveyed the terms of female victimisation much more effectively than Freud ever managed. Explaining that James's governess and Jackson's Eleanor Vance are victims because they have been placed in situations over which they have little to no control, he writes that '[t]he world of desire confounds them' (p. 149). While this seems to suggest a regurgitation of Mary Ann Doane's thesis in *The Desire to Desire* (1987),[16] Haggerty's objective in assessing these female characters as 'abject and isolated', analysing them as unable to 'accept intimacy because intimacy is exactly what haunts them in the first place', is less about the limitations of the representability of female subjectivity and more about Gothic fiction's role in foreshadowing psycho-sexology and really working to formulate our contemporary understanding of the relationship between sexuality and psychology. Haggerty writes that these female characters:

> each understand intimacy as something that threatens to destroy them. Had Freud understood that, the history of twentieth-century psychiatric treatment might have been different. The almost overly familiar gothic trope of the persecuted female imbues these outwardly neurotic women with a depth and a complexity they would otherwise lack.[17]

While Haggerty's argument that modern understandings of psychology and sexuality owe as much to Gothic fiction as they do psychoanalysis, his language choices suggest a certain complicity in the pathologising of the identities that these characters represent, as would a purely psychoanalytic reading of these texts. Queer theory has many inseverable roots in psychoanalysis, but it is not the only theoretical application useful in explaining the richness, complexity and value of its relationship with the Gothic and its relationship to female subjectivity.

Contemporary adaptations of Jackson's fictions exist in the form of radio plays, musical theatre pieces and feature-length films. The original 1963 adaptation of *The Haunting of Hill House*, Robert Wise's *The Haunting*, is a crucial text to the canon of lesbian film. It develops a lesbian subtext between Theodora's and Eleanor's characters, played respectively by Claire Bloom and Julie Harris, which builds on the subplot established by Jackson.[18] Jan de Bont's 1999 remake of *The Haunting* sees Theodora's character, updated to Theo (Catherine Zeta Jones) played as an openly bisexual woman: Eleanor, or Nell (played by Lili Taylor), asks her if she has commitment issues, to which she replies, 'My boyfriend thinks so, my girlfriend doesn't'. The hammy acting is perhaps the most memorable aspect of this particular adaptation, which was received as ripe for parody, evidenced by the subsequent 2001 release of spoof-horror film *Scary Movie 2*, which revised many of its iconic scenes.

While there is no overt visualisation of desire in Wise's film and no explicit 'lesbian scene' in the book or film to establish or confirm Theodora's sexuality, queer readings of the narrative hinge on scenes most suggestive of same-sex desire. Such scenes are set, both in the book and the 1963 film, in the instances where Eleanor and Theodora share a bedroom, as Patricia White explains:

> The process whereby the apparition of lesbian desire is deferred to the manifestation of supernatural phenomena is well illustrated by a sequence depicting the events of the first night spent by the company in Hill House. Theo accompanies Eleanor to the door of her bedroom, and offers to come in and arrange Eleanor's hair. Although Eleanor refuses Theo's advances, the women end up in bed together anyway, but not according to plan. (White, 'Uninvited')[19]

The pair become on-screen examples of 'queer spectators'[20] when they witness the house's first show of disruptive supernatural activity; loud banging surrounds and terrorises them. After an initial frightened embrace, Eleanor later clings to what she thinks is her companion's hand as loud blows sound through the walls and, in both the book and film adaptation, flickering lights return to the room to reveal that the two women are not close enough together, that Eleanor sits alone on the bed, crying 'God! God! Whose hand was I holding?' Commenting on this, Haggerty notes of this that '[t]he point seems to be that although she imagines she is gripping Theodora tightly, she is actually gripping something out of a nightmare of confused identity that the house has become for her'.[21] This scene therefore establishes and inflects subsequent adaptations with the notion of Gothicity thwarting queer desire, of 'confusion' and introspection prevailing over jouissance.

The most notable example of critical analysis given to the Wise film appears in White's book, *Uninvited: Classical Hollywood Cinema and Lesbian Representability* (1999), where White lists it among the films responsible for 'unleash[ing] an excess of female sexuality that cannot be contained without recourse to the supernatural, or indeed the unnatural'.[22] White's analysis is largely psychoanalytic, but the representational politics that it expounds is very effective. On modes of spectatorship, White uses examples of classic films with queer subtexts to challenge the ubiquity of mechanisms such as Mulvey's male gaze:[23] 'the epistemological doubts that stalk both the cinematic look and assertions of heterosexual mastery are uniquely mobilized in horror films that imply nightmarish alternative realities'.[24] White thereafter addresses the equation that continues to pervade criticism surrounding female and queer spectatorship, which always amounts to that character being represented as a confounding version of subjectivity and desire. White summarises here:

> In asserting the female spectator's narcissistic over-identification with the image (Doane), in describing her masculinization by an active relation to the gaze (Mulvey), or in claiming that the film's fantasy encourages identifications that disregard the viewer's gender and sexuality (Bergstrom), feminist film theory has been unable to envision women who looked at women with desire. (p. 73)

This builds on the ideas set out by Doane in *The Desire to Desire*; that 'female spectatorship . . . can only be understood as the confounding of desire'.[25] Doane argues that the figuration 'of female subjectivity in the women's film is characterized by a deficiency in relation to the gaze, a metonym for desire itself'.[26] If her deficiency defines her, her only hope and chance for representation lies in the Gothic contexts of classic women's films.

While the 1963 film adaptation develops on existing suggestions made in the novel about Theodora's forwardness, her bohemian brashness and confidence, these are presented in stark contrast to Eleanor's conservative, measured manner, and the audience are encouraged to regard the characters in parallel. Whereas White describes Theodora as 'the invited researcher who is definitely a dyke' (p. 79), and Haggerty reads her as 'the fashionable and self-possessed lesbian',[27] Michael Koresky reads Theodora's 'probable homosexuality' as existing 'largely as it relates to Eleanor and her demons'.[28] The function of this representation of same-sex desire, arguably presented by Jackson and expounded by Wise, problematically connects psychological trauma or disorder to queer sexuality. At the time of its publication, homosexuality existed in the public consciousness and in US law as criminal and pathological; at the time of the film's release these ideas were shifting but still lingered.

White makes the most astute observation, pertaining to the scene discussed, though it can be applied to many examples of female Gothic, particularly in their representation of queerness: '[i]n fact the scene most literally transforms homosexuality into homophobia by replacing sexuality with fear' (p. 86). Furthermore, as White notes, the Production Code Administration recommended that the film rethink a scene depicting two women on the same bed for its 'imprudence' and consider instead placing the characters on twin beds. Readings emanate around the (impossible) touch, proximity and shared experiences of these women. Jackson, the cinema and the haunting spirit seem to be, as White suggests, accomplices in maintaining a rather counterproductive, almost seductive distance between them. It is curious then that the very latest incarnation of this queer narrative, produced in the twenty-first century without the limitation of censoring codes, exaggerates the parallel between pathology and sexual identity in the character of Theo, and it does so in relation to touch. *The Haunting of Hill House*, the 2018 Netflix series, is inspired by the novel and film, as well as by the biographical information about Jackson.[29] However, instead of characters brought to together to visit the house, characters in the series belong to one family who try to make Hill House their home. The family's matriarch (Carla Gugino) is an architect, like Jackson's real parents, one of the siblings is named Shirley (Elizabeth Reaser), her sisters are Nell (Eleanor, played by Victoria Pedretti) and Theo (Theodora, played by Kate Seigel). Theo is played as openly gay, shown bringing women home from bars, freely expressing her attraction and desire; Koresky celebrates that by 'making subtext text, history gets the last laugh'.[30] However, while the contemporary lesbian has no need to dwell in the shadows, she remains tied to pathological representation.

In an elaboration on the original character's power of extrasensory perception, Theo wears gloves and cannot touch directly those she encounters without establishing a psychic connection that she is unable to ignore. The hands provided the queer Gothic crux of Jackson's novel and Wise's film: in each, Eleanor at least imagines she grasps Theodora's hand, 'holding so tight she could feel the fine bones of Theodora's fingers'.[31] Hand imagery, for Rebecca Munford, 'returns again and again in the narrative, most notably when the tangibility of the body (and its relation to the body of the

Other) is being called into question'.[32] For the hands to reappear as the site of weakness for this queer character as well as a new locus of supernatural ability, they function to return the spectator to thinking about how queer female subjectivity is figured in relation to wider society, suggesting an inherent precarity in queer identity, as well as a disconnect from others. White, however, offers a different theory on the original character's talent for extra-sensory perception in connecting it to the mode of 'paranoiac spectatorship' with which *The Haunting* has been read:

> In developing a feminist film theory that would incorporate Theo, we might recall the model of spectatorship she offers the film. Telepathy, to lesbians and gay men as actual readers and viewers, has always been an alternative to our own mode of paranoiac spectatorship: 'Is it really there?' The experience of this second sight involves the identification of and with Theo as a lesbian.[33]

The question then remains, if, in latest adaptation, Theo has no need to hide her sexuality, if it is 'really there', then what is the significance of continuing her pathological and physical disenfranchisement? Munford concludes that in *Hill House*, the 'problem [that] has no name' appears ghostlike 'at the heart of the patriarchal scenes, [as] lesbian d-sire'.[34] In twenty-first-century adaptations of texts significant to the genealogy of lesbian representation, the associations between 'ghosts' and 'girl-loving', as Terry Castle discussed in 1993, prove enduring. What I aim to investigate in this book is whether this tradition has been continued by contemporary authors and filmmakers. I argue that the apparitional status of queer women in Gothic fiction and visual culture remains and sometimes appears as an aesthetic romanticised stasis. However, I will show that the relationship between ghostliness and girl-loving has shifted in the New Queer Gothic to encompass a proliferation of meaning.

Gothic Times with Angela Carter

In 1974, in the afterword to *Fireworks*, Angela Carter wrote 'we live in Gothic times'[35] and since then this quotation has appeared as an epigraph in countless articles and chapters on the value of the Gothic genre. Linnie Blake recently used this quotation to inspire the theme of the 2019 Gothic Manchester festival symposium, 'Gothic Times', which stated in its call for papers that the phrase could not be more apt for times of political uncertainty as currently experienced in the United Kingdom and United States. Fred Botting discusses Carter at length, referring to her famous comment as accounting for the way in which genres like the Gothic, which have been historically relegated to cultural margins, come to be taken more seriously. Botting develops Carter's summation in writing that 'Gothic figures and fictions now circulate with greater visibility to manifest the absence of strict, prohibitive mechanisms or a strong, exclusionary force'.[36] Botting notes that where once the 'restoration of symbolic, normative boundaries was celebrated in the violent climaxes to older tales of terror, monstrous figures are now less often terrifying objects of hate or fear, monstrous others become sights of identification, sympathy, desire, and self-recognition' (pp. 285–6). This certainly speaks to the plots of Carter's subverted fairy tales in *The Bloody Chamber* (1979), while *The Magic Toyshop* (1967), *The Infernal Desire Machines of Doctor Hoffman* (1972), *Nights at the Circus* (1984) and *Wise Children* (1991) all attend to female subjectivity and desire with much use of pastiche and parody, which is crucial to the ways in which postmodernity and the Gothic relate in contemporary literature. Critical attention around how Carter's work has impacted on the Gothic genre tends to figure Carter as changing its form and destabilising its traditional construction. Carter's postmodernity is not only obvious in the style that she uses, but in the playfulness and irony with which she treats Gothic convention and gender politics. The marginalised, maligned and malevolent are rendered, by Carter, as sympathetic and humane, and the systems or institutions that oppress or exclude them are exposed as monstrous, taking on, as Botting describes, 'terrifying, persecutory, and inhuman shapes . . . Transgression becomes just another permitted social activity' (pp. 285–6). This idea really subverts what has been appreciated in the previous century as a generally conservative genre of fiction. Many of the impressions that Carter has made on the world of Gothic studies crucially concern her foregrounding of female subjectivity and the female experience.

Carter's work does not engage explicitly with queer politics because it predates it; she cannot be called a queer feminist, but she is an interesting feminist with a brand of feminism that has famously courted controversy. Carter's novels and short stories are chiefly concerned with presenting female subjectivity as complex and her use of the Gothic mode in relation to representations of gender and sexuality establishes much of theoretical and generic identifiers used to critique contemporary queer Gothic fiction. Works of Carter's that characterise her impact on a study that focuses on female subjectivity and representation, queer sexuality and identity and the Gothic mode include *The Magic Toyshop* (1967), *The Infernal Desire Machines of Doctor Hoffman* (1972), *The Passion of New Eve* (1977), her collection of Gothic fairy tales *The Bloody Chamber* (1979), her long essay *The Sadeian Woman and The Ideology of Pornography* (or, *The Sadeian Woman: An Exercise in Cultural History* – also 1979) and *Nights at the Circus* (1984).

Carter's fiction explores the historical, literary and artistic frameworks through which female subjectivity has been represented. Throughout her oeuvre, the Gothicity of such mechanisms is highlighted by her use of imagery, one example of this can be noted in her deconstructions of the Sleeping Beauty myth in *The Infernal Desire Machine of Doctor Hoffman*. The titular machines, which replay depictions of Pre-Raphaelite subjects; 'images of somnolent and corpse-like femininity', are recognised by Rebecca Munford to recall the imaginings of the Marquis de Sade in their sadomasochistic framing of the Sleeping Beauty and their foregrounding of 'deathly eroticism'.[37] Carter's fiction works to challenge metanarratives of femininity and sexuality by using Gothic themes to describe unequal power structures and subvert the politics and traditional gestures of the Gothic. Munford makes the observation that Carter's Gothic settings, particularly in 'The Bloody Chamber', recalls Sade's *Justine*: she writes that Sadeian Gothic castles are spaces in which women 'become part of the paraphernalia of the Gothic *mise-en-scène*' (p. 53). I would elaborate on this to argue that Carter's reaction to Sade connects her theories on feminist politics and literary form in a very postmodern and playful way; by providing a parody of Sade in her subverted folktales and transgressive fairy-tale narratives, and by working pastiche into the highly stylised prose, Carter calls attention to the Sadeian as both menacing and ridiculous. Carter creates a paradox with which to view women in a Gothic context.

Integral to this book's appreciation of queer feminist politics is the culture created via the Gothic fiction of the female authors discussed in this chapter. There is an argument that Carter's fiction perhaps made more problematic incursions into questions of queerness than it raised questions of interest but does not to her body of work providing textual opportunities to reflect on a time in which ideas about sex, gender and sexuality were very much in flux. Rachel Carroll has analysed the tensions present in *The Passion of New Eve* (1977) between feminist politics and transgender identity, directing readers to the contentions that this particular novel provoked based on its narrative use of violence and rape suffered by the transgender body, the problematic questions of authenticity provoked by the textual contrasting of the two central trans figures, and the novel's presentations of reproductive (hetero)sexuality. Many of these problems, Carroll explains, rely on essential binary constructions of sex that necessarily problematise claims that Carter's fiction can be described as queer. Carter, was, however, pivotal in shifting ideas about female sexuality and agency. Her presentation of desire in some of her later novels is valuable to queer subjectivity, particularly her representations of incest in *The Magic Toy Shop* and *Wise Children*, which each work to deconstruct heteronormative nuclear family constructs and offer nuanced representations of girlhood. Her impact was not, however, limited to the world of fiction. As Jackson did with her memoirs, Carter popularised her ideas about the gender and sexual politics of women in society in non-fictional form as well as in her novels and short story collections.

The Sadeian Woman was written after Carter developed an interest in pornography while living in Japan. The 1970s was a decade characterised by the strong momentum of the women's movement, which gained traction throughout the West; Feminist circles were, however, fraught sites for debate. Chief among the topics for debate were pornography and violence against women. When Carter published a long essay that aimed to demystify pornography so that it might be appreciated as useful to women and to feminism, using the Marquis de Sade's extreme ideas and depictions of explicit sexual violence against women, reactions among other feminist, literary critics and commentators of the time were incredibly polarised. One example of strong criticism came from Susanne Kappler's *The Pornography of Representation* (1986). Kappler believes that Carter dressed up the validation of pornography as the celebration of equal opportunity with literary aesthetics to thrill the intelligentsia and harm real women in society. Linda Williams, on the other hand, claimed to understand Carter's intention not to harm but to take an opportunity in reading the undoubtedly misogynistic Sade and re-appropriating his works. In *Hard Core* (1990), Williams used *The Sadeian Woman* to argue for pornography having positive potential for women. Describing Kappler's and Williams's responses as 'symptomatic and illustrative of the significant role Carter's work has played in the debate'.[38] Sally Keenan qualifies that neither argument does Carter's intentions justice: 'Carter was not looking to Sade for a model, but rather to provide a speculative starting point' (p. 135). Keenan goes on to describe *The Sadeian Woman* (1978) and *The Bloody Chamber* (1979) as 'contrasting sides of the same genre' (p. 136), which is a crucial way of thinking about how Carter used metaphors of meat, anthropomorphic imagery and Gothic aesthetics to synthesise a statement about female agency and power, and the project of emancipating women from the role of victim in patriarchal cultures. Margaret Atwood summarised this point effectively when she wrote: 'It is Carter's contention that a certain amount of tigerishness may be necessary if women are to achieve an independent as opposed to dependent existence; if they are to avoid – at the extreme end of passivity – becoming meat.'[39] Carter was incredibly influential on how female subjectivity connects to metaphors of meat, and these ideas will be returned to in Chapter 5, when this book turns its attention to queering the cannibal in Julia Ducournau's 2017 film *Raw*. Lorna Sage describes the most obviously scandalous implication of Carter's project: 'her conviction that the pornographer de Sade can be made over into an ally in the task of demystification'.[40] With an apparent support for pornography and of perpetuating of some of its themes, Carter was criticised by some critics for the way that her fiction corresponded to Sadeian depictions of graphic violence. Sarah Gamble observes that this kind of reception 'conclude[d] that, in spite of the feminist opinions she started expressing from the late 1960s onwards, she actually only furthers reactionary portrayals of women as nothing more than the objects of male desire'[41] (Gamble, 'Angela Carter'). While many arguably misread *The Sadeian Woman* as an attempt to refigure an archetype of misogyny and pornography as a proto-feminist, Gamble argues that this is an unsurprising and forgivable reaction, commenting on the contentious, challenging and teasing tone that suggests the intention to court controversy, or rather a turn to satire as a pre-emptive tack predicated on inevitable hostility to the subject matter. For example, Gamble describes the 'Polemic Preface' of *The Sadeian Woman* as:

> on one level a perfectly correct summary of Carter's analytical intentions, to a certain extent it also wilfully misrepresents the spirit in which such an analysis is being undertaken, veiling its seriousness in an elaborate display of its own contentiousness. Although Carter later engages in a more rigorously critical anatomisation of de Sade's intentions, here she make sweeping generalisations in language calculated to shock and offend. (p. 101)

This foray into non-fiction writing might have been her most divisively received output, but the debate it provoked has had a lasting effect on the ways in which feminist politics inflect contemporary fiction and Carter's project of demystification has been noted across all the novels that she published in the 1970s. Although the popularity of Carter's work has surged decades after its publication, she can certainly be credited with shaping the culture of textuality in postmodern Gothic fiction dealing with female subjectivity and sexuality. Of *The Passion of New Eve*, *The Sadeian Woman* and *The Bloody Chamber*, Merja Makinen writes:

> [They] engage in extremely complex ways with feminist debates about femininity that were very much of the time. They represent violent women for positive ends, shifting myths of femininity away from passive stereotypes that uphold suffering and victimisation, suggesting instead that there are alternatives . . . the confrontation with female violence creates a productive opportunity to transgress cultural codes. Depictions of women wielding violence can be both demystifying and cathartic. In the 1970s, Carter took the

initiative to show the exhilarating thrill of women's sexual and textual aggression.[42]

This sexual/textual aggression was often bound up in narratives of transformative retribution or metamorphosis. For Gamble, *The Bloody Chamber* is an important text that encompasses gender and feminist politics in the motif of metamorphosis. In Carter's short stories, metamorphosis 'works both ways, for these are not just stories where the once so submissive, so passive, fairytale heroine gets her own back. On the contrary, by giving as good as she gets, the heroine works towards a utopian space where both male and female benefit from the transformation of old power relations.'[43]

British novelists such as Sarah Waters (whose work this chapter also discusses), Jeanette Winterson and David Mitchell have all claimed Carter as a great influence on their own fiction. Her influence can be felt in the way in which she inspires others to write from the margins, inflecting texts with themes of transgressed boundaries and with subversive narratives, but it can also be felt in her hallmark style; magical realism allows for so many of these ideas to be explored. Citing Latin American authors such as Gabriel Garcia Marquez and Alejo Carpentier among her major influences, Carter welcomed the 'magical realist' label that became attached to her work.

Carter's brand of magical realism has become synonymous with transformation and metamorphosis, particularly of the female or androgynous subject. The highly aesthetic, phantasmagoric and the corporeal intersect in Carterian magical realism, this is a tradition followed by the texts that this monograph claims as New Queer Gothic. Carter has become synonymous with phantasmagoria, and this connection has been analysed as linking the cinematic world and the literary world. Laura Mulvey describes such an observation:

> The aftermath of the Enlightenment saw the birth of the Gothic and a proliferation of phantasmagoric technologies. For instance, ghosts were summoned up in special performances in Paris after the Revolution; and magic lanterns and ghost photography fascinated the nineteenth century. Just as the materialisations of irrational fears were swept away from the external world and came to haunt the

interiority of the human psyche, they were re-created through screen images.[44] (Mulvery, 'Cinema Magic')

Here Mulvey writes about Carter having been inspired by films of the 1950s, 'their last decade of supremacy in the Western world' (p. 241), and also discusses the Neil Jordan directed film adaptation, *The Company of Wolves* (1984), which drew on the wolf stories of *The Bloody Chamber* as well as some narrative and characterisation elements from *The Magic Toyshop*, which Carter also adapted into a screenplay for a film of the same name, directed by David Wheatley in 1987. Other adaptations include radio plays based on her various short stories, though *The Company of Wolves* remains her most famous and engaging adaptation. Some criticised *The Company of Wolves* for its overly ambitious use of intertexts, enveloping nods not only to Carter's fiction but to the genealogy of fictional and cinematic werewolves that came before it (see Martin, 2001). Maggie Anwell, in particular, rejected the decision to alter the ending of the film, where the image of a girl sleeping soundly in the arms of a wolf is swapped for the image of two wolves running off together into the forest, calling this a 'coy reluctance . . . to allow an image of successful sexual initiation'.[45] Others have praised its intertexuality and consider it a faithful homage to Carter's text, using it, as Kim Snowden has, as a text for 'cultural pedagogy' purposes. Exposing her undergraduates to the film has allowed Snowden to discuss the feminist contexts and themes of the film, drawing as it does on the complexity of female subjectivity and the expectations impressed on young girls and women, as a means of challenging the ubiquity of postfeminist ideology which obfuscates her students' thinking; Snowden writes, '[p]ostfeminist ideology wants my students to believe that they must choose between being a babe or a feminist bitch',[46] and uses the Carter adaptation in conjunction with other contemporary examples of feminism in contemporary media such as Joss Whedon's American supernatural drama series, *Buffy the Vampire Slayer* (1996–2003) to suggest otherwise (Snowden, 'Fairy Tale'). Carter's Gothic works, especially those with feminist themes, have proved themselves prescient, considering the longevity of their afterlife via adaptation and continued critique.

Maryse Condé's reclaimed Black Witch

While Carter's work performs much postmodern irony in its portrayal of Gothic tropes and figures to give her narratives a feeling of being outside of time and space, Maryse Condé's use of Gothic magical realism is postmodern in its task of reimagining historical figures to give voice and recognise the humanity in maligned people who, in their lifetimes, were denied such agency. In this way, *Moi, Tituba, Sorcière . . . Noire de Salem* (1986) has inspired other works of bio-fiction, such as Rachel Holmes' neo-Victorian biography of Saartje Baartman, *The Hottentot Venus* (2007). *Moi, Tituba* was originally published in 1986 and translated into English in 1992 as *I Tituba, The Black Witch of Salem*.

Condé is best known for her novel *Segu* (1984), which not only provided an important representation of Black excellence but also offered something rare, insightful and powerful to the African diaspora in providing a historical novel about the African content that encompasses a great expanse of time, exploring Africa beyond its associations with slavery. In this way, her novels aim to represent the scope and horror of colonialism rather than the limited depiction often conveyed by fiction. She wanted to understand Africa, and, like many African American authors piqued by the rhetoric of Marcus Garvey's 'Return to Africa' movement in the early 1920s, Condé felt a similar urge to return to where her ancestors lived and be 'reborn' or 'find herself' in Guinea. Like many attempting to retrace heritage and family lines, Condé found that the contemporary Africa she visited was at odds with the mythic idea of the continent represented in fiction and impressed on the minds of those belonging to the African diaspora, as well as the rest of the world. She discusses the impossibility of finding oneself when so few accurate depictions exist to construct a complete picture of African history and culture because of cultural and racial hegemony privileging the colonisers' perspective. Condé's postcolonial literary voice champions polyphonous techniques of narrative and representation, especially when depicting Caribbean culture, which is synonymous with plurality in identity, language and culture.

Having completed her PhD in comparative literature in 1975, which examines Black stereotypes in Caribbean literature, Condé began her literary career later in life and published her first novel at the age of forty. Her novels speak to a mature and well-conceived approach to reclaiming Black history via figures who have been grossly misrepresented in existing historical fiction. Using historical documents from the Salem Witch Trials, Condé offers a postcolonial reimagining of the version of events that casts Black subjects as invisible, peripheral and monstrous. Removing Tituba from racist, colonialist representation, Condé gives voice to a woman previously condemned to silence or to the monstrous representation offered in texts such as Arthur Miller's play *The Crucible* (1953). *The Crucible* presents Tituba as a black magic or Obeh Priestess, whose rituals – which include animal sacrifice, African language incantations and wailing – facilitate the collective hysteria of the Salem women who begin accusing one another of consorting with the devil and practising witchcraft. Miller's Tituba was rarely seen on stage or screen in any of the play's outings or adaptations, yet she is always blamed for whipping up the frenzy with her black arts. The Tituba of Condé's novel is powerful and influential; she is moved from the periphery or off stage to the centre of the narrative where her power and influence can be seen to foster a strong sense of solidarity and support among the slave community or other groups of female characters throughout to novel. Condé herself attributes her appreciation of postcolonial, neo-slave narrative to her Caribbean and Creole identity:

> if you are a creolized person, you have a lot of influences in you. You have the African coming through you because of the science of the magic, the respect for the invisible. But you have been trained by Europeans, so you adopt some of their values. You realize that faith in magical realism is faith in social realism, socialist realism. With all these different influences your inner self is always in a kind of turmoil. You believe in this or that, which seems to contradict another kind of belief, but they can cohabitate in your mind. The words that you are producing are a reflection of all the elements, all the influences that are in you. If you reduce a human being to one single line of thought or opinion, it is petty. Maybe the advantage of being a colonized person is the realization that you have so many things that belong to you: your tradition, something coming from the West, something indigenous to the area where you have been

living – you have to blend all that to express yourself. I don't see a fight, I just see a kind of complexity.[47]

Here Condé presents her reparative approach to postcolonial fiction like hers and underlines the value in recouping narratives of historically maligned figures towards an appreciation of dynamic characterisation; she breathes life into Tituba using magical realism and other 'irrealist' modes to represent the subjectivities of colonised people more accurately, as living beings. In this way, Condé speaks back to the absence of Blackness in white-authored fiction, which speaks volumes to that racial hegemony of whiteness as default central and Blackness as peripheral, and connected to the unconscious, as Richard Dyer argues. *I, Tituba* is a speaking text wherein the reader is encouraged to suspect that its narrator, Tituba herself, is unreliable. As Maha Marouan notes, the effect of the autobiographical narrative is that Tituba functions as both 'the narrator and the narrated . . . speaking directly to readers and establishing a close intimacy with them',[48] but it also poses the question as to whether Tituba's voice can be trusted, since Tituba's autobiography may be read simply as another 'confession' that is meant to manipulate the readers, echoing historic record of the trials.

Interestingly, Condé was not the first to attempt a recouping of the Tituba figure, a woman who, in historical fact, was likely an enslaved Indigenous South American woman whose 'magic' had nothing to do with African Obeh practices. Historical records show her alleged practices were identifiably English, but her racial misidentification corresponded better with American stereotypes of the Black slave woman, and Miller's representation endures in the popular imagination and has shaped public memory and popular culture surround the Salem Witch Trials (p. 113). Since *The Crucible*, at least one other attempt has been made to re-record Tituba's story. In 1964, the African American author Ann Petry wrote a children's book called *Tituba of Salem Village*, which presents an intelligent oppression-battling slave, and transforms her into an aspirational role model figure for children (p. 104). Condé's reimagined novelisation makes further empowering inroads by addressing the impossibility of a full and true recuperation; instead, leaning into the African American identity socioculturally imposed on her to give her, inventing a parentage in giving her Abena, Tituba's Barbadian mother who was raped by a sailor on her journey to the Americas. Marouan describes this assertation as addressing the impossibility of full recuperation 'and locates Tituba's traumatic tale of displacement and enslavement within the larger historical context of the African diaspora' (p. 110). Other critical responses have noted Condé's use of dualities to illustrate 'patterns of mistrust and concept that weave the fabric of racism and cultural misunderstanding in slave societies', as well as her paralleling of modern science and psychiatric ideology replacing the institutional power of the Church and the practice of witch-hunting (p. 116). The queerness that she imagines in Tituba's identity translates textually as a same-sex romance while incarcerated; however, it speaks to Condé's political revisions of the narrative according to historic record. Lizabeth Paravisini-Gebert makes the point that the 'juxtaposition of Christian bigotry and the mysteries of African spirituality that the Salem witch hunt developed' are Condé's key contention.[49] However, I would extend this to include her queerness because of the ways in which her engagement with other women, particularly the white women of Salem, has been historically misrepresented and is in need of redressing. Condé's project of humanising and reclaiming a maligned 'witch' thus functions to furnish contemporary understanding of intersectional identity in narratives of the past and challenges tyrannically authoritative discourses.

Queer Vampires from Anne Rice and Jewell Gomez

Anne Rice's fiction comprises fantasy sagas that draw on the Gothic genre, fairy tales and religious Christian tradition. Her sagas include her series *The Vampire Chronicles* (1976–2018), *The Sleeping Beauty Quartet* stories (1983–2015), *The Mummy, or Ramses the Damned* books (1989–2017), *Mayfair Witches* books (1990–4), *Christ the Lord* books (2005–8), *The Songs of Seraphim* books (2009–10) and *Wolf Gift* chronicles (2012–13). Of all her stand-alone novels and sagas, Rice's vampire fiction is her most popular and is renowned as the first of its kind, sparking an enduring trend in popular vampire fiction, sometimes referred to as contemporary horror or urban

Gothic. Some of the more contemporary examples belonging to this trend show crossovers in genre, mixing elements of contemporary Gothic with detective fiction, science fiction, fantasy and romance, and appeal mostly to a young-adult audience. The list of sagas and series that Rice's work has inspired include, but will unlikely be limited to, the following: L. J. Smith's *The Vampire Diaries* series (1979–2013), Charlaine Harris's *The Sookie Stackhouse* books (2001–13), Kelley Armstrong's *Women of the Otherworld* series (2001–11), Stephenie Meyer's *Twilight* saga (2005–8), J. R. Ward's *The Black Dagger Brotherhood* series (2005–), Rachel Caine's *The Morganville Vampires* series (2006–16), Patricia Briggs's *The Mercy Thompson* series (2006–), Richelle Mead's *Vampire Academy* series (2007–10) and Jeaniene Frost's *Night Huntress* series (2007–15). Rice's *Vampire Chronicles* certainly inspired the burgeoning trend for fantasy fiction writers to reimagine the vampire trope and continue inserting classic Gothic figures – such as vampires, witches and werewolves – into contemporary narratives over the past forty years and has thus proved integral to encouraging Gothic readership into the twenty-first century.

Rice's vampire chronicles centre predominantly on the lives of gay male vampires, Lestat, Louie and Armand, and, while the third book in her series, *The Queen of the Damned*, might be expected to foreground the titular 'mother of all vampires', a pre-Egyptian Queen named Akasha, most of the narrative continues to serve the male characters. In *Interview with the Vampire*, however, Louis and Lestat create for themselves a queer Gothic family by siring a five-year-old girl. Claudia has a firm and necessary place in the genealogy of queer Gothic children and is an important figure for this book. She is gravely overlooked, however, by meaningful criticism, and, as with most child characters who appear in Gothic fiction, she has been engaged with predominantly in psychoanalytic terms. As a child vampire, her corporeality remains unchanged though her subjectivity ages, and the great tragedy of her existence extends beyond the usual precociousness attributed to queer Gothic children. Critics favour reading Claudia as Louis's double, as Sandra Tomc here explains:

> [A]s with Louis, the expansion of Claudia's self generates a radicalized consciousness – a more radicalized consciousness, since her

hunger for plenitude is greater. In the process of her 'growth', Claudia acquires an awareness of her own potential and integrity that culminates in the recognition that she has been 'enslaved' by her 'fathers'.[50] (Tomc, 'Dieting and Damnation')

As a character with so much potential, Rice's development of Claudia is pinned to her relationships with the two male protagonists. This idea relates to Rice's treatment of female characters in the narrative generally: there is often a configuration of attachments predicated on the Sedgwickian triangulation of desire. Tomc agrees with the majority of criticism that has delineated Rice's fiction as ushering in the vampires' domestication, something that she suggests was compounded with the casting of Tom Cruise: a 'squeaky-clean icon of normative masculinity, in the role of the amoral, sexually ambiguous Lestat' (p. 96). What Tomc adds to the criticism surrounding Rice's *Chronicles* is her observation of the problematic deficit of female characters, which she connects to its project of 'bland domestication', facilitated by what might be perceived as the 'revolutionary potential of gender and corporeal metamorphosis [that] liberated Rice's vampires from the stocks of their heritage' (p. 96). While others celebrate Rice for her use of risqué, erotic interplay, reminiscent of homosexuality, Tomc notes that:

> the sexuality of her vampires, in fact, bears little resemblance to the forms of gratification conventionally associated with the interactions of men's bodies. Rather, the vampire's body is something entirely new. It represents a type of polymorphousness and androgyny founded on the disappearance of the markers of sexual and reproductive difference. (p. 98)

Tomc suggests that Rice's narrative actually reads as rather misogynistic, evidenced by such scenes, which exist in both the novel and its film adaptation, as when Lestat dances around with the corpse of Claudia's mother, before they transform the five-year-old girl into their undying daughter: 'This violent demystification of maternal power, centred on the mother's body as something dead and obsolete then opens the conceptual space for the alternative represented by vampire sexuality' (p. 99). Rice's misconceptions of queer identity are suggested by this quotation, alluding to a highly troubling and damagingly stereotypical version of queerness that privileges male homosexuality, where women and female queers cannot occupy the same spaces. Tomc writes that women characters are 'not absent in this novel to just to make a metaphoric point. They present a problem, and to avoid confronting that problem in ways that could compromise the gender-free ideal, Rice simply gets rid of them' (p. 99). Indeed, they are all got rid of, but it is my contention that they only ever existed in essentially gendered roles and in relation to male characters. Rice predominantly wrote mothers and daughters rather than women and girls. Claudia burns to death in the arms of her surrogate mother, and later in the series when Lestat transforms his own mother, Gabrielle, in *The Vampire Lestat* (1985), only to have her depart to travel alone, beyond the main narrative. Gabrielle's transformation reads as a highly eroticised scene with lots of blood and forceful tongue kissing, though this seems only to be included to beat readers over the head with Oedipal inference. Rice hints at the idea of androgyny being afforded to this female character; soon after becoming a vampire, Gabrielle swaps the new dress that her son-turned-maker has brought for her for the masculine clothing of her first male victim. Rice does not, however, develop any queer potential in women beyond this character.

As well as inspiring a whole canon of serialised contemporary Gothic and horror fiction, Rice's *Vampire Chronicles* are important to the subject of *The New Queer Gothic* because of the ways in which they engage with and represent queer characterisation and relationships. As the first popular vampire franchise not only to feature but to foreground homosexuality, Rice's vampire novels continue themes present only in the subtext of classic Gothic works. The tumultuous relationship between protagonists Louis and Lestat, whose sexual attachments are homosexual, first feature in the novel *Interview with the Vampire* (1976). The 1994 film adaptation of the same name, directed by Neil Jordan and starring Brad Pitt, Tom Cruise and Kirsten Dunst, provided an interesting text that achieved cult status and provided a watershed moment for the Queer Gothic genre. However, the fiction on which it is based has been criticised for representations of queerness that implicate conservative values and homophobic ideology. Other vampire fiction franchises have provoked similar criticism in their presentation of right-wing conservatism, gender essentialism and normative sexual mores, all donning the expansive cape of traditional family values.

Some critical engagement with Rice's *Chronicles* notes it as the first progressive depiction of homosexual vampires in contemporary Gothic literature, celebrating the romanticism of the characterisation and sensational plot. The expansive fandom of Rice's vampire fiction revels in the intertextual markers that cultivate the cult of erotic Gothic masculinity. Gail Abbott Zimmerman makes the claim that 'Rice's characters have the ability to transcend gender'[51] in the way that they present gender identity and sexual preference as fluid and malleable (Abbott Zimmerman, 'The World of the Vampire'). As well as representing the homoerotic, Rice's novels belong to a genealogy of Gothic kinship in their entrenchment of the trope of the queer and fractured family, which, 'incestuous and blurred as it is, presents a subversive alternative model to the nuclear family'.[52] The limitations of this, however, invite singularly psychoanalytical readings of the family acting as a signifier for one individual's psyche, usually the patriarch, while other characters languish in existential crises owing to a long-lost autonomy: a decidedly un-queer interpretation of the family and something Rice cannot seem to overcome. Sensationalised family drama, masquerading as nuanced Gothic fantasy, is the reading some prefer, and Rice's flirtation with queer politics is understandably frustrating. George Haggerty writes that '[t]he family has hovered behind all the action of these chronicles, and it emerged in *Memnoch the Devil* as if to mock those who imagined Rice might really give credence to alternative sexualities'.[53] William Hughes has described 'the fractured vampire families of Rice's *Vampire Chronicles* [as having] been eclipsed by the supportive and thoroughly domestic vampire clans of Stephenie Meyer's teenage America',[54] which might suggest that Rice is not wholly to blame for the current popularity of conservative politics in vampire fiction aimed at teens. However, Haggerty argues that Rice's Chronicles have:

> long managed an uneasy relation with conservative politics and the cult of glamour. If not the record of the cultural experience of the United State since the 1980s, they at least offer a precis of some of the nation's deeply held cultural assumptions and an overview of the

banality of transgression in the later twentieth-century. The novels have all the topical urgency of popular fiction as well as the peculiar air of decadence in which Rice specialises. The *sin qua non* with which Rice mesmerises readers, however, is homoerotic desire.[55]

Haggerty explains that the homoerotic relationships that surface throughout Rice's *Vampire Chronicles* function as little more than a symptom of the self-consuming culture that has produced them. Haggerty uses Lauren Berlant and Elizabeth Freeman's notion of 'Americana nervosa' – a means of describing American society's habit or condition of gorging on images of eroticised male bodies as one of many images ritualistically consumed in late twentieth-century capitalist culture (p. 191). Haggerty's reading of the narrative circulates around the 'Glamour' of Rice's vampire characters and how it relates to their eroticised, commodified status in the context of late twentieth-century's cultural conservatism (p. 186–7). For Haggerty, the representation of homosexuality in Rice's *Chronicles* is always culturally determined. Queerness is engaged with via its relation to capital, as well as through its connections to psychoanalytic narratives such as the Oedipus complex.

Jewel Gomez's debut speculative fiction novel *The Gilda Stories* challenges many of the common assumptions, narrative tropes and characterisation that Rice's fiction is guilty of perpetuating. Published in 1991, in the interim between the publication of *Interview with the Vampire* and the release of its glossy Hollywood adaptation, Gomez's vampire novel presents an African American queer female vampire protagonist and a more dynamic and considered iteration of the queer family. Converse to Rice's same-sex parents who wander around devouring Creole and Caribbean sailors and sex workers, Gomez's characters group together with multiple constellations of queer kinship, as discussed in Maria Holmgren Troy, Elizabeth Kella and Helena Wahlström's book, *Making Home: Orphanhood, Kinship, and Cultural Memory in Contemporary American Novels*, which takes *The Gilda Stories* as one of its key texts in exploring orphanhood. Gomez's novel is often critically situated within a small group of texts written by African American women that 'epitomize the outspoken engagement with feminism, art, and racial equality that began in the 1970s but gained impetus in the

1990s and later'.[56] It provides an important counter-narrative to more mainstream works of fantasy fiction; it reflects my intensions in this book of reconciling the marginalisation of certain identities within queer fiction and criticism, but the novel has broader significance as 'literary counter-memory that works forcefully against the pathologization of the black family, in the past, the present and for the future' (p. 195). The novel's speculative projections see the United States as uninhabitable in the future thanks to Euro-American greed, over-consumption and exploitation, and the difficulty of enveloping white Europeans or Americans into an ethical and equal kinship collective speaks to the necessity of having other voices speculate about the world's past, present and future. In this way, *The Gilda Stories* is very much a speaking text, in the vein of Henry Louis Gates's theory of signifyin(g), because it can be observed to be in conversation with other neo-Slave narratives and Black-authored texts, as well as responsive to mainstream works.

Christopher Lewis places Gomez's novel alongside Octavia Butler's *Kindred* (1979) and Toni Morrison's *Beloved* (1987) on that basis that they all:

> engage the antebellum system of enslavement and its legacies as horror in order to emphasize slavery's 'mundane horrors that aren't acknowledged to be horrors' (Sharpe 3) in dominant historical narratives, as well as to demonstrate how white slaveholding society's unwillingness to see enslaved black people as human beings and fellow citizens positioned them as social monsters. However, rather than challenge the association between blackness and monstrosity, as much antiracist writing powerfully and importantly does, these neo-slave narratives interrogate the terms under which one becomes recognizably human in U. S. culture.[57]

Gomez makes the subversive quality of her narrative overt from the outset, having Gilda's mother tell her at the beginning of the novel that the slave-owning whites are 'just barely human. Maybe not even. They suck up the world, don't taste it.'[58] This reveals the politics of the novel as a counter-narrative and a postcolonial talking back, particularly to colonial Gothic texts that cast the non-white racial Other as a symbol of parasitic monstrosity. In subverting this colonial representation, Gomez highlights the terrible conceit of slavery: that the master-slave relationship is, as Orlando Patterson describes it, a matter of 'total parasitism'[59] that enacts the premature death of the slave in the exhaustive extraction of labour.[60] Lewis discusses the legislative practices of slavery as enabling the institution of normative whiteness, reading the default citizen as heterosexual and the Black subject as queer, inferior and, legally, only three-fifths human. He argues that 'Gomez positions white-determined humanity as a terrifying force in *The Gilda Stories*' that functions to challenge 'the utility of aspiring to gender and sexual normality, a social compulsion that emerged in the United States as a means of defining whiteness as superior to blackness' (p. 450). What this subversion does is speak back to existing literature that defers the parameters of personhood and humanity to white privilege and supremacy; Gilda's longevity can be comparable with Rice's vampires, but the radical potential of this enduring queer Black vampire woman provides a direct contrast wherein the notion of living free is facilitated by Black determinism and queer kinship.

For my purposes in this book, I recognise Gomez's novel as ground-breaking to the project of unearthing the origins of the new mode and reading practice of the New Queer Gothic. The Neo-Slave novel is interesting to this project because it demonstrates the sociogenic rather than ontic positioning of slavery, as Sarah Kent describes:

> This echoes the geneses of vampires in popular lore who result from a contaminatory socialization rather than a biocentric reproduction. Vampires are not born vampires; vampires are made. Both 'slave' and 'vampire' struggle between the competing directions of human and other-than-human and are forced to occupy the liminal space in-between.[61]

Like Condé's Black witch, Tituba, Gomez's Gilda can also be appreciated as speaking back to a canon of texts where white hegemony effects Black representation, particularly since white authors dominated vampire fiction. Gomez's Black lesbian vampire protagonist was inspired by the poets of the Black Arts Movement, as well key feminist thinkers at the time, via the literary journals of lesbian activists. She recalls her impulse to mould Gilda into a heroic figure as a further means of transforming 'the pain of oppression into art'; their 'calls to action', Gomez writes, shaped 'Gilda's every act and observation as well as her personal development'.[62] *The Gilda Stories* belong to a group of texts that use neo-slave narratives to engage the legacies of horror from antebellum slavery in the United States and its enduring impact. Lewis appreciates Gomez's novel alongside Octavia Butler's *Kindred* (1979) and Toni Morrison's *Beloved* (1987) to argue that 'rather than challenge the association between blackness and monstrosity, as much antiracist writing powerfully and importantly does, these neo-slave narratives interrogate the terms under which one becomes recognisably human'.[63] *Beloved*, especially, is another text essential to the foundations of the New Queer Gothic since it demonstrated queer kinship and love, focusing on the subjectivities of African American women and escaped slaves in a narrative that whorls through Gothic conventions – with its haunted house and poltergeist – to construct rich tapestries of 're-memory' and collective as well as individual trauma. Paradigms of identity politics were shifting dramatically throughout the late twentieth century and this is reflected in relevant literature of the 1980s and 1990s. We can see the cultural afterlives of Gomez and Condé's in contemporary Queer Gothic television, particularly in the cosmic horror drama series *Lovecraft Country* (2020) and migration narrative series *Them* (2021). I will return to these texts in the Conclusion.

Sarah Waters and Queer Gothic

Sarah Waters is the author of six novels and writes predominantly historical fiction in the Gothic mode. Waters's neo-Victorian novels have received the most attention, both popularly and critically. Her first novel, *Tipping the Velvet* (1998) is set in the 1890s and follows the developing sexuality of its young female protagonist who falls in love with a male impersonator in London. *Affinity* (1999) sees another young, Victorian, female protagonist experience same-sex desire; this time, a middle-class woman falls in love with an incarcerated spiritualist and becomes embroiled in a plot laden with betrayal and malleable identity. *Fingersmith* (2002), the last of Water's Victorian-set novels, follows the burgeoning romance between a maid and a lady whose lives are bound up in a twisted plot with more betrayal, and further explorations into sexuality, agency and subjectivity. The unexpected interweaving of characters' lives is a narrative device that Waters continues to use in her next novel, *Night Watch* (2006), which also features lesbian themes, although it is set in the 1940s. *The Little Stranger* (2014) sees Waters return to the Gothic tone she established in *Fingersmith* and *Affinity*, although this time the plot focuses on the domestic drama of an affluent Warwickshire family in the post-war era and does not concern queer plot or subtext. *The Paying Guests*, Waters's most recent novel, is set in the 1920s and sees a mother and daughter involved in love affairs and crime after they take in lodgers in order to keep their London home. It is clear, then, that Waters's is not an exclusively Gothic author but rather returns to the Gothic throughout her oeuvre, and her most popular novels see her employ an explicitly Queer Gothic tone.

The reinsertion of queer female characterisation into Victorian settings in Waters's historical fiction has provoked fascinating debates on the uses and limitations of neo-Victorian fiction's project of 'writing back' to the Victorian era with regard to contemporary identity politics, particularly the intersections of class, gender and sexual representation. While some critics (Lucie Armitt and Sarah Gamble, 2006; and Cora Kaplan, 2007) have suggested that Waters representations of queerness do not succeed in presenting characterisations of identity and desire that are unbound by heteronormative scripts demonstrative of patriarchal power struggles, other critics celebrate Waters's neo-Victorian fiction for its complicated representation of power and agency, noting in particular its envelopment of Judith Butler's notions of performativity.

Sarah Parker is an example of a critic who believes that writers such as Sarah Waters and neo-Victorian novels such as *Affinity* effectively 'write the lesbian back into tangible existence [by] "repossessing" the spectre of the lesbian towards their own emancipating ends'.[64] Parker begins her article with the 'Queer Victoria principle' – a term coined by Terry Castle relating to the story that Queen Victorian could not believe such a thing as lesbianism existed. Parker frames this as a joke, but a less than jovial punchline follows: that it 'is one of the most powerful discourses distorting the representation of lesbianism to date' (pp. 4–5). She continues in her analysis of lesbian desire and the Gothic genre in Waters's *Affinity* by calling on Patricia Smith's theory of 'homosexual panic'[65] and Gayle Rubin's theories of women losing meaning and value in a patriarchal system.[66] She describes the intersecting politics of class and sexuality in the Victorian setting of the novel:

> [W]hat is at stake for a woman under such conditions is nothing less than economic survival, as the object of exchange is inevitably dependent on the exchanger for her continued perceived worth . . . lesbianism frequently lacks a name, much less an acknowledged or acceptable identity. Accordingly, the fear of the loss of identity and value as object of exchange, often combined with the fear of responsibility for one's own sexuality, is a characteristic response; it is from precisely such fears that lesbian panic arises.[67]

However, Parker argues that this is circumnavigated by the queer characters in *Affinity*, as Waters uses the Gothic genre to challenge the narrative of lesbian panic (p. 7). Parker's reading sees the working-class character Selina use her more marginal status and the 'ghostly lesbianism' with which she is figured to 'escape the patriarchal economic system that the middle-class Miss Prior, to her detriment, remains trapped within' (p. 11). Furthermore, of Margaret Prior's final diary entry and the novel's close, Sarah Parker reads Ruth and Selina's expression of desire as freeing them and enabling them to start new lives together abroad, while Margaret is confined to remain, treated punitively by the novel for her inability to express same-sex desire and break from the bonds of 'homosexual panic'.

Stefania Ciocia makes similar claims about the novel's 'subtle' success in critiquing patriarchal rules and values; although she also writes that if we want to argue that Waters's ultimate goal is to provide positive models of homosexual behaviour, then her critique of 'the double restrictions that [the patriarchy] imposes on homosexual women' is supplemented by her 'unprejudiced representation of her heroines as less than perfect'. In this way, Ciocia reads Waters's queer characters as realist, forgivable, human characters whose defiance may remain only 'skin-deep, while the conservative rules of society get slowly reinstated'.[68] While Waters is celebrated for the act of bringing sensationalist novels in the style of classic Gothic texts to a wider, more diverse audience, and for successfully producing fiction with a cross-over popularity that attracts the attention of popular and academic readers and commentators, there is no universal consensus on how the novel illustrates female sexuality. However, I would argue Waters's deft use of academic research functions valuably as exemplary Queer Gothic fiction, written after and mindful of contemporary queer politics, which is enveloped into its historical setting. The setting allows for avenues into some of the most intriguing mores of lesbian and queer feminist fiction, particularly the Victorian fascination with mediumship and spiritualism, which connects to the cultural legacy of the queer women's representation.

Rachel Carroll has described the representation of late nineteenth-century spiritualism in *Affinity* as 'a performative space in which the incoherence of normative sexual identities are materialized',[69] which allows readers the opportunity to rethink 'the "origins" of both sexual desire and of modern sexual identities' (p. 136). Carroll suggests that *Affinity* is bound by its relationship to the conventions of the sensation novel and the nineteenth-century sensibilities enacted therein. What Carroll refers to as a 'revisionary feminist historiography' becomes, therefore, the aperture through which readers are privy to a reconstruction and representation of the past. Carroll uses the example of the ways in which Waters appropriated the term 'queer' throughout her novel to expand on how such a reconstruction depends on the accounts of the past changing with every endeavour to return to it in the 'complex temporalities of knowledge' (p. 143) in her writing:

> While Waters is no more unknowing about the 'modern usages' of the word queer than her readers, to read queer as simply denoting lesbian would be to evacuate it of its most radical meanings. More interestingly the recurrence of queer moments in *Affinity* have the effect of evoking meanings prior to and subversive of its derogatory meaning; it is placed simultaneously within the late-nineteenth-century continuum of the peculiar and within a

late-twentieth-century continuum of desire, both pre- and postdating its abusive appropriation. (p. 145)

This consideration of the term 'queer' reads Waters's appropriation of it as attached to the praxis of spiritualism in a Gothic refocusing. Rather than restating its attachment to the historical criminalisation of homosexuality, Carroll reiterates its potential to expose the incoherence of normative sexuality. Indeed, Carroll's is one of very few critiques of the novel that offers such a broad reading, where so many have attached *Affinity* very specifically to lesbian subjectivity. The most Gothic contexts of the novel prove to be the prison house and the seance scenes. Therein, the relationship between darkness and sexuality pertains, for Carroll, to the performative nature of all sexual identity: 'The masquerade of heterosexuality staged by the dark circles is not a mask beneath which is concealed a "true" sexuality, whether same-sex or heterosexual; rather it foregrounds the performative nature of sexual identity, the mobility of desire, and the instability of its objects' (p. 142). Although representationally important for lesbian identity, Carroll's argument here persuasively cements *Affinity* in the Queer Gothic mode.

Marie-Luise Kohlke has said of both Carter and Waters that they present a 'metafictional impulse' towards the 'narrativity of history', arguing that 'by centralizing extremely socially marginal characters – a prostitute-turned-circus-star-freak and a closet-lesbian-ugly-spinster-sister – as primary narrators and historical commentators, they metaphorically give voice to the historically silenced and forgotten who have no history'.[70] It is Kohlke's contention that the paltry ways in which marginalised people were 'imagined' out of history warrants historical fiction, and specifically neo-Victorian fiction, a licence to 'imagine' them back in again. However, with regard to the efficacy and value of writing these characters back into settings from which historic record has omitted them, one phrase recurs across criticism: 'utopian promise' (p. 163), something attributed to Waters's historic fiction. This term drives at what is on offer to the queer reader, or the spectator of Waters's adaptations, and gives us pause to assess what transformative or subversive potential such projects have. It is my argument that Waters's queer narratives are most effective when the Gothicity for the Victorian sociocultural setting reflects the power inequalities in contemporary society; without their Gothic furnishings, same-sex romance would read as rather utopic and twee.

Helen Davies's analysis of Waters's fiction focuses on ideas of agency and voice via her central thesis of ventriloquism in neo-Victorian fiction, which works to question the extent to which the project of 're-voicing' actually constitutes a transformation, considering the ways in which *Tipping the Velvet* and *Affinity* can be appreciated as re-presenting some of the narrative mechanisms and politics of their Victorian intertexts.[71] Davies considers the prison visits, mediumship and seances in *Affinity* as 'ventriloquial exchanges' and suggests the two roles that are composite in such exchanges – the 'ventriloquist' and 'dummy' – are 'available for appropriation and resignification' (p. 117). While Carroll reads the use of a male-gendered spirit guide, in Peter Quick, as an opportunity to parallel Ruth and Selina's encounters with enactments of 'heterosexual rituals of desire',[72] Davies contends that '[a]ltering the sex of the ventriloquist does not change the script of objectification and manipulation of women'.[73] Herein lies the failure of Waters's attempts at that 'utopian promise' that most critical perspectives agree on: her framing of queer subjectivity within narratives restricted, historically, by patriarchal and heteronormative scripts fundamentally problematises easy assimilation.

Concerns for how some of the pornographic elements that feature is Waters's fiction might be appropriated by different audiences is noted by Ann Heilmann and Mark Llewellyn in their 2010 book, *Neo-Victorianism: The Victorians in the Twenty-First Century, 1999–2009*. Discussing the serialised BBC adaptation of *Tipping the Velvet* (2002) and the attention that it attracted for a notably erotic scene featuring a Victorian sex toy, leads the authors to conclude that the adaptation 'will be remembered as much for the golden phallus/dildo as anything about the narrative of women's rights presented in the novel'.[74] Davies develops this, arguing that whereas Waters may be appreciated as 'deploy[ing] neo-Victorian ventriloquism to "talk back" to the hetero-centric tropes of pornography, this re-voicing comes perilously close to being recited as an instrument of the very patriarchal script it attempts to re-articulate'.[75] Indeed, this notion also applies to the erotic scenes of same-sex love in the BBC's subsequent adaptation of *Fingersmith* (2005) and has been at the centre of further debate after director Chan-wook Park transported the action of the neo-Victorian novel to 1930s Korea with *The Handmaiden* (2016). While stylised and beautifully shot, the questions of spectatorship and hegemonic gaze continue to pervade Waters's adaptations. However, as this book testifies, these questions provoke an ongoing conversation about the ways in which queer female subjectivity is represented in contemporary fiction and visual culture. I will speak to the functions and politics of pornography because it is a crucial topic of discussion to the study of sexual representation encompassing notions of female subjectivity and queer sexuality.

Like *Affinity*, Water's subsequent novel, *Fingersmith* (2002), also presents lesbian desire and characterisation in the context of Victorian England, and investigates sexuality alongside class, gender and questions of power and agency. Paulina Palmer has described Waters's rich crafting of the neo-Victorian narrative as successful because of its intertextual envelopment of aspects and episodes from classic Gothic texts, like Wilkie Collins's *The Woman in White* (1859) and Charles Dickens's *Bleak House* (1852). Palmer observes the reparative effects of Waters's transformative engagement with these texts that marginalised the female attachments in focusing on the 'heteropatriarchal family', where Waters foregrounds the sexual aspect of Sue and Maud's relationship as the prime narrative that works to 'challenge and eventually supplant the masculinist-inflected narrative'.[76] Kaplan refers to the significance of Waters's use of intertextuality, describing her references to other texts as bold and self-confident pastiche, and explains that Waters conveys her political message well: Waters wrote her PhD dissertation on historical lesbian fiction and it is clear from her own fiction that this research led her to discover a great deficit in representation, and so she imagined one instead. In challenging the metanarrative of Victorian literature, Waters presents a reserved authorial persona in writing pastiche.[77] Rather than the lesbian utopia attributed to *Tipping the Velvet* in much of its criticism, Kaplan describes *Affinity* as a Victorian dystopia 'portraying at every class level a female world of large and small tyrannies and injustices, where even the women who escape are bound together by forms of domination and submission' (p. 112). What is important to remember in this reading of Water's neo-Victorian novels, and what highlights their appeal to queer readers, is, as Kaplan notes, the nuances of desire and betrayal in very complex female characters: 'In all three novels the Victorian setting provides a space for Waters to emphasise the sadistic – if not necessarily the masochistic – side of masculinity and femininity' (p. 112). Not only is same-sex subjectivity explored in her fiction, but the complicated economy of gendered and class identity is given space as well, with the effect of subverting character stereotypes found traditionally in the Victorian novel, which have been embedded in our culture and broadly made the representation that Waters imagines a difficult undertaking. Kaplan writes that Waters 'deliberately makes it hard for her readers to distinguish between what is disturbing and what is comfortable in her writing, what disrupts or confirms subjectivity or historicity'. Much of this encouraged discomfort hinges on the paradox of the Victorian context, 'simultaneously a site of social oppression, subjective development [and] literary exuberance' (p. 115) in relation to queer erotics. *Fingersmith*'s ending is an ambivalent re-purposing of that which was used throughout the narrative as a tool of systemic oppression for women and particularly lesbians, where their sex acts were appropriated by and for the gratification of men. The final scene sees Maud teaching Sue literacy with her uncle's pornography collection; her aim is to continue the family business of collecting, forging and circulating pornography. While this ending has divided critics, it symbolically reflects Waters's intentions in her choice of form and subject matter to present a reparative pastiche where necessary questions about agency, subjectivity and authority are raised.

In this chapter I have provided an overview of the ways in which a selection of women authors from the twentieth century and the twenty-first century have shaped the landscape of contemporary Gothic literature. Each of these authors has provided texts that explore the subjectivities of women, girls and queer characters via Gothic narratives. Jackson's legacy provokes us to be cognisant of the ways in which women in Gothic fiction relate to domestic spaces. With *The Haunting of Hill House* and its film adaptation, Jackson and Robert Wise provided queer culture with a richly psychoanalytic image of desiring women not only restricted by the Gothic house and plot but also given the opportunity to touch a firmly established locus of queer expression. Jackson's writing has also encouraged us to think about the apparitional and supernatural status of the lesbian in contemporary adaptation and representation of Gothic texts. Because the representation of same-sex desire has been historically connected to ghostliness and the apparitional, as discussed by Castle and White, Jackson's legacy reminds us to recognise this trope and wonder at the mechanisms and politics of representation through which we view queer women in the Gothic. While Jackson's oeuvre certainly brought female subjectivity and desire to the fore in post-war Gothic literature, Carter's fiction carried on this tradition with a stronger focus on subverting meta-narratives of femininity and sexuality. Carter's influence is significant because she developed a Gothic aesthetic replete with Sadeian pastiche, inflected by her own brand of feminist ethics concerned with re-positioning Gothic heroines as aggressors as opposed to victims. Carter's writing was foundational to the New Queer Gothic in the way in which it introduced an overt feminist politics to contemporary postmodern Gothic literature. Rice's *Vampire Chronicles*, however, suggest a post-feminist ethics with the sparse and limited characterisation of girls and women. Despite girls and women figuring predominantly in relation to the queer male protagonists, Rice did provide the Queer Gothic canon with an important Gothic child in the character of Claudia, and sparked a whole subgenre of gothic literature. Vampire fiction has since become one of the most popular subgenres of popular Gothic literature among young adults and adults alike. Rice's writing, and the criticism it provoked, leaves a legacy of discourse on the relationship between fetishised homosexuality and role of Gothic literature within mainstream and popular culture. While Rice's fiction provides examples of queer desire and kinship that marry neatly with Sedgwick's early theories of homosocial desire and the triangulation of desire, Sarah Waters is the only author whose writing can be said to have been influenced by queer theory. Waters's project of writing queer women into a Victorian setting is an important one, without which my investigations would not be possible, not least because *Fingersmith* is the source text of one of this book's exemplary New Queer Gothic texts – the postcolonial transformative adaptation *The Handmaiden* – but also because of the deft way in which Waters introduced an ambivalent re-appropriation of sexual mores like pornography. The ways in which Carter and Waters have threaded themes of pornography into their literary aesthetic has set a tone of radical feminist politics in a Gothic context. Because Waters's fiction relates explicitly this to lesbian and queer subjectivity, it is appropriate to situate these women authors within the same genealogy as the texts that I explore in the six subsequent chapters of this book.

2

Miles away from Screwing? The Queer Gothic Child in Florence and Giles

The rectum may be a grave, but that hardly keeps it from speaking. The catachrestic lips, by contrast, can only speak as that which they are not ... they both mark the abyssal negativity the rectum names and, at the same time, dramatize the necessity of speaking otherwise.[1]

Florence and Giles (2010) is a transformative reworking of the 1898 Henry James novella *The Turn of the Screw*. English author, John Harding, sets his neo-Victorian novel in 1891, in a New England mansion called Blithe, and provides consistent homages to the classic Gothic novella. Harding's tale centres on the lives of orphan titular children, whose situation and characterisation are inspired by James's characters, Miles and Flora. Ellis Hanson has dubbed the children in *The Turn of the Screw* 'literary milestones ... in that they mark a most distinguished beginning to the tradition of the sexual child as gothic conundrum in the English novel'.[2] The critical attention given to James's Gothic children is plenteous, with Shoshana Felman (1977), Beth Newman (1992) and Agnieszka M. Soltysik (2008) giving fascinating readings that focus on the artful crafting of ambiguity, unease and paranoia. Hanson notes the complicity foisted upon the reader following the paranoid mania of the governess. She believes that Miles and Flora were altogether 'too close' with their now deceased guardians – a valet named Peter Quint and a governess named Miss Jessel. This couple, who are assumed to have been having a sexual affair, are feared to have corrupted the children with knowledge of their activities and to continue such corruption posthumously, with the governess implying that their spirits haunt and even possess the bodies of the children. There is no doubt that *The Turn of the Screw* presented readers with a Gothic tale about queer children, as have adaptations of the text in the twentieth century, most notably Jack Clayton's 1961 film *The Innocents*.[3] In *Florence and Giles*, a similar narrative unfolds as the reader is invited to walk a tightrope between the worlds of paranoid fantasy and moral panic. Florence becomes increasingly fearful that her new governess, Miss Taylor, plans to kidnap and eat her brother, Giles. While the assumption of cannibalistic paedophilic desire might suggest phantasmagorical embellishments in Florence's tale (or perhaps a history of sexual abuse suffered and internalised by Florence), they also reflect her own queer desire and notions of identity as she continues to build evidence to support her theory of Miss Taylor's malevolent agenda. Florence strives to protect what I shall describe as her 'queer family unit' by stowing away her little brother and murdering Taylor. As with the 'accidental' murder of Miles in the crushing embrace of James's governess, this murder is presented as a necessary means of protecting children who are presumed threatened by supernatural and sexually malevolent forces.

The Queer Gothic girl of New Queer Gothic fiction is a critically and symbolically potent and dynamic figure. It is the aim of this chapter to explain the significance of this figure to the overall politics of representation and theoretical debate of the New Queer Gothic, and to start to discuss what opportunities for critique this recognisable figure and her aesthetic motifs induce. The child, more broadly, is a provocative figure and symbol that is often used in nineteenth, twentieth and twenty-first century literature to convey a paradox of sexuality and innocence. The adolescent girl is a more provocative and complicated figure still; this is because of the contexts within which she has historically been represented.

Florence, of *Florence and Giles*, seems to be a product of the fictional Gothic characters who came before her, as well as a product of the discourse around the specific gendering of erotic childhood, which this chapter argues evolves into a defiant queerness in its contemporary incarnations. Through looking at the historical representation of same-sex desire as something that could be taught, and investigating the attitudes around gender and child sexuality in the nineteenth century, this chapter will work to unpack the queerness of the novel's protagonist, arguing that a queer reading of this Gothic transformative text allows an investigation into the troubles and fissures replete in queer feminist critique.

Before continuing with this chapter's readings of the novel's use of form and genre, as well as its demonstrative use of queer themes, it is important to highlight some contextual theory. There are two types of 'Queer' (at least) that need careful consideration when offering any kind of queer reading of any text. Lynne Huffer delineates mindful consideration towards the types of 'queer' in the introduction of her book *Are the Lips a Grave*, charting the rise and institutionalisation of intersectionality happening in the academy and various feminist circles since the 1980s. This process, Huffer recognises, meant that identity and difference were more fraught, troubled, contested and shifting than ever: 'this well-known problem of difference produced shifts in feminist scholarship that were nothing short of paradigmatic'.[4] With the emergence of queer theory, which became part of this process in the 1990s, Huffer notes its import has two axes or perspectives:

> It can be seen either as a part of the larger intersectionality paradigm shift within feminism or, alternatively, as the birth of a discrete field separate from feminism . . . If conceived as one of many possible pre-existing paths that meet at an intersection, queer sexuality can be and is attached by some to a subject with an identity: a fraught, contested, troubled, performative, unstable, shifting, marginalised identity, but a subject with identity, nonetheless . . . If, one the other hand, one conceives of queer theory as following the cracks in subjectivity's foundations all the way down, queer theory's relation to intersectional feminism becomes more fraught. In this version of queer theory there are neither selves not intersections, just an abyssal undergrounding that not only troubles identity but undoes subjectivity itself. (pp. 14–16)

The latter perspective of queerness repudiates the terms that make intersectional feminism a comprehensible possibility in establishing itself an anti-foundational and poststructuralist means of thinking about sexuality, divorced completely from the foundational feminism that undergirds intersectionality. To put this more simply, queerness can inform identity and subjectivity, but it is, at the same time, a means of rejecting identity and of seeking alternative desubjectivation. The anti-foundational and anti-relational branch of queer studies is usually associated with terms like 'negative' and 'antisocial', and queer critics such as Jack Halberstam and Jose Munoz critique anti-relational queer theorists like Leo Bersani and Lee Edelman for perpetuating an exclusive canon of white masculinity that foundational approaches lament. However, Huffer agrees with Edelman's stance 'that the differences between the intersectional and the antisocial strands of queer theory revolve more around differing investments in subjectivity that they do around success or failure in diagnosing an unjust present order' (p. 17). Mindful as she is of anti-foundationalist queer theory's problems when it comes to canonisation, exclusion and marginalisation, Huffer uses this 'anti-relational' strand of queer theory to intervene in rifts occurring between feminism and queer studies: 'to suggest that the institutionalisation of intersectionality as the *only* approach to gender and sexuality that takes difference seriously masks intersectionality's investment in a subject-making form of power knowledge that runs the risk of perpetuating precisely the problems intersectionality had hoped to alleviate' (p. 18).

To help salve rifts, Huffer calls on a combination of Michel Foucault's and Luce Irigaray's notions of ethics and genealogy to develop her own queer feminist ethics. Irigaray believes that Western culture was founded on the murder of the mother, thus producing an absence of maternal genealogy at the level of the symbolic. She has claimed that Western metaphysics both produces and masks the constitutive absence at its source, stating that such a constitutive absence is sexed: 'In light of this absence, women are always residual and derivative: they can only appear as defective copies of men or as the objects of exchange that secure masculine homosocial bonds' (p. 4). The absence that Huffer discusses is a violent one, which, following Irigaray, she claims produced sexual difference.

Considering this diagnosis of genealogical absence, Huffer chooses a queer feminist genealogy as a means of resistance to the idea that queer theory and feminism should part ways entirely. The themes in *Florence and Giles* reflect these troubles, fissures and desires. It is significant that Florence's queerness is first represented by her isolation; she literally lacks any kind of maternal genealogy and is both 'residual' in her apparitional characterisation and 'derivative' in her very status as a transformative adaptation of the Gothic or the Queer child.

'Getting to be quite the young lady':
The Queer Gothicity of Neo-Victorian Girlhood

Louisa Yates uses the term 'queer' to describe non-traditional family units and elaborates on Weston's (1997) notion of 'families of choice' to include 'lesbian and gay families, single parent families, families with adopted or fostered children, or any familial unit that may not contain anyone strictly related to one another but who nonetheless maintain kinship-like relations'.[5] Yates links the figure of the neo-Victorian child to contemporary debates around 'civil partnerships, adoption rights, and child protection issues' (p. 94). She argues that 'rather than a turn to marriage, neo-Victorian fiction tends towards the articulation of non-reproductive sexual practices outside the state of matrimony'. She describes her chosen texts (*Tipping the Velvet* (1998) and *The Crimson Petal and the White* (2002)) as those which 'seek to "deprivilege" marriage as the optimum environment for the child' (p. 97). Using Lee Edelman's polemic against 'reproductive futurism', to which this chapter will return, Yates concludes that 'the ability to reproduce – especially in a nineteenth-century system that had neither artificial insemination nor effective birth control – does not equal an investment in reproductive futurity; the opposite may be just as true' (p. 115). This significant reading of neo-Victorian queer families and narratives supports my argument that *Florence and Giles* presents a new and exciting figure in the New Queer Gothic girl. Unpacking the queer challenges posed to the genres and theoretical frameworks this Queer Gothic girl straddles will be the objective of this chapter.

As a contemporary neo-Victorian novel that plays so overtly with the gender of the archetypal queer child, *Florence and Giles* raises many questions about how girlhood has been perceived historically and how it continues to be perceived. Of course, *The Turn of the Screw* already belongs to an established tangent of Gothic studies that I described in the Introduction; namely, the female Gothic. The term was first coined by Ellen Moers in her 1976 book *Literary Women*. What began with Moers's definition – 'the work that women writers have done in the literary mode that, since the eighteenth century, we have called Gothic',[6] pertaining to such women authors as Sophia Lee, Ann Radcliffe and Mary Shelley – can now be recognised to encompass other Gothic works not limited to female authorship. Gothic heroines such as James's governess, Brontë's titular *Jane Eyre* (1847), Cathy in *Wuthering Heights* (1847), Mrs de Winter in *Rebecca* (1938) and Hitchcock's film adaptation (1940), and, more recently, Edith in Guillermo del Toro's *Crimson Peak* (2015) all feature women as protagonists and prime investigators of the unsettling or macabre plots that envelop them, usually within big Gothic mansions populated by various kinds of ghost. Rather than choosing the curious and astute young women in search of truth and explanation, Harding offers us Florence, a very lonely girl of twelve. Her precocious intelligence and active imagination place her in the same predicament as most girls her age growing up in nineteenth-century middle and upper-class households; they have no proper outlet to express themselves:

> I lonelied my way around the big house, opening doors and disturbing the dust in unslept rooms. Sometimes I would stretch myself out on a bed and imagine myself the person who had once slumbered there. Thus I peopled the house with their ghosts, phantomed a whole family, and, when I heard unidentified sounds in the attic above me, would not countenance the idea of mice, but saw a small girl, such as I must once have been, whom I imagined in a white frock with a pale face to match, balleting herself lightly across the bare boards.[7]

This melancholy account of her life at Blithe House suggests that Florence understands her own subjectivity as rather arbitrary and ephemeral. She positions herself as a ghost, attempting to assuage her own loneliness with a dissociative fantasy that enables her to people the house all by herself, in turn shirking her own non-identity to become those other phantom people. Her framing of herself as apparitional not only calls attention to the great sorrow of her orphaned and overlooked childhood – she has never met her uncle and benefactor and is told that he has no desire to ever meet her – but also establishes her supernatural status, something that she exploits to bolster her confidence and precocious power over the adults in her life.[8]

One significant deviation from the narrative of the source text is the omission of the ghosts of Quint and Jessel. With the absence of any suggestion that the children in *Florence and Giles* are influenced by the ghosts of a dead valet and governess, an alternate reason for Florence's malevolence towards her new governess and her arbitrary attitudes to the lives of others is offered to the reader as singular and inherent lack of empathy. Qualities like these appear as common tropes of the Queer Gothic child, especially one who is depicted as losing innocence in gaining knowledge, rather than possessed by other entities. Steve Bruhm uses Anne Rice's Claudia of *Interview with the Vampire* (1976) as an example. Owing her knowledge of activities such as hunting and feeding, and her awareness of erotic desire, Bruhm describes her as 'like the other children who are not possessed by evil but just are evil', Claudia proves that the 'Gothic child is not only not blank, but the information buried in the layers of the unconscious will return from its grave to destroy the stability we enjoy'.[9] The corrupting, destabilising force described here perhaps suits the vampire child, but Florence is human and all too adamant about her own innocence, even in murder.

Of course, the notion of inherently 'evil' children, a product of religious and medical discourses becoming ever-more fixed meta-narratives in nineteenth-century Western societies, is a theme that Harding intentionally plays with. By insinuating that Florence's actions might have a lot to do with developing anxiety disorders, an anachronism imposed by Harding, and malformed social behaviours brought about by neglect and extreme isolation, Harding tempers the image of Florence as a supernatural child, with the equally objectifying assumption that she is pathological. The status of her mental health is mentioned when Florence explains her somnambulism and recurring nightmares early on in the text:

> After I had nightwalked three or four times and it had began to be a pattern, they called in Dr Bradley . . . He pronounced me fit and well and told them it was likely the manifestation of some anxiety disorder, which was only natural considering my orphan status and the upheavals of my early life. This was confirmed, he said, by my fears focussing upon Giles, who was afterall, the only constant person in my life.[10]

In her glib understanding of her condition, Harding shows Florence to be aware of her own psychology and in doing so begins weaving the threads of the narrative together to offer an image of Florence's Queer Gothic characterisation: her anxieties manifest themselves slowly from the world of her dreams to her subjective reality. From nightmares to paranoid delusions, these manifestations reflect anxieties about losing her little brother and being totally alone in the world. Harding employs a textual mirroring between Florence's reflections of herself and her visions of the new governess, Miss Taylor, as a witch or a ghoul. Her obsessive need to be close to Giles brings on a jealousy that leads her to suspect Taylor of the incestuous and cannibalistic drive to possess and keep her brother. This is exposed as the core of the anxieties about herself that she projects onto her governesses, ultimately to justify her murder. With this gloss of the queer reading, this chapter looks at a number of concerns: the first pertains to the relationship between the theoretical frameworks used to analyse a text and the fictional text itself; the second to the problem of conflating discourses of pathology and queerness. Shoshana Felman (1977) makes the astute observation that because James's novella lends itself so well to psychoanalytic readings, these have dominated its criticism. Moreover, the Gothic child is typically read through psychoanalysis as a kind of metonym for 'a certain version of the unconscious', as Sue Walsh reminds us.[11] She connects the Gothic child's relation to the unconscious with its uncanniness, explaining that it is in being given the role of securing adult selfhood that the child has its connection with the 'Gothic', since both have been read as embodying the unconscious as something there waiting to be revealed by the critical act (p. 190). Virginia Blum calls psychoanalysis 'the story of the adult's relationship with an internalised, repudiated, but nevertheless ceaselessly desired child'.[12] *Florence and Giles* is indebted to a that which has already facilitated crucial dialogues between how critics relate text and theory. Following Walsh (2007), it is my intention to provide different ways of thinking about the Gothic child in order to open new dialogues.

Harding positions his neo-Victorian novel as a direct descendent of the Jamesian Gothic, though the form of the novel differs considerably from the source text. In James's novella, a frame narrative structure is used that suggests that the main events have been told and retold as a ghost story. The first narrator is unnamed, but then introduces the second narrator, Douglas, who tells the tale of *The Turn of the Screw*. Thereafter, the governess is the principal narrator, describing events through flashbacks and in dialogue with a confidante character, Mrs Grose.

James's novel is famous for the world of ambiguity, doubt and paranoia that it creates. In Harding's novel, the narrative apes the governess's subjective viewpoint, though it offers a playful, self-referential and intertextual knowingness of the unreliability of that single subjective viewpoint. At intervals, Florence will admit her fanciful imagination – 'At least I think that's what happened'[13] – though showing no real concern for her inability to discern between reality and fantasy: 'I misremember how much of the above I eavesdrop and how much my mind just made up, as it is wont to do' (p. 14) In Harding's novel, roles are reversed and the story is told from the child's perspective, as she becomes ever watchful and suspicious of her new governess. Where James's governess would divulge her fears to her confidante, Mrs Grose, Florence's concerns are shared with a new confidante character in the form of Captain Hadleigh, one of the few original characters in the transformative text and not inspired by one of James's existing players. Captain Hadleigh was chief inspector investigating the death of the children's previous governess, Miss Whitaker, who Florence often reminds the reader 'tragicked upon the lake'. Hadleigh is also a plot device whose purpose is to affirm readers' reasonable doubts about the veracity of Florence's narration; he suggests a version of events in which Whitaker's death was not an accident, but an unprovable murder committed by the child. Later in the novel, Harding shows Florence practising the manipulation of adults, where flattery and flirtation are heavily implied: 'he had knight-in-armoured me . . . he looked at me as if I were his special study, an enigma only he could solve' (p. 130). Suspected by Hadleigh as a child murderess, his willingness, nevertheless, to assist Florence suggests his attraction to her and her queer self-awareness: 'his face was close to mine. His breath smelt of milk and cinnamon, which somehow comforted me' (p. 142). Here, Harding suggests to the reader Hadleigh's extreme proximity to the child, the child's apparent sensory pleasure at that proximity, and choice to include such an expression of warm feeling in her narration. As established, Florence's unreliable subjective is much like the governess in *The Turn of the Screw*; however, where the former incited moral panic in the reader and even a complicity in thinking the children into scenarios of sexual abuse and spiritual possession, Florence's subjective aligns the reader with a little girl who desires company, of all things, and who seems particularly interested in the company of intelligent adults.

While it is important to critique the relationships between child and adult figures through various theoretical perspectives, some writers, such as James Kincaid, err on a problematically anachronistic form of reading, which Catherine Robson sidesteps:

> The beginning of widespread cultural interest in the child and the recognition of the figure of the pedophile are not simultaneous events, but are separated by over a hundred years. The point is not to deny that sexual desire may be present in the gentleman's obsession with the child, but to ask questions about the cultural origins of that desire, to consider what else that adult interest might be signifying in the period before the pronouncements of medicalized discourse effectively closed down all explanations other than the diagnosis of individual pathology.[14]

The nuances of child-loving culture present in Victorian fiction are undermined by some contemporary understandings dominated by a pathological discourse that simply did not exist in the nineteenth century. Something was happening in the social psyche during the nineteenth century that catalysed yet prefigured much of the moral panic around child sexuality occurring in the twentieth and twenty-first centuries. Child-loving in the nineteenth century, according to Kincaid, was essentially genderless, the erotic child as it entered representation via visual culture, through comics and serials, whether nominally depicted as male or female, merge 'toward (though not duplicating exactly) an androgynous oneness, the perfect erotic child'.[15] However, girlhood in the 1890s was certainly in cultural flux, and the relationship between Florence and Hadleigh recalls the numerous cases of girl-loving present in nineteenth-century literature. Robson charts and analyses this 'idealisation and idolisation of little girls', which she describes as 'long acknowledged features of the Victorian era'.[16] Robson argues that this phenomenon 'cannot be thought of without reference to a pervasive fantasy of male development in which men become masculine only after an initial feminine stage. In this light, little girls represent not just the true essence of childhood, but an adult male's best opportunity of reconnecting with his own lost self' (p. 3). The little girl of Harding's novel sits in a genealogy of the 'ideal' little girl written by Ernest Dowson, John Ruskin or Lewis Carroll: little girls who have always been critiqued through the binary frame of innocence and subversion. With the death of these three authors at the turn of the century, Robson marks the death of the fetishised little girl, which ushers in a new figure to represent the erotic child: the little boy.

Robson explains that as early as 1884, with the impact of journalist W. T. Stead's account that influenced the ages of consent amendments, there was a new need 'to satisfy the desire to establish an all-inclusive realm of protected girlhood', therefore, 'all girlhood, paradoxically, has to be viewed through the lens of sexuality' (p. 14). Cast in this light, girls no longer play the same role in Victorian psyche and their pinnacle status representing idealised innocence becomes obfuscated. Robson describes the girl's innocence as being 'discussed and legislated out of existence', which led to her fall from grace at the close of the nineteenth century (p. 15). It makes some sense then, to follow Robson, that the idealised gender of the quintessential eroticised child that graduated from little girl in the nineteenth century, to little boy in the twentieth century, would in twenty-first century fiction require another transformation or re-evaluation contingent on how contemporary society appreciates the gendered and sexual identity of children. However, Robson's argument is not beyond problematisation. Perhaps Dowson, Ruskin and Carroll are not representative of the general picture of masculinity in the Victorian period, but they are certainly voluble examples.

Kincaid writes that by the Victorian period, the new dividing lines in the construction of childhood seem 'to have achieved general currency under the name of puberty' signalled by developments in 'liquidity': menstruation for girls and 'nocturnal emissions' for boys. 'The dividing parameters,' he states, were 'like the child itself . . . first of all constructed, and second, often constructed sexually.'[17] Carol Mavor develops this conceptualising of parameters, comparing those of the child – 'the solidly false, as solid as they are false', as proffered by Kincaid – to those of the less definable adolescent. As opposed to 'the fantasy of the child', which she describes as 'pure tabula rasa . . . ripe and ready for our own pre-determined inscriptions',[18] Mavor argues that adolescence is 'smudged by sexuality, changing bodies and bodily fluids' (p. 21). In her measuring of descriptions, Mavor uses the 'blank page' metaphor, suggesting that the adolescent us no longer defined by notions of innocence, or lack of knowledge. She is talking about constructions in the nineteenth century, but the logic links to Claire Kahane's assessment of differentiating between boys and girls in Gothic fiction:

> While the male child can use the very fact of his sex to differentiate himself from this uncanny figure, the female child, who shares the female body and its symbolic place in our culture, remains locked in a more tenuous and fundamentally ambivalent struggle for a separate identity. This ongoing battle with a mirror image who is both self and other is what I find at the centre of the Gothic structure.[19]

Kahane discusses how Gothic child characters are figured in relation to an uncanny mother and suggests the girl's subjectivity, her independent sense of self, to be contingent on her relation to this figure. Harding certainly dramatises this dynamic, as will be made evident later in this chapter's analysis of the doubling that occurs between Florence and her new governess.

The Queer Gothic Child

Investigating the figure of the Queer Gothic girl through the theoretical lenses of feminism and queer theory attends the contested and abstruse topic of the sexual liberation of children. Abigail Bray writes that much of the literature around this expresses the persistent theme 'that the social construction of childhood innocence erases children's sexual rights and subjectivity in the name of protection while intensifying the eroticisation of innocence'.[20] Bray makes the case that feminist perspectives on narratives of child sexuality have been marginalised; that the idea that 'paedophilic desire [as] a mainstream ex-nominated heterosexual norm remains largely unspeakable' and writers prefer to imagine the child as a highly theoretical object: 'reduced into a malleable third person singular: "children" become "the child" who becomes "it"' (p. 177). Bray accuses Hanson of this very objectification in 'Screwing with Children in Henry James', the article that first inspired this chapter, due to his genderless reference to children as a synecdoche of sexual freedom and new sexual beginnings. Bray argues that 'it is precisely this very exclusion of the abject history of sexual harm against children that enables the glamorisation of child/adult sex as a heroic transgression of repressive sexual norms' (p. 178). Rachel Carroll elaborates on these notions and illustrates the landscape of disparate stances on how our culture appreciates and represents child sexuality:

> Age of consent laws have constructed what counts as an intergenerational relationship in different ways for heterosexual and homosexual people regardless of actual consent by individual agents. For feminists the sexuality of girls is in need of protection from abuse by adult men in a patriarchal culture; for gay rights and queer activists the campaign is against the repression of queer children's sexuality in a homophobic world. The confluence of different contextual influences and political priorities has constructed intergenerational sexuality as the site of specific tensions between feminist and queer perspectives. The term itself is contested and originates in queer contexts where it fore-grounds ambiguities of generational and sexual identity – ambiguities which feminist frameworks for the analysis of child sexual abuse might see as problematic.[21]

Carroll clarifies that 'the use of "cross-generational" as a signifier for transgressive sexuality seems to risk the elision of the consensual and the coerced' and this is one of the key concerns of feminist perspectives (p. 85). It is possible to infer child sexual abuse might have been experienced by Florence and induced in her the fear of paedophilia, the trauma of which is omitted in the text, as can also be inferred from *The Turn of the Screw*. However, as this chapter will develop, Harding suggests more of an independent, uninitiated and isolated formation of queer and sexual subjectivity in his protagonist. As I will show, this framing of the sexual child as a Gothic trope risks the sensationalism of real children's vulnerability. What could be read as a queer rebellion might also read as exploitation.

'She got herself booked . . . and all ideaed up': Queerness in a Girl's Education

The starkest deviation that *Florence and Giles* makes from its parent text is the re-gendering of its child protagonist; in *The Turn of the Screw*, the most critically queer character proves to be Miles. As the elder sibling he communicates the most precociousness and is believed to have spent much time being altogether 'too free' with the supposedly salacious Peter Quint.[22] Harding's Giles is more alike to the infantile and endearing Flora (of *The Turn of the Screw*) and in this narrative the reason for his expulsion from school is no sexually conspicuous mystery but simply a matter of his being a slow learner and a victim of bullying. The abuse at the hands of his peers is described as something he does not 'mind much'. Unable to empathise with such meek antipathy, Florence catches herself thinking that Giles must enjoy the pain somehow. Hanson observes the relation between sadomasochism and homosexuality:

> As with homosexuality, sadomasochism excites the most horror when it is observable, as if through demonic possession, in the children. Historically, it has occupied much the same social status as homosexuality, in that it is an unjustly pathologised, sometimes criminalised, sexuality.[23]

Elsewhere James's preoccupation with sadomasochism has been identified to centre on the relationship between adults and children,

The Queer Gothic Child

or, more specifically the teacher/student dynamic. In another of James's novellas, *The Pupil* (1891), Kathryn Bond Stockton reads the queer child student and the 'quasi-queer child' adult tutor: 'we watch the tutor learn to love the boy or how the boy defeats the assumptions of his innocence'.[24] Stockton discusses how sex appears in James's fiction through notions of delay, mobilised through conflicts with other themes such as family and money. Without the paranoid hysteria of a governess whose 'obsessive voyeurism' doubles the eroticisation of child characters, *The Pupil* is decidedly not Gothic; instead, 'James turns the screw of what could look like same-sex paedophilia in the direction of brotherly masochism' (p. 64). *What Maisie Knew* (1897) showcases more of these narrative themes of children growing up queer through their navigations around notions of innocence and their disillusionments or affinities with adults. But it is this didactic relationship that entwines sadomasochism and sexuality that is most intriguing in the work of James. *The Turn of the Screw*, especially, can be placed in a history of sexual induction via older peers and adults. Importantly, this theme maintains a predominant focus on moral anxieties about boys and same-sex initiation, which supports the claim made by Bray that there seems to be no real concern for girls' early initiation into sex as that is simply a 'mainstream ex-nominated heterosexual norm'.[25] In his essay 'Fear of the Queer Child', Clifford J. Rosky offers a comprehensive study of how queerness has, until very recently, been culturally assumed as something that can be taught through exposure. His taxonomic genealogy provides historical perspectives to conclude that fearing the queer child is a persistent ideology in our culture, but all his examples pertain to male homosexual initiation. The 'fear of the queer child', Rosky writes, 'is a remarkably old, pliable, and enduring thought, which has proved capable of conforming itself to times and places in which people held starkly varied ideas about homosexuality and childhood . . . they touch upon several themes that anticipate the fear's evolution in the modern period'.[26] Rosky develops this idea by separating types of fear; qualifying them as sexual, educational and universalising. Early versions of the 'seduction fear' describe homosexuality as something that one is initiated into, particularly during childhood and often by teachers. Being a pre-nineteenth century paradigm,

Rosky asserts that the men and boys would not yet be understood as 'homosexuals', yet sex acts would be believed to be habits and behaviours passed on 'from one generation to the next'. The 'fear' of a child whose queerness is a contracted or learned 'corruption' is an idea that has formed the fabric of contemporary understanding, refractions of which can be noted in contemporary Queer Gothic fiction.[27] Rosky's account of this phenomenon refers predominantly to men and boys, so it is limited in its summation of homosocial male cultures but is interesting nonetheless when tracing the reflection of such an idea in the nineteenth-century work of James. Rosky's genealogy also speaks to the idea that the 'seduction fear' has simply not applied to little girls, and their premature sexualisation, as Robson and Bray argue, has historically been accepted as a norm rather than a concern. The queer little girl, then, is a rather unexplored and untheorized figure. The habits passed on in *Florence and Giles* are decidedly non-sexual on first inspection. However, the child protagonist's precociousness in matters dark and queer is suggested to be greatly influenced by her interest in eighteenth and nineteenth-century Gothic literature; having taught herself to read, Florence squirrels away stashes of literature in various hiding places and turns into a rather neurotic bibliophile: 'I timed myself reading a few pages by the grandfather clock, to determine exactly how far four minutes would take me.'[28] Harding very quickly establishes the literature to which Florence cleaves as her most erotic pastime: the act of teaching herself to read is described as embarking on the 'sneakery of [her] life' and the candles used to facilitate such 'sneakery' are connotative to a secret sexual affair as Florence 'scrape[s] their guilty drippery from the floor' (p. 8). The bibliophilic turn that Harding gives his protagonist gestures to the novel's status as a neo-Victorian pastiche of traditional eighteenth and nineteenth-century Gothic fiction. Some of the novel's intertexts are reflexively described as items on Florence's reading list; these include the Gothic classic, *The Mysteries of Udolpho* (1794) and *The Woman in White* (1859) – her declared favourite writer is Edgar Allan Poe, which speaks to her frequent use of raven imagery. Many of these works provide intertexts that encourage dialogues between past and present incarnations of the Gothic and seem to lay claim to a place within the genre. Moreover, her bibliophilia firmly establishes her precociousness and deviant hunger for 'forbidden knowledge'. Mair Rigby states that 'for early twenty-first century readers, the Gothic preoccupation with "forbidden knowledge" is likely to suggest more than a hint of dangerous sexual possibility', explaining that 'the close tropological proximity of the term "forbidden" with the term "knowledge" engages the cultural productions of sexual deviancy as a kind of prohibited knowledge, something so tempting that it must be kept secret less it spread'.[29] The allusions to the sociopolitical representations of queerness in children here are overtly connected to normative assumptions of gender binaries. That Florence is shown to have a blurred perspective and an attenuated ability to differentiate between reality and an imagination fed by Gothic novels seems to suggest Harding's intention to prove correct the absent sexist uncle who forbids reading in girls due to the corrupting potential of knowledge. The reader, in turn, is encouraged to see her literary self-education as having the most influence on her development over the interventions of any adult.

Novels become Florence's teachers in lieu of any formal education. They jar, however, with what Florence has been told is expected of her sex. Her prohibition from reading is thought to be a result of her uncle's scorned love-loss after the women he was engaged to marry enrolled in a New York college:

> She wasn't there long before she got herself booked, and musicked and poetried and theatred and philosophied and all ideaed up, and pretty soon she offrailed, and most probably started drinking and smoking and doing all other sorts of dark deeds, and the upshot of it was that she ended up considering she'd overtaken my uncle and intellectually down-nosed him, and of course then it was inevitable but that she someone-elsed.[30]

Here the reader sees Harding emphasise the Victorian conservatism of the absentee patriarch, and the young heroine's feminist potential in the way that he contrasts their reactions to the recognisable trope of the New Woman, which hovers tentatively around the whole narrative.[31] The confusion between nouns and verbs here also suggests Florence is still developing her understanding of language, although it might also read as Harding describing her development as queer; isolated as she is from normative systems of education, Florence restructures her reading rhetorically and, with these functional shifts, queers the language she learns to suit her own purposes. Significantly, this confusion of what does what to what, or who, implicates notions of agency and objectification. As an orphan, the only female role models that Florence has are the well-meaning though illiterate and inattentive servants and Miss Whitaker, the children's previous governess who shares much of the naivety and melodramatic romanticism of James's governess: 'a silly young woman who stood and besotted before the portrait of my Uncle on the stairs and twittered about how handsome he was and how when he interviewed her he had been quite taken with her'.[32] Whitaker's 'tragicking' upon the lake is suggested to be have really been a murder committed by Florence. Harding shows her alluding to something like guilt when she admits that she wished her dead after Whitaker had found Florence in the clandestine act of reading, 'co-incidentally' on the day of her demise. Teachers cannot be said to impress a lasting impression nor a corrupting influence on this child who seems so self-sustaining. However, the queer dynamic of same-sex teacher/student arises with the arrival of a new governess at Blithe. Miss Taylor is wholly different from her predecessor:

> 'Pah! Sewing.' She looked angry, but then softened somewhat. 'Well, of course there are things a young lady is expected to learn, but this is 1891. The days when ladies merely played the piano and painted a little – and badly – and embroidered useless things are on their way out. I am of the opinion that all women, and you're no different, need a little more stimulation than that.' (p. 98)

This rousing feminist speech, the likes of which Florence has never heard, offers the chance to celebrate her own self-improvement and to unburden herself from so much secrecy in her bibliophile identity. Taylor effectively 'outs' Florence, offering the freedom to spend the majority of her days unafraid of having her true desires and passions prohibited. However, this does nothing to stay her obsessive concern for the other object of her desires: her little brother,

Giles. Thus, the possibility of recognising a mentor and perhaps another love object in her new (rather capable) governess is passed over in preference for the need to maintain the self-sufficiency that Florence has become used to.

With *The Turn of the Screw*, critics have favoured the interpretation that Miles, especially, has been 'turned' by sexual experiences and knowledge 'given' as tutelage. Eric Savoy refers to Shoshana Felman's reading of the novel that establishes the centrifugal hinge of the plot as the 'hole' in the narrative: Miles's unexplained expulsion from school.[33] Savoy offers:

> If the 'hole' is a critical metaphor that intentionally points to the suppressed content of the headmaster's letter the recessive prehistory at Bly, the gaps in the narrative, and the governess's thwarted or repressed conclusion, then these various formal deployments of the term can be understood as a perseverated recircling around the anatomical 'hole' that is both the site of traumatic initiation and, consequently, the occluded, nonpossessed 'beginning' that initiates the circumlocutions of the story's 'very telling.' That anatomical hole is – if one follows this narrowing spiral of reasoning – Miles's anus . . . It is striking that criticism has been so reluctant to trace the signifying chain of the 'hole' to its eminently plausible origin in the narrative's prehistory of traumatic sexual initiation.[34]

To follow Savoy's reading, then, the centrifugal image of queerness in *Florence and Giles* can be understood as another anatomical hole, one that is seemingly neglected in the Jamesian Gothic and rather more prevalent in later incarnations and tangents of the Gothic: the vagina. In *Florence and Giles*, Giles might be observed as a characterisation of delay and sadomasochism in the style of James. However, he serves no greater purpose here than as the object of his sister's affections and desires. The body of Giles is thus not a hole or a vessel but a small morsel, a piece of familial flesh. Harding first suggests Florence's incestuous desire for her brother in her description of her recurring nightmare:

> I would look up and see a shape bending over Giles's bed. At first that was all it was, a shape, but gradually I realised it was a person,

a woman, dressed all in black, a black travelling dress and with a matching coat and hood. As I watched, she put her arms around Giles and – he was always quite small in the dream – lift him from the bed . . . and she would always say the words 'Ah my dear, I could eat you!' and indeed her eyes had a hungry glint.[35]

This imagery is overtly Gothic in its allusions to cannibalism but is nevertheless an image of maternal anxiety or sexual abuse, both on the part of Florence who sees Giles as smaller and more vulnerable in her dream, and on the part of the hooded figure who cradles the sleeping Giles. Foucault explained that:

> in a society such as ours, where the family is the most active site of sexuality, and where it is doubtless the exigencies of the latter which maintain and prolong its existence, incest . . . occupies a central place; it is constantly being solicited and refused; it is an object of obsession and attraction, a dreadful secret and an indispensable pivot.[36]

With a wholly absent patriarch in the form of an uncle that neither child remembers ever meeting, as in *The Turn of the Screw*, *Florence and Giles* offers a cautionary tale pregnant with nineteenth-century sexology and cultural discourse; of course, sexual chaos reigns, a patriarch does not preside. Moreover, with the omission of the Quint character, this domestic unit made up only of women and children emphasises the lack of traditional family wholeness for Florence. Even with the option of a heteronormative suitor in the guise of asthmatic neighbour, Theo, Harding takes every opportunity to align her queerness, or her 'growing sideways', as Stockton would term it, with stunted development and criminality. Florence's extreme isolation and her desire to keep her brother and single love-object close, situate her as always already condemned in the hypocrisy of patriarchal law. As Foucault explains, 'If one considers the threshold of all culture to be prohibited incest, then sexuality has been, from the dawn of time, under the sway of law and right' (pp. 109–10). However, while incestuous queerness is suggested as the aim in *Florence and Giles*, the means, or the catalyst, of that one hunger emerges as another: same-sex desire.

'The bad thing was a rook in a snowdrift': Queer Destruction and Death Drives

From the first meeting between Florence and Miss Taylor, the children's new governess, Harding shows Florence doubling herself with this uncanny stranger. This is made obvious through a metaphor that appears in the novel with accelerating frequency, building towards the climactic scene of murder. Initial Gothic imagery describes the governess's appearance:

> Her skeletal figure was dressed all in black and I thought how strange that was, for Miss Whitaker had been told my governesses always wore grey, but I noticed how well it matched with the rooks which were even now circling above us, as though they too had turned out specially to welcome her.[37]

Here, the inclusion of rooks, as well as recalling Florence's penchant for Poe, recalls the corvidae metaphor used in early scenes to denote her sense of self and, often, the status or measure of her innocence: 'As far as my early life went, it was all a blank, a white field of snow, without even the mark of a rook.'[38] As Florence's suspicions of Taylor begin to mount and her paranoia transforms her nightmares into delusions that remove the threshold, for both Florence and the reader, between fantasy and reality, this metaphor stitches together Taylor's predatory or malevolent potential with Florence's own moral self-assessment. The image of a rook on a field of snow slaloms throughout the novel, its meaning becoming more attached to Florence's notions of subjectivity. In one scene, it connotes her return to extreme isolation when Giles remains at school and Theo's ill health stops him visiting: 'it was the rook and the virgin snow all over again' (p. 55). Yet, when she suspects Taylor to be possessed by the ghost of the dead governess, Whitaker, 'the bad thing was a rook in a snowdrift' (p. 99). With crude uses of light and dark to suggest innocence and corruption Harding deploys a child-like leitmotif of anthropomorphised emotional ethics.

Another way in which Harding employs the corvidae metaphor to double Florence with Taylor appears when Florence highlights the carnivorous nature of the rook and crow, these carrion birds that peck at flesh. When Florence recalls the embarrassment of Whitaker's brother shouting out his derision at the trial, placing some blame for the death with her, Florence describes her anxiety 'with everyone's eyes feeding off me, like crows on a dead rabbit' (p. 129). This fear of flesh-eating becomes the locus of her spiralling suspicions over what the strange new governess wants with 'her Giles', and Harding shows this through paralleling cannibalism with sexual threat. She resolves to 'observe Miss Taylor', thus beginning an obsessive voyeurism in the vein of the Jamesian ever-watchful 'hand-wringing governess' (p. 123). Her findings include more allusions to the carrion bird image. When eating, she sees her peck at her food 'like some demented bird' (p. 83); thereafter, every touch and caress of Giles is associated with cannibalism: 'It seemed as if she could scarce look at Giles without licking her lips' (p. 100). Of course, this fear of cannibalism/paedophilia suggests that Florence has experienced or witnessed sexual abuse herself, though Harding only suggests this through her knowledge and concern, which induce complicated negative feelings, especially when she begins to believe that Taylor's tactile affections are requited by Giles:

> I near expected him to lick her hand . . . I well imagined that's how he had responded to those bullies at his school, not with resentment, but with gratitude when, during those intervals when they did not tease or hurt him, they showed him a little act of kindness no matter how trivial or even unconscious on their part. (p. 97)

This quotation shows the intense voyeurism that Florence commits herself to, while also suggesting more diversions from her own queer desires, situating herself as the normative spectator looking in at queer, intergenerational erotic play and enflaming what she sees with the assumption that Giles is a little masochist and a flirt who encourages his own exploitation and courts sexual danger.

Not only does the transference of the devouring carrion bird carry from Florence to Taylor, so too does her frustrated desire to be close to him as she had been when they shared the bedroom from which she has since been ousted on the grounds of her maturation: 'Mrs Grouse said I was getting to be quite the young lady and ought not to be in a room with my brother any longer' (p. 43).

Hereafter, Harding shows that Florence use any excuse to sneak back to her brother's bed: 'I so frighted myself with these thoughts that I worried for Giles and had to rise from my bed . . . I stretched myself out beside him and fell straightaway into a deep and heavy slumber' (p. 82). Projections of guilt are implied when Florence believes that she catches her looming over the sleeping boy (as in her recurring nightmare): 'She wouldn't want anyone to know she had middle-of-the-nighted in Giles's room' (p. 94). Robson writes that this period of being ousted from the nursery was typical for most Victorian girls; while 'trousers and school . . . marked the end of the first phase of existence for boys', girls of the middle and upper classes would remain in petticoats and pursue whatever education was allowed at home, experiencing none of the 'division between early and later childhood', which would have been possible if they were boys. The androgyny with which Harding has Florence describe Giles confirms him as part of her own identity, which is further enabled by the neo-Victorian style of the novel, as Robson qualifies: 'the first six years of male life in the nineteenth century carried a clear stamp of femininity', since the garments and the world left behind by boys continues to be distinctly feminine. Robson continues, 'while it may be a critical commonplace that the Victorians adhered to a rigid system of gender separation, in this particular instance it seems that young boyhood crosses the line, and actually looked more like girlhood'.[39] While this might suggest that the anxieties expressed by Florence around being separated from Giles are wholly normative, her subsequent act of projecting those anxieties onto the adult caregiver in order to oust her from the equation are queerly malevolent.

Ironically, Harding chooses to use the word 'queer' to mobilise Florence's anxieties; it is the only way she can describe the situation she observes: 'There was something queer about all of this.'[40] Yet the projection of her own desires continues as a suggested compulsion of her paranoid conclusions. Taylor, to Florence, becomes a supernatural being who imbibes no food, while she apparently saves room for devouring young Giles: '"She evidently gets her fun out of cutting rather than eating." I shivered at this. *Ah, my dear, I could eat you!* sprang into my mind, the memory of her greeding over Giles in the night, as if she could scarce resist the temptation to sink her teeth into his tender flesh' (p. 123). That tender flesh that Taylor would scarce be able to resist betrays Florence's fetishisation of her brother. However, rather than solely provide a canvas screen refracting the spectrum of Florence's queer desires and greedy malevolence, Taylor is also suggested as another adult that Florence is attracted to. In the same scene in which Florence's appearance seems to have transformed completely into that of the governess, her weight loss suggesting an aping of the governess's strange and frugal eating habits, the connective bird metaphor is used again, but this time it describes the disappointment of being found unattractive:

> I saw a tall, gangling crane of a girl, all long limbs and extended neck, with a complexion so pale as to not look well. My eyes were marooned in great saucers of black, my white frock and apron hung from my bones as if I were getting smaller, not growing, and all in all I scarce recognised myself, I looked so ill. There saddened a movement behind me and Miss Taylor appeared in the mirror, staring over my shoulder at me. 'You are not pretty, Florence,' she informed me and inside me a white dove fluttered and dropped injured on the ground. 'But you have a certain attractiveness that is much more important than prettiness.' We both stared at my reflection. (p. 145)

Florence misses the glimmer of empowerment in this back-handed compliment and Harding shows the confidence knock in a renewed frequency of delusions. Florence now avoids and covers the mirrors in the house as a part of Taylor's witch soul dwells there, infecting the whole house with its uncanny laughing reflections.

The desire to kill this physical manifestation of all that is bad and queer and hungry in herself, to erase the rook from the virgin snow, becomes the only solution if Florence is to 'save' Giles. An obsessive need to be close to him, to sneak into his bed at night, is the first behaviour projected onto the governess, followed closely by a desire to physically enjoy his flesh or to eat him, a manifestation of her compulsion to realise the desire of incorporating into her own being, corporally enveloping him within in her much like the crushing embrace with which James's governess kills little Miles. All this relates back to that notion of (w)holes. Florence so wished to be a 'whole' – believing Giles to be as much a part of her corporeal and psychic identity as a limb:

> I had once torn in two a playing card – the queen of spades it was – straight across the middle, thinking to make the two queens from one, the picture at the top and its mirror image below, but found instead I did not even have one, the separate parts useless on their own, and it struck me this was me without Giles, who was part of my own person. (p. 28)

What better way to incorporate him than by consuming him? Where the hole in *The Turn of the Screw* might pertain to the unascertained sexual knowledge passed onto Miles, revolving around the anus, this hole is much more oral and vaginal, recalling Barbara Creed's work on the 'monstrous feminine'. Creed describes how in contemporary horror film, the repeated image of 'the mysterious black hole that signifies female genitalia as a monstrous sign threatening to give birth to equally horrific offspring as well as threatening to incorporate everything in its path'.[41] She calls this 'the generative archaic mother, constructed within patriarchal ideology as the primeval "black hole". This, of course, is also the hole that is opened up by the absence of the penis, the horrifying sight of the mother's genitals – proof that castration can occur' (p. 46). Creed argues that gender constitutes monstrosity in female monsters far more than in male monsters but that this does not equate to a presentations of feminist power or agency, rather it is more indicative of male anxieties. It is precisely this analysis of the monstrous feminine that parallels Harding's twining of maternal orality with the threat of castration that culminates around the 'black hole' of the well, down which Florence's uncanny enemy is dispatched. While Creed's analysis helpfully describes the misogynistic tropes of the Gothic mode, which are obviously present in this contemporary Gothic novel, the monstrous feminine is itself not a thesis that encompasses queerness. This can be noted in its preoccupation with the reproductive threats or potentials replete in vaginal imagery. The central queer female image of *Florence and Giles* bears more of a likeness to Lynne Huffer's thesis in *Are the Lips the Grave?*, a queer feminist response to the oft-labelled 'negative' and 'antisocial', but also male-centric, theses of queerness disseminated by Leo Bersani and Lee Edelman. *Lips* provides an important intervention into the fields of feminism and queer theory and the ongoing debates found at their intersection with Huffer's thesis focusing on the ethics of sexuality, gender and difference.

Where the queer crux of James's novella may have been the 'hole' in the narrative centring on the passivity and malleability of a little boy and his anus, Harding's novel opts for a little girl's ravenous maw of a vagina. This, in turn, suggests that the queer crux of this Gothic transformation has more to do with the maintenance of a 'wholeness', rather than lack of information and the gaps in the accounts of children that become filled by suspicious adult minds. Florence's narrative reads as especially candid towards the novel's climax. The kidnapping of her brother, plying him with chloroform and stowing him away in the tower; the baleful neglect of Theo as he suffocates during an asthma attack; the brutal murder of the governess – these are details that might have been omitted if the narrative style at the beginning of the novel had continued. Where the novel began with the overt unreliability of Florence's narrative, not least due to the gaps in information surrounding her first governess's death, the novel's conclusion is given a new wholeness; warts and all.

Before I relate this to Huffer's queer feminist ethics, it is important to first recognise how this text diverges from the traditional genealogies in which its source text and intertexts exist and how this supports the need to read the novel as a New Queer Gothic text. Harding's imagery of vaginal holes representing wholeness is the key metaphor used by this text to suggest a fuller picture of female subjectivity in a way that was not representable the female Gothic genre. The villainous governess threatening maternal care and compassion imagined by Florence as the worst sort of fiend, connects the queer and the Gothic along a similar trajectory recognisable from female Gothic texts and Queer Gothic criticism following psychoanalytic reasoning, but it also works to trouble the female Gothic continuum. Florence's subjectivity is as contingent on her relationship with this or any maternal figure as it is on the reproductive capabilities of her sexual organs: it has nothing to do with either. However, it is no coincidence that the mouth/vagina plays such a vital role in affirming this Gothic girl's queer subjectivity. Marie Mulvey Roberts explains that in the traditional female Gothic novel, patriarchal systemic and institutional controls such as 'the Freudian Law of the Father and institution of marriage' were imposed on the female body. She lists the driving forces for these controls as 'power, possession and patrimony' and qualifies that they manifest through the 'policing of the female body and its constituent parts, particularly the open mouth and vulva'.[42] These were the parts considered carnivalesque in contrast to the classical body.[43] To reclaim them as a site of agency, queered language, and as a whole rather than a void, is an incredible subversion of the way in which the body of the girl has been used in Gothic literature and criticism.

Huffer's thesis analyses the other ways of thinking about Foucauldian ethics that drive much queer thinking; she is interested mainly in debating the status of morality and ethics within queer theory, specifically what can be learned from Foucault's later works, post-Levinasian thinking and the work of Luce Irigaray. Her thesis in *Lips*, as the title makes overt, involves reconfiguring Leo Bersani's argument in 'Is the Rectum the Grave?' In *The Turn of the Screw* the governess's paranoid assumptions around Miles's anus reflect Bersani's thesis starkly:

> If the rectum is the grave in which the masculine ideal (an ideal shared – differently – by men and women) of proud subjectivity is buried, then it should be celebrated for its very potential for death. Tragically, AIDS has literalized that potential as the certainty of biological death, and has therefore reinforced the heterosexual association of anal sex with a self-annihilating originally and primarily identified with the fantasmic mystery of an insatiable, unstoppable female sexuality.[44]

Here, Bersani discusses anal sex as being irrevocably related to death in historic representation and critique; he stresses this relation is made all the more pertinent in the 'literalising' effects of the AIDS crisis. With the transformative project of *Florence and Giles*, to re-gender both characterisations and the narrative queer crux, it seems logical to apply theory that builds on Bersani. The Bersani quotation above is used by Lynne Huffer to launch her queer feminist response to 'Rectum' through coupling it with Luce Irigaray's 'When Our Lips Speak Together':

> When Bersani writes 'the rectum is the grave in which the masculine ideal of proud subjectivity is buried' we can't help but see that he and Irigaray are going after the same phallogocentric, self-replicating target. To put it in philosophical terms, the force of the negative – figured by Bersani as a rectum – both exposes and shatters the false ideal of the other-destroying Western subject. It is the antifoundationalist, poststructuralist force that also powers the engine driving the antisocial thesis of queer theory, from Bersani through Edelman to Halley, in a nonredemptive, nonreproductive, anal-erotic sexuality.[45]

While following this idea of the vagina – or 'the lips', Huffer's choice of term connecting queer feminist iconography to notions of orality and communication – as a locus of poststructuralist, non-redemptive and non-reproductive sexuality and subjectivity, it is important to note the differences as well as the similarities shared between the rectum and lips. Significantly, Florence's queer desire to envelop her brother, to ingest him and be whole, her precocious knowledge of her power over Hadleigh (a trait that signals queerness in the vein of James's Gothic children Miles and Flora) and her same-sex attraction to her governess all communicate her queer desires to the reader. This not only links to Bersani's death drive – 'The suicidally aggressive nature of desire: the subject not only seeks to assimilate the other but, like a bird paralyzed by the serpent's gaze, will itself be devoured'[46] – but also to Huffer's assessment of how the lips speak:

> The rectum may be a grave, but that hardly keeps it from speaking. The catachrestic lips, by contrast, can only speak as that which they are not. And yet, in doing so, they both mark the abyssal negativity the rectum names and, at the same time, dramatize the necessity of speaking otherwise. Simultaneously inscribing both a self-shattering undoing and a making – what Jane Gallop calls the lips as *poiesis* – the lips articulate an ethics of relation that differentiates them from the pure negativity of queer antisociality. For it is in their catachrestic, heterotopian attempt to speak otherwise that the lips are

simultaneously here and elsewhere, now and not now: not a pinned-down figure of the Other of the Same, but a hovering, catachrestic Other's Other. The lips name a heterotopian *ethopoisis*, an ethical remaking of the erotic relation.[47]

Through relating Florence and the Queer Gothic narrative within which she exists, it is not my intention to define her by what she is not, but to stress the ways in which this character can be read as engaging with and embracing the forms and figures without which she could not have come to be. Positing her against the contexts that *Florence and Giles* suggests requires a means of understanding new methods of reading female subjectivity in a New Queer Gothic. Where James's hole was an unspoken gap that suggested child sexual abuse and 'learned' sexual behaviour, Harding's speaks to the complex nature of Queer Gothic girlhood as a whole *Other* thing. Huffer aligns 'Queer theory's embrace of undecidability . . . with poststructuralism's embrace of performativity and the concomitant undoing of narrative' (p. 66). This chapter's analysis of *Florence and Giles*, while appreciating it as a New Queer Gothic text, has found its reconfiguration of concepts of girlhood as they exist in multiple genealogies and contexts, to have been successful. Through situating Florence within Victorian constructs of childhood and girlhood, within criticism on historical representations of queerness in children and within criticism on girls and women in the Gothic, I have argued that this representation suggests the potential for a complex, not fetishised or idealised, reworking of queer child subjectivity, which is erotic and dangerous and tragic, but also defiant and powerful.

Where the source text had the effect of interpolating the reader to eroticise the children, the ending of *Florence and Giles* instead aligns us with the queer child's perspective, and readers are invited to understand events as precipitating from the 'human malevolence or neglect' that Florence speaks of early in the novel.[48] Florence has been written with Jamesian motifs of taught queerness, yet she lacks a teacher or indeed any obvious abuser. Her queerness is a paradox, represented as tantamount to Gothic villainy and rebellious antisocial subjectivity, yet she ultimately proves a transgressive antiheroine who does succeed in protecting her brother from what she perceives to be the threat of sexual objectification. She does so by killing anyone who disturbs the very small queer world that she has built from nothing. In the vein of patriarchal sexual economy – as relevant today as in the nineteenth century – clearly the novel treats Florence punitively for her transgressions in developing forbidden knowledge and queer sexual subjectivity. Her identity is initially presented as apparitional, a status that connotes the history of queer female (in)visibility and evokes her meta-status as derivative. However, over the course of this novel, Florence's characterisation flourishes into a solid, whole identity, the likes of which should not be used as metonymic of anything else. With important changes made to the central figure and the narrative, swapping rectum for lips allows Harding to create a nuanced representation of contemporary queer girlhood via the neo-Victorian genre. While it is very tempting to read Florence as Miles has been read, to treat her as an analysand and fall into the psychoanalytic traps set by James more than 100 years ago, I have instead shown that *Florence and Giles* is truly transformative in that it offers an excellent aperture through which we can better understand the troubles and values of intersecting queer and feminist critical perspectives, an approach that will continue to prove essential in any future analysis of queer girlhood, not least the chapters to follow.

Part II

3

'What happened to my sweet girl?': Conventions of the New Queer Gothic and Queer Subjectivity in Black Swan *and* Jack & Diane

ം

Queer subjectivity, explored using the Gothic mode, is the most intriguing feature of New Queer Gothic films. In Darren Aronofsky's *Black Swan* (2010) and Bradley Rust Gray's *Jack & Diane* (2012) the anxiety of queer subjectification is shown as a drama played out on the body with horrific results. This chapter will frame its comparative analysis of *Black Swan* and *Jack & Diane* around the two key motifs. The first involves corporeal horror, focusing on the theme of metamorphosis and visual presentations of monstrosity on the Gothic body. The second motif to be introduced is the technique of mirroring, relating the signification of the visual doubling and multiplying of characters to the notion of queer subjectivity. My analysis of these motifs will draw on the theme of abjection as a common affective visualisation of the anxiety over monitoring the borders of identity. After using a comparative analysis built around motifs, this chapter will then complicate that analysis's conclusions by offering a framework with which to read these New Queer Gothic films as an avenue into better understanding the representational value, political relevance and original perspective made available by this new mode. This chapter recognises that the representability of queer women is a contested area of criticism, and it makes this intervention of demonstrating these texts as New Queer Gothic and debating the uses of reading queerness in the contemporary Gothic in order to ask whether mechanisms of visibility still effect or obfuscate the representation of queer women.

In her book, *Film Bodies: Queer Feminist Encounters with Gender and Sexuality in Cinema* (2018), Katharina Lindner recalls the invisibility and 'negative' stereotyping that has defined the history of homosexual representation in American mainstream cinema due largely to the legacy of the Production Code (also known as the Hays Code), which censored any depictions of 'sex perversion' with reference to homosexuality. Lindner highlights, however, the important body of scholarship that explores 'how, despite, or perhaps because of the (relative) absence of explicitly gay and lesbian characters or narratives, the cinema and its stars significantly aided the formation and cultivation of gay and lesbian identities and communities'.[1] As this book's introduction and first chapters made clear, the question of invisibility pervades the historical culture of representing lesbians and queer women. Patricia White was singled out in the introduction as a pioneer of lesbian cinema scholarship and is also referred to by Lindner as playing an important role in foregrounding the potential of the Production Code towards motivating spectators to read what then becomes coded by the gaps and ambiguities; what is left unsaid and, importantly, unshown. Lindner makes the point that censorship, ironically, served to produce sexual meaning and encouraged these to be read by critics such as White, arguing that this limitation actually 'highlight[ed] the impossibility of clearly separating visibility from invisibility' (p. 22). While this chapter will not be debating the production of meaning via codified representations of queerness, it will develop this idea of finding ways to subvert perceived negativity or limitations when it comes to available methods of reading New Queer Gothic films.

Directed by Bradley Rust Grey, *Jack & Diane* was arguably marketed as a romantic horror. The film centres on the developing romance of two girls (played by Riley Keough and Juno Temple). The narrative is broken up by Diane transforming sporadically into a cannibalistic monster and by arrestingly grotesque animations of plaited hair snaking through intestinal workings. *Black Swan* follows the journey of ballerina, Nina (Natalie Portman), from infantilised and innocent 'White Swan' to the monstrously queer and uninhibited titular 'Black Swan'. This thesis recognises Aronofsky's film as incorporating pastiche as it relates to Richard Dyer's definition of the term, meaning: 'a knowing form of the practice of imitation which itself always hold us inexorably within cultural perception of the real and also, and thereby, enables to make a sense of the real'.[2] The introspective paranoid gaze of the film, however, crucially complicates this sense of the real and a hyperbolic construction of the cult of femininity, which at times borders on camp,[3] works to skew attempts to read a political perspective in the film. Dyer connects this to pastiche:

> Pastiche embraces closeness: it accepts the possibility of being seduced, penetrated, dependant or ventriloquised, without seeing this as a significant and anxiety-producing loss of autonomy. As a result though, pastiche is unstable in relation to a fixed or certain point of view.[4]

Used effectively in *Black Swan*, pastiche allows for ambition, gendered and sexual subjectivity, madness, freedom and death to become themes that interweave and conflate. Aronofsky is known for works that explore the extremes of human experience, building narratives of darkness and unease that nod towards shades of horror and Gothicism.[5] *Black Swan*'s focus circles tightly around the desperate insularity of its protagonist, offering an immersive subjective paranoia. In each film, anxiety around the dematerialised self is illustrated by paranoid and reparative uses of body horror and mirroring and abjection.

The Horror of the Gothic Body in Jack & Diane

Body horror might be considered by many as a purely cinematic trope, though it has clear origins in the literary Gothic; the various aesthetics of on-screen body horror today owe much to the novels and short stories of such authors as Ann Radcliffe, Mary Shelley,

Edgar Allan Poe and H. P. Lovecraft, to name a few. The term 'body horror' did not enter academic criticism, however, until 1986, when *Screen* journal dedicated essays to its use in contemporary horror film, among these was Barbara Creed's pioneering article, 'Horror and the Monstrous-Feminine: An Imaginary Abjection', which she later developed into her 1993 book *The Monstrous-Feminine*, an invaluable springboard for thinking about New Queer Gothic cinema and queer female subjects. Often used in horror cinema for its powers of shock and repulsion, body horror's mutated, grotesque aesthetics challenge corporeality and connect to Julia Kristeva's notions of abjection in which the signs of bodily purge, of leaking borders of the self, alert a subject to a fear of mortality. Since the 1980s, body horror has become the topic of much psychoanalytic, feminist, queer and Gothic criticism but has not often been read reparatively. The first examples of body horror that this chapter discusses are the monstrous bestial metamorphoses experienced by the titular protagonists in *Jack & Diane* and Nina in *Black Swan*. In *Jack & Diane* the audience expects to see Juno Temple reflected in the bathroom mirror but is instead shocked by the sudden appearance of a black, bear-like beast in place of the actor. This instance of transformation is less drawn out than the former, which lingers over its grotesquely painful transformations. However, each use mutilated and transformed human bodies to connote a form of dematerialisation.

In *Jack & Diane*, Diane has two personas, one innocent, naïve and infantile, the other desiring and passionate. When Diane's queer-coded desires surface (either in the presence of Jack or just while Jack is on Diane's mind) they manifest in the very sudden appearance of the monster, which symbolises the feelings associated with that persona as, at best, frightening and, at worst, monstrous, cannibalistic and pathological. The monster is characterised by its ambiguity, its appearance on screen is abrupt and fleeting, making what it is hard to discern; animalistic noises, and its thick black fur obscures any distinguishable features. The monster suggests that Diane has an Other, dissociative self, which is represented as having little to no control or sentience – it is only ever seen in fleeting glimpses smashing objects. After the two meet and fall in love, Diane leaves Jack to keep a promise to her sister and attend a fashion school abroad. *Jack & Diane* does give problematic attention to traditionally paranoid stereotypes of the monstrous feminine and the killer queer; however, because these representations are relegated to an unconscious zone, to the abstract appearances of a monster that might only exist as a metaphor, the queer subjectivity cannot be considered wholly pathologised by this representation. Although the film cannot be said to be a wholly negative and paranoid text, neither is its representation of queer subjectivity something that easily induces enjoyment. Throughout the film Rust Gray uses the motif of nosebleeds, which increase in frequency in each protagonist and suggest notions of trauma and transformation in an abject sense – each woman's experience of falling in love is shown via this expression of leaking borders and personal vulnerability. While this chapter will return to the significance of mirroring in *Jack & Diane*, it is important to first note that this doubling of nosebleeds connects monstrous transformation to the body and ideas of abjection. Julia Kristeva's notion of abjection describes questions of mortality and identity being challenged by the appearance of bodily fluids that have breached their corporeal boundaries signalling a disruption to 'identity, system [and] order'.[6] Placed immediately before or after the monster appears on-screen, the nosebleeds suggest an anxiety of queer desire signalling a loss of boundaries as the phantasmagorical infects reality and induces physical bleeding, much like the boundary-crossing horror of queer 'Sinthhome' villain, Freddy Kruger, in the *Nightmare on Elm Street* franchise, whose ability to perform violent acts on victims in their dreams travels into and impacts on their waking lives.[7] Rust Gray encourages this uncertainty and leaves the boundary between the real and the imaginary or the conscious and subconscious liminal. In one scene, Diane is masturbating alone in her room when, alongside her climax, a monstrous limb flashes into the frame, smashing her lamp and leaving the scene in darkness. This exacerbates the connections between sexual desires, fantasy and monstrosity.

Bodily horror that engages with ideas of the dematerialised or a disassociated self via visual transformation into something monstrous is the crucial motif which connects the queerness and Gothicity of *Jack & Diane* and *Black Swan*. Images of women's bodies undergoing such a process is very much connected to the gendering of spectatorship conducive to the mechanisms of cinematic representation. Linda Williams makes the sobering argument that 'there is not that much difference between an object of desire and an object of horror as far as the male look is concerned'.[8] This has much to do with how women have historically been connected to Gothic coding; even when framed outside the immediate context of Gothic or horror films, women have been used as spectacle-objects until they are, as Williams notes, too old, and thus 'persevere as horror objects in films like *Whatever Happened to Baby Jane?* [1962] and *Hush . . . Hush, Sweet Charlotte* [1965]' (p. 23). The notion of recognising the on-screen woman as always already signalling monstrosity, or at least the threat of becoming monstrous, is owed to what Williams called 'the strange sympathy . . . between the monster and the girl', which 'may thus be less an expression of sexual desire (as in *King Kong, Beauty and the Beast*) and more a flash of sympathetic identification' (p. 23). What *Jack & Diane* expresses is a continuation of the trend to parallel monstrousness with the female, particularly the sexual and desiring female.

The horror of the body is of course contingent on how it is framed in the film's use of space. Pauline Palmer notes that a common trope in both traditional and contemporary Gothic fiction and film is 'the construct of the uncanny city'.[9] In her book, *The Queer Uncanny*, Palmer writes that this is frequently portrayed 'in terms of a maze of streets and alleys, in which the protagonist, unable to locate the correct route and distinguish between reality and illusion, loses his way both geographically and morally' (pp. 121–2). In *Jack & Diane*'s opening sequence, Diane wanders around an unnamed American city, seemingly lost, trying to find her sister who she was expecting to meet; she asks to borrow the mobile phones of strangers, and crosses busy streets and ends up entering a skate shop. Blossom Dearie's twee 'A Doodlin' Song' plays over this opening scene, emphasising a tone of infantilised femininity. Diane's dress is also childish; she is completely out of place and immediately coded as naïve and lost in the busy city. She asks to use the telephone in the skate shop and soon meets Jack – in that moment, her nose begins to bleed. This first occurrence of spontaneous bleeding suggests an arrival at anxiety or becoming 'lost'. The uncanny city exists in *Black Swan*'s subterranean walkways and hall-of-mirrors interiors (a discussion to which I shall return, when this chapter focuses on the theme of mirroring). In each film there exists a strong parallel of ingénue protagonists (Nina and Diane) picking a route through the uncanny city, usually led by the hand of a more 'experienced' woman who is knowledgeable of the space (Lily and Jack).

In both narratives the same-sex couples end up in a nightclub. The nightclub space in *Jack & Diane* provides an anonymity and the appropriate sensory deprivation to allow for their awkward social interactions to give way to purely passionate ones: the red washes of light bathe their features, and when they kiss they are almost completely hidden. In *Black Swan*, the painfully sheltered Nina has never factored nightclubbing into her gruelling dance schedule, and Lily encourages her to drink and take ecstasy so that she can practise losing herself in dance in a much less formal context. In both films, the same-sex couples dance, the display in *Black Swan* is more overtly erotic with Nina and Lily's lesbian spectacle, attracting the lustful lingering of men on the periphery to highlight the effect of the gaze: the capital of Portman's and Kunis's bodies is made explicit via such signalling of their appeal to the heterosexual male spectator. Indeed, both films are reminiscent of the disco scene in *Basic Instinct*.[10] Significantly, that scene, and the film more generally, courted controversy for its representation of a queer character (Sharon Stone) seeming to perform or exaggerate her bisexuality for the sexual gratification of the leading male (Michael Douglas) whom she encounters on the dancefloor before abandoning her 'prop' same-sex dance partner in favour of the stationary man, who stares at her with a kind of aggressive sexual disbelief. More recently, *Black Swan* has attracted very similar criticism for the sex scene that it depicts between Nina and Lily, which Amber Jacobs believes borrows from the 'standard iconographies of soft porn'.[11] For Jacobs, rather than representing her specific desire, the sexual scenes in *Black Swan* perform only male fantasy. It is difficult to divorce any notions of sexual self-discovery from the very patriarchal direction of the film (both in the sense of Aronofsky as auteur and of the film's narrative) because the horror of *Black Swan* truly exists in its depiction of internalised misogyny and the self-destructive implosion of subjectivity that it causes. These nightclub spaces, with strobe lighting and red washes, create spaces of ambiguity, salaciousness and discovery.

While in both films the charged atmosphere builds towards a kiss, in *Jack & Diane* it is the titular queer couple who find one another, whereas *Black Swan*'s Nina is shown suddenly to be kissing an unknown man. Confusion around the representations of desire multiply when Nina later discovers that her sex with Lily was only a delusional dream: Lily mocks her the next day with 'Did you have some kind of lezzy wet dream about me?' The nightclub space in both films acts as a threshold space, a space of sexual experimentation that precedes a transformation: Diane kisses Jack then springs into her monster form in the toilet; Nina dances with Lily then has a very lucid sex dream about her, replete with suggestions of metamorphosis. In each case, paranoid sexual dramas are explored through the motif of Gothic space.

The Horror of the Gothic Body in Black Swan

The bestial metamorphoses in each of these films is more nuanced than in certain body-horror titles that use similar themes to convey the threshold-crossing and sexual awakening involved in female adolescence. For example, lycanthropy is one such metaphorical metamorphosis, associated with the encroaching puberty and alternative sexual desires, as seen in such films as *Ginger Snaps* (2001).[12] In *Jack & Diane*, however, queer 'becoming' takes precedent over any coming-of-age metaphor and pervades the monstrous transformations. The ursine quality of Diane's bestial self suggests emergent queer desire being equated with something big, uncontrollable and dangerous. The traumatic swan metamorphosis of *Black Swan* is more nuanced still, perhaps signalling pastiche more than any one specific paranoid or reparative reading. Aronofsky shows Nina massaging her gnarled dancer's feet. The hyperaudible cracks and pops of bone are repeated later in the torturous transformation process. While alone in her dressing room, a sudden and ridiculous backwards crack of the legs leaves Nina struggling to steady herself in an impossible flamingo-stance; it is body horror made carnivalesque. As with *Jack & Diane*, the inability to distinguish between moments of fantasy and reality in *Black Swan* seems intentional. Permeating the latter, however, is a continuous use of explicitly foregrounded body horror in the form of bodily change. Rather than the sudden appearance of Diane's enormous black furry hands over the bathroom sink, Nina first notices a pocked rash on her shoulder, like plucked chicken skin. Later, the sprouting of swan feathers becomes more prominent; during her (fantasy) sex scene with Lily, a vibrating wave of pimpled skin, monstrously sexual goosebumps, undulates like an electric current between the two women's bodies denoting a sexually driven dark energy. The same effect rushes around Nina's skin in the final scenes when the 'Black Swan' has fully taken over, and she dances her set perfectly. The implication is that her sexual awakening has allowed her abandon to the malevolence and chaos of the role. Visual transformation of the body depicted during the sex scene marks the moment of consummation as a climactic moment in the film. Clara Bradbury-Rance takes issue with the trope of the transformative sex scene in queer cinema and uses it to hinge her argument that lesbianism in popular films such as *Black Swan* and, more recently, Nicolas Winding Refn's *The Neon Demon* (2016), features as little more than a plot device. Having compared *Black Swan* to David Lynch's *Mulholland Drive* (2001), where the sex scene provides the film with a 'climatic feature of narrative transformation emphasised through literal character transformation',[13] Bradbury-Rance reads *Black Swan* as 'another film featuring the illusory duplicity of the performer's narcissistic desire', and as yet another 'example of lesbianism's deployment as a tool of generic climax . . . the transformational cliché of lesbian sex as a mere vehicle confirms it as both reality and dream, both artifice and spectacle' (p. 33). While transformation at the point of same-sex intercourse has already been highlighted as a clichéd trope, it is my contention that New Queer Gothic films are all the more engaged with such a cliché, and that body horror is often used to suggest a psychosexual dematerialisation and queer epiphany in the plot.

In *Black Swan*, problematically and predictably, hypersexuality is equated with queer sexuality, which is figured as monstrous and all-consuming. The power radiating from Nina as the 'Black Swan' suggests a sexual climax in the last movements of frenzied fouetté turns where her arms transform into majestic wings. The price, however, for a perfect performance is a steady escalation of self-harming practice, something that cements the reading of this film as a pastiche embracing other examples of narratives in which the desiring female faces a punitive trajectory. Among its intertexts, Hitchcock's *Rebecca* (1940) and Powell and Pressburger's *The Red Shoes* (1948) are the most palpable with respect to female subjectivity contingent on replaceable roles and narrative persecution via 'madness' or death on any deviation from the highly prescriptive and gendered role. The scratching of her rash that draws blood, the ripping strips of skin from cuticle to knuckle, the apparition of herself as Beth, the previous 'Swan Queen' (Winona Ryder) stabbing her own face with a nail file, provide accelerated tension building towards the final scenes of self-harm where Nina, thinking that she has stabbed her 'alternate' Lily with a shard of broken mirror, plucks forth the glass from the growing blood stain in her plumage and swan dives to a 'perfect' death after her dance is complete. Sakshi Dogra offers a Lacanian reading of Nina's suicide, describing it as 'the price for a sense of narrative closure and also a cause for synthesis [with the ego's external image]',[14] and this might feed queer readings that invoke the death drive in celebrating the radical queerness of *Black Swan*'s ending. However, the literal and fantastic dematerialisation of Nina's body and psyche offer an overwhelmingly paranoid notion of queer female as dehumanised crisis.

Body horror and mirroring together create a world in which women are homogenised and expendable. In Mark Fisher and Amber Jacobs's debate about *Black Swan*, Fisher makes the case for his interpretation of *Black Swan* as an 'Irigarayan Horror',[15] whereas Jacobs argues that it 'reproduces the terms of Western male imaginary that Irigaray describes and critiques' (p. 58) but offers no alternate escape from those. Jacobs goes on shrewdly to account that:

> relations between women [are] reduced to pathological variant[s] of a mother-daughter bond characterised by merging or hate and competition ... Under the patriarchal conditions *Black Swan* replicates, women's attempts to achieve subjectivity invariably result in madness, breakdown, self-destructivity and premature death. (p. 59)

While I agree with Jacobs, Irigarayan horror seen evidenced in such a film that is so consumed by its objective of Othering women runs the risk of overlooking other Others. It is not only to the detriment of female subjectivity, as Jacobs has it, that *Black Swan* attempts to show the danger of patriarchal control, it is, furthermore, to the detriment of *queer* female subjectivity. Nina tries to make herself attractive to Thomas (Vincent Cassel), her chauvinistic choreographer who condescends the company's prima ballerinas (first Beth, then Nina) in bestowing them with his 'little princess' pet name.

Thomas constantly mocks Nina's restrained and controlled manner, telling her explicitly that she must present herself as sexualised. He gropes at her body: his hands squeeze her petite frame as if she were a sculpture and he the artist. He holds her in place, leering over her, forcing a kiss onto her twisted wincing face. He commands, 'open up your mouth', then stalks out of the dance studio disappointed: 'that was me seducing you'. Later, when Nina has been consumed enough by the 'Black Swan' to dance the performance perfectly, exuding dark vibrating power and sexuality, she leaps offstage between acts to force a kiss upon Thomas. However, this does not mark a straightforward role reversal: with Nina's transformation into a hypersexual alter ego, Aronofsky shows her behaviour to present as increasingly transgressive. Problematically, female agency, female sexuality and queerness all fall into negative representation in the process. The film remains ambiguous as to whether Nina is a lesbian, possessed queer desire, or indeed whether she ever desired her choreographer. What is interesting is that what makes her seem queer to other characters in the film is her obvious disinterest in sex (Thomas asks how 'fuckable' male dancers find Nina, which is met with sniggering). Arguably, the film codes this asexuality as related to her immaturity; that she 'frigid' because she is infantile. Thomas sets her the 'homework' task of touching herself, as if he held the key all along to her vagina – as though Nina requires an authoritative male to permit her to masturbate. As those around her continue to pair sexual passion with performance, notions of artifice and reality begin to blur for Nina. As she watches Lily (Mila Kunis) dance, with her hair loose, her skirt long and flowing, Thomas commentates in her ear, his words acting as her subconscious: 'Look at the way she moves. Not technically perfect but effortless. She's not faking it.' With an obvious conflation of Lily's sexual persona and her dancing, Nina is offered an image of femininity that she, the frigid 'un-fuckable' 'White Swan' cannot achieve without 'letting go'. Thomas asks her to show him more of that 'bite', referring to Nina's attempt at securing the part by donning the guise of the retiring prima ballerina and sporting her stolen lipstick. Nina feels shame for her animalistic defensive reaction to bite the lips he forced on her, but he mistakes the bite as vampirically sexual. Pastiche comes to mind again with this bite that encompasses connotations of hungry ambition and castrating female power. The questions *Black Swan* raises about bodies that signify the subject, suggest it as an Irigarayan horror, as theorised by Butler:

> The body that as reason dematerializes the bodies that may not properly stand for reason or its replicas, and yet this is a figure in crisis, for the body of reason is itself a phantasmic dematerialisation of masculinity, one which requires that women and slaves, children and animals be the body, performing the bodily functions that it will not perform . . . [Irigaray] fails to follow through the metonymic link between women and these other Others, idealizing and appropriating the 'elsewhere' as the feminine.[16]

Here, Butler takes Irigaray's notion of female mimesis to task in arguing that some expressions of feminism neglect the othering of some Others. I argue that this same trend is evident in Aronofsky's film, which tracks the implosion of subjectivity through internalised misogyny by way of overt queerphobia. Nina is clearly fascinated by Lily, and their sexual encounter seems to triumphantly, if reductively, mark her transition from controlled 'little girl' to an impulsive and independent woman. However, hopes for a reparative reading narrow when it is revealed that this scene occurred only in dream. Aronofsky thus relegates any notion of queer sexual awakening to the realm of the unconscious, reflecting the attitudes of any repressive patriarchal society.

Mirroring in Jack & Diane

Unlike the Black/White Swans and Lily/Nina dichotomies in Aronofsky's film, Jack and Diane are not obvious doubles and mirroring is less overt in the queer couple, although the theme remains a significant trope elsewhere in the film. Diane is very infantile and stereotypically 'girly'. Her fronds of blonde hair and sullen pout, coupled with her frilly, flamboyant outfits, set her apart from Jack's more traditionally masculine cropped brown hair, skater shorts and baggy shirt. The binary representation of feminine and masculine gender performances is undeniable and the 'butch/femme' lesbian stereotyping is overt. Keough's character is very sure of herself, and the film suggests that she is more mature and sexually experienced; this is emphasised when Jack is shown to pay a visit to an older woman (Kylie Minogue) for sex. Diane, however, is presented as a character with questions about her own subjectivity and identity. From the opening scenes, Gray places Diane in search of her twin sister Karen, who, it is revealed, encouraged Diane to move away so that they could be apart and the more overbearing Karen would not feel as though she were holding her sister back. In one scene, the twins have a phone conversation in which Diane tells her sister about meeting Jack. Later, Diane gets grounded by her aunt, so Karen agrees to call Jack and pretend to be Diane. This goes horribly wrong when Jack tries to engage Karen in phone sex that forces her to come clean, professing that she is 'not gay'.

The uncanny figure of the doppelgänger and the Gothic motif of mirroring clearly inform much of *Jack & Diane*'s narrative and visual presentation. One scene sees Jack's friend, Chris (Dane DeHaan), photoshopping Jack's face into pornographic pictures to sell over the internet. After Diane visits him and offers the image of her face to be used, a buyer informs them that that face is already circulating porn sites in a viral video. It is here that Jack learns that Diane and Karen are not only twins but identical twins. The doubling here is a cause for Gothic trauma and sexual paranoia, which is very much connected to heterosexual and non-consensual sex acts. The video shows Diane's twin (also played by Juno Temple, with auburn hair) being drugged by some men at a party. In it, she is led to a room and laid on a mattress on the floor where she is sexually abused. One of the men can be heard 'reassuring' Karen that nothing penetrative will happen – 'It's just a shower' – referring to their subsequent act of ejaculating on her prone body. Jack immediately runs to Diane's apartment to tell her about it. Karen fears that getting the police involved would only serve to increase attention for the video; instead, Diane says, 'I told her she could say it was me'. The twins have thus swapped again, suggesting an ease and familiarity with this shared knowledge of their likeness as problem-solving. This presentation of malleable identity between the sisters suggests that the homogenisation of women, as a paranoid trope of the Queer Gothic, is open to reparative repurposing. This is evidenced by Diane's ability to protect Karen via accepting any harassment on her behalf since she is not subject to the same degree of heterosexual exchange.

Female corporeality is made monstrous, but only through reflection. Discussing the monstrous feminine, Barbara Creed argues that horror does not emerge from the 'fact that woman has broken with her proper feminine role', but from the fact that she has 'made a spectacle of herself'[17] to herself, and projects that anxiety by enveloping another subject within it. In the final scenes, before the star-crossed lovers are wrenched asunder by circumstance, they try to navigate a dark, claustrophobic locker-room space together. With only the intermittent visibility from a camera flash, Diane leads the way while a nervous Jack follows.

This scene features the monster's final appearance, and in the fleeting flash we see that it is not Diane that has been possessed by the transformation this time, but Jack. Whatever the monster represented is now something that has been passed on in the vein of sexually transmitted disease, or, more specifically in the context of paranoid Queer Gothic, of AIDS panic. The last that images audiences are left with are the animations of internal workings, the moist sound of intestinal machinations continues along with something resembling a heartbeat. To me, this ending evokes the transformative potential of queer desire and love on each woman's sense of subjectivity. However, it is my argument that *Jack & Diane* works to represent the ambivalence of this potential: queer desire is at once paranoid and reparative in its effect on one's subjectivity.

Mirroring in Black Swan

Black Swan is no such queer love story. The Gothic elements of its narrative come from an internal turmoil similar to that portrayed in

Jack & Diane, but rather than reaching any new understanding about her own queer subjectivity, Nina's journey hurtles towards the final fouetté turns of her dance, frantically snatching at an impossible desire to be perfect, in a way that is extreme and wholly destructive. As this section will demonstrate, the existing scholarship on this text's engagement with mirroring suggests that there is a great deal to be explicated. Katharina Lindner laments that most:

> gender-focused debates tend to lack an acknowledgement of *Black Swan*'s intensely tactile and visceral register and the ways in which this might undermine understandings of subjectivity grounded in disembodied, specular and symbolic relations (and the gender norms intrinsic to these relations, in cinema and beyond).[18]

This chapter's contention is that there is a disjuncture in *Black Swan* between the queerness and the Gothic horror of destabilised identity and that this disjuncture operates around the film's use of mirroring. Mirroring in *Black Swan* is never a reflective exercise on keeping subjectivity borders in check, it is hyper-introspective and encourages a haemorrhaging of all that Nina tries to control, as her body, mind and certainly her sanity, are laid to waste by the film's end. Kristeva connects the uncanny to the abject in describing how the subject's encounter with unsettling and *unheimlich* phenomena serve as a reminder of mortality and to disturb identity. Through Aronofsky's use of mirrors, post-production overlays of Portman's face onto other peripheral female characters, and the constant suggestions of comparisons with the doppelgänger 'alternate', Lily, mirroring is explicitly evident as a queer as well as a Gothic theme. Used as an overt technique to dramatise the fractured sense of self in *Black Swan*'s subjective protagonist as well as her homogenisation within the dance company, mirroring catalyses Nina's ever-slackening grip on reality; she becomes pathologised and objectified by her visual transformation from girl to swan. As Jacobs suggests:

> The mirrors crudely hammer this point home; the infinite image of the reflected, homogenous bodies and faces of the ballerinas represents a construction of femininity that has no life outside the terms

of the mirror/gaze of the male symbolic . . . *Black Swan* proceeds as if feminist film theory never happened.[19]

Crucially, however, the misogynistic messages courted by the doubling of two women, and the peripheral homogenisation of all women, not only succeeds in showing women as part of one ensemble (one swan as only part of the composite bevy) but it also refuses queerness. Holding the prima role in the production requires playing the two 'Swan Queens', each a varying image of the prince's affection. Trying to force herself into these roles, in this heteronormative romance and tragedy does not marry neatly with Nina's personality and lifestyle. She is a young woman whose two main concerns in life are her dance career and a co-dependant relationship with her mother (Barbara Hershey). Aronofsky uses mirrors as one of many recurring motifs that create a composite metaphor of the feminine. Time and again, mirrors play tricks on Nina: a female giggle sounds, for example, as Nina turns to see her reflection scratching her shoulder while she remains still. Female competition is represented as a part of her subjectivity, while these competing selves are causing physical harm. Moments of paranoia like this are crafted, as Clara Bradbury-Rance argues, through the film's use of CGI, with camera and editing techniques that make visual the 'recognisable historic trope' of the double who signifies and characterises 'excessive female competitiveness, violence and the threat of lesbian sexuality'.[20] As is evident throughout this thesis, such a trope has been established by historic cultural representations of queer women as predatory, promiscuous and cruel.

Bradbury-Rance observes that 'the female characters in Aronofsky's film are always mediated in some way', and she concludes that via its 'relishing a turn to cliché cloaked (and read) as arthouse creativity' *Black Swan* is doubly problematic: 'the lesbian is doubly dangerous to conventional systems of representation because she not only multiplies the existing threat of women's sexual desire, but also reduces it' (p. 25). This is exactly how the homogenisation, pathologising and vilification of women is achieved in the film, and exactly why its misogyny hinders reparative reading.

The mirroring between the diegesis of the ballet and the film's plot is consistently and compulsively returned to with the many various mirroring techniques. Aronofsky demands a paranoid spectatorship by encouraging confusion between narrative threads. Following a play-within-a-play format, *Black Swan* presents the behind-the-scenes action of lead Nina 'becoming' the titular 'Black Swan', mirroring the metamorphosis that she must perform in her New York ballet company's production of *Swan Lake*. To the perceptions of space in the film, this form immediately insists on the ambiguity of both physical and psychological space. Aronofsky uses extreme close-ups either of Nina's face or scrutinising shots of her anatomised body, the grotesque habits of which are also given special voyeuristic inspection. Shots intent on establishing a morbidly fascinated yet repulsed gaze oscillates around the body of this tortured dancer whose feet and joints crunch and crack. Regularly holding the camera invasively in Nina's face or at her eye level encourages a subjective viewpoint of her insular experience in which fantasy, delusion and delirium bleed from the world of Nina's art – from the artifice of the theatre and magical realism of the ballet – into every contour of her life. Spaces Nina occupies include the stage, rehearsal spaces, the apartment she shares with her mother, and the walkways and metros between these public and domestic spaces. There is a confluence of doppelgänger illusions occurring in all these spaces, whether Nina recognises her own face on a passing stranger or misrecognises her face as another in her own reflection.

Bookending the film are two scenes of Nina dancing the 'Black Swan', the first is a dream or prophetic fantasy that she will become the company's new prima ballerina and will dance flawlessly. The final scene sees Nina's dream realised, though the 'reality' of any success is made ambivalent when Nina's wound begins to bleed, showing her to have fatally conflated perfection and death in very literal obedience to her choreographer's direction to 'lose' herself.

Mirrors are used in *Black Swan* to reflect the extreme self-scrutiny, narcissism and insularity specific to ballet culture; more broadly, however, they are used to relate women's subjectivity to appearance, beauty ideals and self-policing. Moreover, mirrors act as multifunctional spaces *and* objects connecting to motifs of horror and abjection in the Gothic body. The most horrific scenes of abjection in the film occur when Nina visits the hospitalised Beth after she has walked out into traffic after being ousted from her prima role. Nina peeks under the sheet at a sleeping Beth's grizzly injured leg. Abject horror is marked by the sudden shock of orchestral music. During another hospital visit, with the intention of returning the stolen lipstick and other items from Beth's dressing table, Nina sees Beth plunge a nail file into her own cheek. The image of Beth haunts Nina and she later appears in her kitchen performing the same violence on herself; Nina sees her own face in place of Beth's, disfigured by the nail file. The items used in these scenes are all significantly feminine, and prove transitory from woman to woman, their uses subverted to destroy rather than maintain beauty. What Jacobs calls the 'laughably crude symbolism'[21] at work in Aronofsky's palette, black and white marking out the simplistic binarism with red lips, eyes and wounds, can be extended to recall the paranoia that swirls around an axis of woman reduced to sex and monstrosity. This notion is succinctly expressed when Nina leaves the toilet cubicle after calling her mother to tell her about getting the part. The word 'whore' scrawled in red lipstick across the bathroom mirror confronts Nina and she winces while smudging it away with her hands. Mirrors, crudely but significantly, thus become a mechanism for paranoia to feature constantly. They allow Nina to try on other women's faces and perform other queer selves. They are complicit in marking femininity as a series, as a collective, internally and externally policed and persecuted by the culture in which it exists. It is with a shard of broken mirror that Nina makes a corpse of Lily, sweeping away the abject horror of her bloody crime into a closet space. Here, an obvious entwining of mirroring and body horror reflects the overarching tone of hyperbolic parody, as Nina sweeps the queer catalyst of her Gothic ravenesque transformation into the closet.

Reading the New Queer Gothic

Queer and Gothic fiction has been critiqued historically using paranoid reading gestures. I have applied rather paranoid readings to the New Queer Gothic films discussed in this chapter that I will now develop into an extended commentary on how to engage with these texts via different reading approaches. A purely paranoid reading of a text might uncover whatever harmful representation, political or problematic undertone exists both in the text and subtext. The act of looking for paranoid gestures in the narrative as well as the action of paranoid reading are debated by Eve Kosofsky Sedgwick throughout her oeuvre. The paranoid is 'something inextricably linked to Gothic tradition, specifically Gothic fiction's historical (mis)treatment of repressed and vilified sexualities'.[22] Ellis Hanson stresses that queer theory's 'powerful investment in the Gothic' is owed to its main critical contribution being 'close analysis of the often-paranoid shame-addled pleasures of gothic epistemology and hermeneutics' (p. 175). Hanson, a key figure in applying Sedgwick's theories of reading to Queer Gothic, wonders at 'how we might understand the queer pleasures of paranoia and horror without limiting our responses to pathologizing, moralising or just giggling'. Hanson asks, 'Is there a reparative reading of the Gothic that does not seek to redeem us from the genre? A reparative reading of paranoid reading?' (p. 188). I would argue that Heather Love answers this when responding to Sedgwick's 'call for reparation' with the challenge, 'we need to answer the call to paranoia and aggression',[23] presenting the seemingly binaristic readings as codependant. Thinking of the paranoid and the reparative as equally significant in the New Queer Gothic allows for a psychoanalytical criticism and investigation into where seats of Gothic anxiety or sexual paranoia lie. Furthermore, this thinking allows more scope for analysing instances in which traditional registers might be subverted, leading to a reparative reading of the still paranoid diegesis. It remains true that the most common gesture of criticism in queer studies of the Gothic is, as Hanson says, 'to find the queerness, the deviant sexual pleasure, occluded by its monstrous or villainous representation in a paranoid narrative'.[24] What this chapter is interested in is the finding of queer subjectivity, via mainly queer desire and pleasure, which exists in spite of monstrous representation. With these ideas in mind, this chapter will now revise its comparative analysis of *Jack & Diane* and *Black Swan* and the demonstrable Gothic themes that permeate their narratives of queer subjectification to uncover what new, valid, reparative effect they possess.

Sedgwick's queer readings of Henry James's works recur as an intersecting point for sexuality, paranoia and narrative. Indeed, some of Sedgwick's readings of James could be considered paranoid, as she offers, for example, the singular argument that a certain passage conveys homosexual anal sex. The form of paranoia that Hanson and Love discuss follows Sedgwick's definition in her final book, *Touching Feeling* (2003). Here, Sedgwick writes that if paranoia is about the repression of same-sex or queer desire then what is exposed by that paranoia is not the queer sexuality or desire but the systems of oppression under which it might exist. 'What is illuminated by an understanding of paranoia', she writes, 'is not how homosexuality works, but how homophobia and heterosexism work.'[25] Paranoia, Sedgwick clarifies, is only one of many ways of seeking out and organising knowledge. It can, at times, merely express delusional suspicions, but at others, it offers possibilities to 'unique access to true knowledge' (p. 130). In Sedgwick's argument the reparative approach is established as antithetical to paranoid theory when she describes it as being about 'pleasure ("merely aesthetic")' as well as being 'ameliorative ("merely reformist")' (p. 144). Sedgwick's own work, along with many important thinkers of queer theory and Gothic studies, acknowledges a reflexive awareness of its paranoid approach. Her studies, flavoured by a distinctive 'history of intimacy with the paranoid imperative', note the homophobic roots of traditional psychoanalysis: 'Freud, of course, traced every instance of paranoia to the repression of same-sex desire, whether in women or in men.' These associations, she offers, worked time and again to 'pathologize homosexuals as paranoid or to consider paranoia as a distinctly homosexual disease' (p. 126). The paranoid is a comfortable and familiar place for queer and Gothic criticism; it has been crucial to include it as a critical textual tool, but it is even more crucial that we find alternatives.

Earlier in this chapter I examined *Black Swan*'s visual representations of same-sex desire in the dancing scene between Nina and Lily and the subsequent sex scene. There is inherent paranoia encumbered by these scenes from the diegetic context: the love scene might have been a dream or a delirious fantasy.[26] I suggested that one could understand the ghettoisation of Nina's fantasy flirtation with same-sex desire as serving the purpose of titillation for the (male, heterosexual) viewer. On the other hand, a reading of Nina's uninhibited queer encounter with her double and her subsequent ability to assume a new sexualised, wanton, yet fiercely proficient role, might be more reparative. The ending is most engaged with Leo Bersani and Lee Edelman's antisocial queer theories, incumbent of psychoanalytic notions of the death drive.

For Lindner, the effective use of mirrors and mirroring in *Black Swan* equates to a 'blurring of boundaries between representation/ reflection and performance takes place not only in relation to the bodies in and around the film, but also involves the body of the film'.[27] Lindner's argument centres on the film's use of digital effects to transform the skin of Nina/Portman. She argues that when 'Nina's body and image are out of synch' the mirror is the crucial site at which the skin of the film and the skin of the protagonist are aligned. The effect of this phenomenological contact of the skin – '(Nina's and our own)'– leads her to ask, 'can we trust it/them? – and therefore the relations of looking, reflection, surface and image are articulated not as specular but as profoundly tactile – as well as increasingly unreliable' (p. 125). Readings like this suggest that paranoia and negativity are perhaps too intimately bound up with queer representation in the Gothic narrative: metaphors for how the metatextual meanings relate to their being bound to the forms of within which queerness finds itself abound in this example of New Queer Gothic film.

Much of the above criticism of *Black Swan* concerns gender. Lindner argues that *Black Swan* is not a feminist film, claiming 'it might not explicitly engage with feminist (film theoretical) concerns' (p. 138). What *Black Swan* does successfully, according to Lindner, is show the affinity between the film form and the body of the dancing female within the film: 'The film's body is the dancing body's double, mirroring its movements, gestures, stances, attitudes and tendencies' (p. 138). Thinking about Lindner's linking of the woman's (predominantly Portman's) on-screen body and the body of the film is interesting when coupled with Tania Modleski's self-conscious claim that her work involves 'analysing in the context of feminist inquiry the works of a filmmaker whom some would call the greatest practical joker as well as the greatest misogynist'.[28] Modleski is of course discussing Hitchcock though a similar claim could be applied to Aronofsky's work. Interestingly, within Modleski's comprehensive studies of Hitchcock's films, she refutes Mary Ann Doane's claim that female spectatorship is denied pleasure, stating that pleasure is available via anger:

> especially when that anger has been long denied or repressed. This is a pleasure Hitchcock's films repeatedly make available to women. It has long been noted that the director is obsessed with exploring the psyches of tormented and victimised women. While most critics attribute this interest to a sadistic delight in seeing his leading ladies suffer, and while I'm even willing to concede this point, I would nevertheless insist that the obsession often takes the form of a particularly lucid expose of the predicaments and contradictions of women's existence under patriarchy. (p. 27)

Perhaps a way of reading Aronofsky's film reparatively would be to consider it as representative of the (im)possibility of female subjectivity thriving within the panopticon of patriarchal culture, and while I do not wish fully to imply a parallel between Hitchcock and Aronofsky, there is something to be said for the presentation of satirical misogyny in this film that perhaps has more to do with its form as a pastiche rather than suggesting auteur homage.

At the end of *Jack & Diane*, viewers are left with an end credit sequence featuring the stop-motion animation of plaited hair that snake their way into the title of the film after snaking through pulsing organ-like workings. This animation is accompanied by the moist sounds of intestinal machinations that conclude the film, along with something resembling a heartbeat. This end sequence works to convey feelings of ongoing internalised turmoil. Perhaps Hanson's ambition to see the reparative in the paranoid reading can, after all, be achieved with this final animation if it were to be read as illustrative of queer subjectivity as an 'always-becoming' continuous effort. An initial reading of the examples of doubling in *Jack & Diane* seems to glean only paranoid results; there is anxiety about the straight sister being mistaken for the queer one in the first instance. A reparative reading emerges when Diane can be seen 'recognising [her] uncanny strangeness', something Kristeva qualifies as the reparative act of disarming it: 'we shall neither suffer from it nor enjoy it from the outside. The foreigner is within me, hence we are all foreigners. If I am a foreigner, then there are no foreigners.'[29] There emerges a double bind in Rust Gray's use of doubling, here. In the one instance, women's bodies are represented as homogenous through the medium of homemade pornography, with faces and identities becoming interchangeable. However, this scene suggests the redemptive power of doubling or multiplying selves as a means of circumnavigating paranoia.

Since the advent of queer theory in the 1990s, key thinkers who would rely on the repressive and the paranoid to effectively 'queer' a text, increasingly worked to find more reparative methods of criticism. Much of the paranoia encumbered, rightly and necessarily in queer criticism, is bound up with the fraught relationship between queer theory and identity politics. Annamarie Jagose describes how, like Sedgwick's calls to read in both a paranoid and reparative mode, it is important to understand queer theorising as not wholly in opposition to identity politics but to appreciate it as a tool for interrogating the effect and preconditions of identity:

> If the dialogue between queer and more traditional formations is sometimes fraught – which it is – that is not because they have nothing in common. Rather, lesbian and gay (and we ought to add feminist) faith in the authenticity or even political efficacy of identity categories and the queer suspension of all such classification energise each other, offering . . . the ambivalent reassurance of an unimaginable future.[30]

Jagose is one of the theorists used by Lindner to 'put feminist and queer (back) in touch with each other' in her book *Film Bodies: Queer Feminist Encounters with Gender and Sexuality in Cinema*. Lindner proclaims that 'we can be queer *and* paranoid – or so it seems',[31] as she tracks the evolution of queer theory through early Butlerian theories concerned with language and discourse, through to Sarah Ahmed's more corporeal, affect-driven uses of queer theory's genesis, from importantly questioning the material conditions on which identity markers like gender are based, to a more phenomenological, 'sensuous' kind of appellation (p. 28). How queerness relates to the bodies and represents subjectivities on-screen in New Queer Gothic films indicates, as evidenced in this chapter's analysis, this balancing act of critiquing material conditions and reading phenomenologically continues to invoke both paranoid and reparative gestures.

It has, clearly, become pertinent for those reading queerly to move beyond simply identifying the systems of oppression under which queerness exists in order to celebrate or bemoan levels of visibility, as was the case, for example, in the Vito Russo era of queer theory.[32] The Gothic themes that drive the queer narrative in *Jack & Diane* might first induce readings that are wholly paranoid. However, as this chapter has shown, ameliorative readings are made possible through close analysis of how Gothic themes feature in relation to the queer representations that they attend. Each of the films reprise nods to the homophobic roots of interpretative analysis noted by Sedgwick, with their employment of traditional tropes, such as the monstrous feminine, which dehumanise and pathologise female protagonists. While *Black Swan* has proven something of an outlier in the lack of opportunity that this hyper-paranoid narrative allows for reparative reading, *Jack & Diane* does allow ameliorative readings of its Gothic motifs to construct positive representations of queer identification and desire. Whereas any representation of the successful queer female is dealt with punitively in *Black Swan*, *Jack & Diane*'s lovers part changed but unharmed, with new perceptions on love, sex and selfhood and a shedding of the contagious confusion that the monster invited. While it may remain true that the most common gesture of criticism in queer studies of the Gothic is, as Hanson says, 'to find the queerness . . . occluded by its monstrous or villainous representation in a paranoid narrative',[33] what this chapter has worked to develop is an understanding of queer subjectivities that exist in contemporary film despite monstrous representation. It is crucial not only that more work continues this act of reading reparatively and that representations of queer subjectivities continue to be critiqued in this balanced way to uncover what new, valid, redemptive effect they have on things like specific genres and modes such as the Gothic, but also that more work be produced that actively seeks to maintain the relationship between queer theory and feminism.

4

'The Saviour who came to tear my life apart': The Queer Postcolonial Gothic of The Handmaiden

❦

While the previous chapter introduced a model for demonstrating key motifs of New Queer Gothic cinema and explored a critical method with which to read these texts, this chapter will provide a developed application of such a critique, this time focusing on one film text. This chapter will demonstrate how using Sedgwick's model for paranoid reparative reading can build an effective analysis of how the representational and critical value of New Queer Gothic films relate to ongoing debates in feminist and queer film criticism, and intersectional studies more broadly. Considering that the canon of film texts explored currently by critics of queer studies predominantly concerns representations of queer women who are predominantly middle class and white, American or European, *The New Queer Gothic* recognises the importance of looking beyond the Eurocentric mainstream. Park Chan-wook's 2016 film *The Handmaiden* is a South Korean transformative re-working of the 2002 Sarah Waters novel, *Fingersmith*. It offers a nuanced depiction of same-sex desire and subjectivity in the context of a Gothic setting and narrative, where female queerness is figured as rather utopic and a means of breaking a chain of patriarchal abuse.

This chapter has two key objectives. The first is to introduce the ways in which the film engages with notions of identity in relation to colonial identity and queerness. The chapter will return to this idea to situate the film within one of its contexts as an example of Asian Extreme cinema. The second objective involves situating *The Handmaiden* within its context as a film representing lesbian subjectivity, in order to discuss a rationale for claiming it as a New Queer Gothic film.

In *The Handmaiden*, much of the plot and narrative remain close to the source text, *Fingersmith*; however, the action is transported from Victorian England to Japanese-occupied Korea during the 1930s colonial period, focusing on the relationship of Sook-ee (known sometimes as Tamako, played by Kim Tae-ri) and Lady Hideko (Kim Min-hee). Park Chan-wook's *The Handmaiden* is a film steeped in duplicity, falsehood and transgression. As two women's lives become entangled in such a way that they can become interchangeable in their roles as victim and aggressor, exploiter and exploited, identifiers such as gender, sexuality, race and nationality are manipulated by characters to suit various agendas and prerogatives that serve as divisive to the plot. The effect of this is that those identity signifiers that are traditionally thought of as existing in contingency with power prove to be arbitrary and performative. The shifting nature of identity might bolster and embolden the impulse to use the term 'queer'; however, some critics debating same-sex desire and lesbian representation in cinema have maintained a wariness of the term. Most recently, Clara Bradbury-Rance expresses her concern over the infantilising and pathologising rhetoric historically and irrevocably attached to queer women in visual culture:

> Even as they promise to emancipate us, shifting terminologies have the potential to reinscribe problematic mechanisms . . . the productive relationship between queer theory and lesbian film is based on the queerly paradoxical structure of lesbianism itself: a latent potentiality for queerness based on the history of the compromised image.[1]

This 'compromised image' denotes Bradbury-Rance's appreciation of the on-screen lesbian as 'marked by a paradoxical burden of visibility and invisibility produced at the convergence of queer and feminist discourses' (p. 2). Questions of (in)visibility and erasure from relevant areas of critical theory are among Bradbury-Rance's key concerns as she debates the relevance of queer theory to contemporary films about same-sex female desire. *The Handmaiden* features in Bradbury-Rance's analysis, but only briefly – she writes:

> What the film has in common with the principal case studies of this book is a gesturing to the precariousness of the image in a visual field that insistently cites the past. Its contemporary production context enables the mainstreaming of its explicit sex scenes. Yet, its complex narrative unsettles our attachments. We fail to know what the visible image has really offered us. Its chronology threatens to make lesbianism impossible: a misremembering, a figment of the imagination or a misrecognition. (pp. 11–12)

Interestingly, Bradbury-Rance points to the non-linear narrative techniques with which *The Handmaiden* presents its displays of queer sexuality and desire. Where Bradbury-Rance's study, in the tradition of Patricia White and others, seeks to investigate how a range of genre-variant films mediate, produce and represent lesbianism and same-sex desire via what is made visual, this chapter is not wholly consumed with visual coding (or lack thereof in the case of *The Handmaiden*). Rather, this chapter approaches its reading of the queer woman as holistically as possible. By analysing Gothic themes of space, mirroring and abjection, this chapter will draw on *The Handmaiden*'s cinematography, sound, styling and script, as well as contemplating, as Bradbury-Rance does, its stark visual presentation of queer sex acts.

Queer Postcolonialism

The plot and narrative of *The Handmaiden* implicate intersecting concerns of queerness and postcolonialism through the ways in which gendered, sexual, national and class identity are represented. An interchangeability of identities features very strongly in the film, and not only in the swapping of 'mad woman' for lady, or rogue for art teacher. Kouzuki, the *Bluebeard*-esque uncle has divorced his

Korean wife, Miss Sasaki (Kim Hae-sook), though, tellingly, she remains housekeeper of the house and continues to share his bed. Kouzuki had married into a wealthy Japanese family. Since his rich bride died, he plans to marry his niece to secure social ascension, fortune and title. Count Fugiwara is a Korean conman performing the role of a noble-born Japanese man, disgraced for ruining himself with gambling and now working as an art counterfeiter and painting tutor. Notions of swapping and changing national and racial identity and modelling colonial hierarchy on a class system is a problematic area of representation that filmmakers should approach sensitively. Filmmakers should also use caution when conveying the interchangeability and homogenisation of women, particularly women of East Asian descent, considering the dehumanising and homogenising effects of colonial narratives and historical stereotypes. Park Chan-wook manages to counter any such concerns in his depiction of a journey to queer subjectivity, provided by the vehicles of postcolonial Gothic read with a consideration of paranoid reparative reading methods.

A changeling dynamic exists between the characters long before any actual plot to swap identities, and this has much to do with the convoluted narrative of plotting and betrayal carried over from the source text. Count Fujiwara (Ha Jung-woo) is fooled into believing that his plan made with Lady Hideko (Kim Min-hee) to swap the identities of the Hideko and Sook-hee (the common Korean thief that he enlists to pose as her handmaiden) will come off. Fujiwara plans to double-cross the women, interring the Lady's handmaiden into an asylum under her name so that he and the real Hideko can each split the inheritance signed over to him. The central women, however, supersede the faux plot used to dupe Sook-hee (Kim Tae-ri) into believing that she must simply encourage the Lady to fall in love with the Count so they could marry before interring *her* in the asylum. Instead, the two women fall in love and hatch a third plan, which involves rescuing Sook-hee from her incarceration as the Lady Hideko and escaping to Russia, leaving the Count behind to be apprehended by Uncle Kouzuki's (Cho Jin-woong) men. In the film's final scenes, Fujiwara is tortured for information about Hideko. Kouzuki lasciviously asks about their wedding night, about her body and how she responded to the

Count's sexual advances. Fujiwara denies Kouzuki any satisfaction, seemingly out of honour, though flashback scenes reveal the pretence of their wedding night; Hideko is shown to deny his touch completely. She makes some gasping sounds to pretend intercourse before slashing her palm with a knife to leave blood on the sheets as evidence of consummation of their sham marriage. Fujiwara begs to be permitted his cigarettes, which he soon reveals to Kouzuki are laced with mercury. Poisonous in its gaseous form, the smoke kills them both. Meanwhile, Hideko and Sook-Hee sail across the wide, open Sea of Japan. The juxtaposition here speaks to the contrast in space marking the ironic narrative twist to questions of agency and freedom and the reversal in power roles between the central men and the central women. As the film's queer women take control of their own lives, outfoxing the systemic oppression of marriage and inheritance, and the scheming committed by the film's class-aspiring, capitalist men, the men themselves emerge as the architects of their own destruction. Central to their demise is the mercury-laced cigarette, which has, over the course of the film, become a totem of female confinement, exploitation and objectification. In an earlier scene, Fujiwara is shown to sketch naked women on his cigarette skin before he rolls and smokes it, describing that as his 'particular way of possessing beauty'. Sitting in the print-making bowels of the Gothic pastiche house, the deepest recesses where Kouzuki's monstrosity is emphasised by the presence of a giant octopus in a tank, smoke fills the confined, claustrophobic space and kills them. In this way the Gothic trope of space is not used to be read as reparative so much as it to be retributive. The percolation of revenge is to be expected in a Chan-wook Park film. In much of his oeuvre, the plot is driven by characters seeking retribution, and this has come to be identifiable as one of the narrative characteristics of the Asian Extreme (sometimes referred to as 'Extreme Asian') genre, more broadly.[2] Historically, queer women have existed in Gothic culture only as phantasmal, ghostly, barely-there creatures of great ambiguity, marginality and liminality. Critics such as Terry Castle refused to associate their work with queer theory when it entered academia twenty years ago because they believed it to be preoccupied with the masculine. Castle lamented the act of placing lesbian phenomenology under what she calls the contemporary 'fashionable rubric' of queer theory, arguing that the use of such a term 'makes it easier to enfold female homosexuality back "into" male homosexuality and disembody the lesbian once again'.[3] In her pioneering text, *The Apparitional Lesbian* (1993), Castle charts the history of the lesbian's representation in fiction and film, following a path from ethereal and ephemeral appearances and negative representation to her imbrication into the world of flesh, life and desire. In opposition to the 'Sedgwickian incarnation' of queer theory, Castle writes of her unease with the universalising aspirations and language of the field.[4] Other critics, however, hold that one of the main projects of queer theory is its undercutting of stable identities in order to expose the shortcomings of representation and offer an 'account for heterogeneity and opacity as constituents of subjectivity'.[5] Annamarie Jagose, another queer feminist critic who feels very protective of female queerness having its own critical discursive space, writes that compared to male homosexuality 'female homosexuality has been ambivalently constituted in relation to the logics of vision: it is less the subject of prohibition than of an incredulousness that would deny the space of its possibility'.[6] This chapter is informed by the view that queer theory is a crucial and necessary critical framework that acknowledges the important work of lesbian and gay studies but challenges the notions of fixed identity. Establishing and demonstrating the value of claiming this text as important to the field of the New Queer Gothic does not aim at incredulity but opportunity.

In *The Handmaiden*, the historical and geographical context of the film is reflected in the queer relationship that develops between a Japanese woman and a Korean woman. Korea's enforced role as an agricultural annex to sustain Japan is a dynamic played out during a love scene where Sook-hee wishes out loud that she had breast milk to feed Hideko. This could read as an internalisation of the colonial power structures that connect two of this chapter's key Gothic themes – space and abjection – in a crucial scene of queer subjectivity development. There is an unsettling mixture of metaphors here, which, although available to both paranoid and reparative interpretations, threatens to balk notions of queer subjectivity.

This sex scene begins, in both of its tellings, from the perspective of each protagonist, with Sook-hee role-playing and Hideko's feigned naivety about what a virgin bride is to expect on her wedding night. Pretending to be the Count, Sook-hee plays at seducing Hideko but both women soon abandon the pretence of rehearsal. This mimesis of traditional gender performance as an initiator of queer sex is something that the plot reprises from the source text, *Fingersmith*, and it works to exposes how essentialist attitudes and colonial zeitgeists are used to the service of lesbian desire across patriarchal cultures, whether they be in the context of Victorian England or 1930s colonial South Korea. The paranoid reparative gestures of writing the queer woman back into history is an overt concern shared by neo-Victorian novelists such as Waters and revenge film auteurs such as Park.

Uncanny Gothic Spaces

Park sets most of his action within a Gothic house that proves quite postmodern in the way that it uncannily resembles the Victorian English 'grandiose' style of the Briar house of its source text. The housekeeper, Miss Sasaki, bustles Sook-hee through the English and Japanese parts of the house towards the servants' quarters. Sook-hee is directed to her space in the house: a box bed. These beds originated in late medieval western Europe when they would have been used in peasant houses to provide sleeping quarters separate from the sheltered livestock and to provide extra insulation during winter. Later references to the box bed appear in classic Victorian literature such as Emily Brontë's *Wuthering Heights* (1847). The bed becomes a very significant totem of Gothic space in this novel, considering that it begins as a sanctuary space for adolescent Catherine Earnshaw, it is the site where Lockwood's nightmares take place, and finally it becomes Heathcliff's deathbed. A paradoxical space of enclosure, at once a refuge from the outside world (where, for example, young Cathy Linton keeps her journals) and a coffin, the box bed exists in literary memory as a highly symbolic compartment in which to store a protagonist. Charlotte Brontë introduced her readers to Jane Eyre in a very similar space: a cupboard-like window seat. Jane is later tormented by being trapped in the 'red room' with the corpse of her uncle, and Brontë's use of Gothic space becomes even more uncanny when Jane discovers her double, the Other woman in the attic. This leitmotif of queer characters physically closeting themselves, or of sweeping that which is connected to sex or death away into a closet or cupboard space, has already been identified as an apropos signifier of the shame, paranoia and moral negativity that attends the antisocial or anti-relational gestures of queer theory – it is a theme I will return to in subsequent chapters. In this context, it has specific intertextual relevance in bridging classic examples of the female Gothic to contemporary New Queer Gothic fiction.

One scene in *The Handmaiden* featuring the box bed sees Hideko shoving Sook-hee into the bed and shutting her away violently. It is in sudden moments of intensity such as this that suggest the film is itself formally hybrid, with its art-house aesthetics and Asian Extreme techniques. The styling and cinematography of this scene shows a meticulous focus on the movement of the women onscreen, wide angles of the large bedroom emphasise their proximity, Hideko slaps Sook-hee and the rapid thunderous sound of their hurried footsteps as she bustles her handmaiden across the room accompanies a close-up shot of their feet. Park is known for continuous uninterrupted scenes of stylised choreographed violence, his most famous example being the corridor fight scene in *Oldboy* (2002). *The Handmaiden* is no such action film, but the application of genre-specific styling to an already queer source narrative increases not only its Gothic affect, as the style calls for moments of extreme violence, but also its ability to frame 'Othering' as multifaceted. As Eunah Lee explains:

> The branding of the Extreme Asian genre borrows from orientalist fantasies of the West, and, in turn, reinforces exotic stereotypes of the East. In other words, western cultists, collecting specific genres of East Asian films with the expectation of graphic visual extremity and classifying that visual style as distinctively Asian, disclose a recurrent anxiety toward the East, which once again presents the East and its artefacts and commodities as unknown, incomprehensible, and wholly 'other'.[7]

The commodification presented to us is certainly built on these paradigms, with Park crafting stylised exploitation and ironic exploitation at every turn; as with the plot, audiences are never permitted total certainty on who is involved, who knows, who is 'in on' the plot. However, Asian Extreme cinema has not been theorised enough for much in the way of critical purchase and I comment on it here as a context rather than qualify it as form.

In *The Handmaiden*, Hideko gives readings of her uncle's 'poetry' (his collection of erotica), as Maud does for her Uncle Lilly in the source novel. On Sook-hee's first night in the house, Hideko wakes shouting for her mother after a nightmare and tells the new maid that the ghost of her predecessor, her aunt who used to perform her role, still haunts the place and on some nights can be seen hanging from the cherry blossom tree where she killed herself. In this way, while the grounds of the house, its outside space, are attached to the trauma of the aunt's suicide, the hybrid house with its mixed nationalities and grand façade creates such an enveloping metaphor of the villainous uncle who keeps Hideko captive as he did her aunt before her. Benjamin Harvey would deem this indicative of a common use of Gothic space in which 'the grip of the past is figured architecturally'.[8] He observes that films such as *Psycho* (1960) and *Peeping Tom* (1960) 'are about post-tyrannies overshadowing, dominating the present: Mrs Bates' bullying and Dr Lewis's experiments; both parents are like psychic vampires'.[9] *The Handmaiden* follows two protagonists and narrates each of their traumatic pasts in order to inform the tyrannical present in which they find themselves trapped. In Part One of the film, which follows Sook-Hee's perspective, the first protagonist's thoughts are expressed in a voice-over as she familiarises herself with her new home. That Sook-Hee wonders at the old mistress killing herself because the house is so big and drove her mad is very poignant and establishes the house as the seat of much of the film's Gothic anxiety. Much of Park's filmography seems to foreground the relationship of public and private space to comment on the historical sociopolitical contexts of his films.[10] This is something that Homi Bhabha recommends as important to interrelate past and present traumas and events, as it connects 'the traumatic ambivalence of a personal, psychic history to the wider disjunctions of political existence'. He argues that this 'does not merely recall the past' but represents it as a conditional '"in-between" space that innovates and interrupts the performance of the present'.[11] It is especially significant that Sook-hee identifies the house as the seat of Gothic trauma and anxiety considering the paralleled fears that Hideko shares with her about her surroundings later in the film. Her prison is an inherited one, and her experience reverberates with other women's experiences over time; the setting, which folds public and private experiences of malleable identity and colonisation, paradoxically homogenises and queers women in *The Handmaiden*.[12] *The Handmaiden* expresses this same postcolonial impulse, a gothicising of colonising power, the antithesis of the West's appropriation of other cultures where subjectivity is neglected; with the Gothic trope of possession, the house metonymically represents the colonising of the mind.

The postcolonial Gothic hybrid house is the site of much psychic trauma; as in most Gothic narratives, it exudes paranoia, uncanniness, supernatural glimpses and claustrophobia. The dark, enclosed setting inside the house is offset by later scenes that see the women, having escaped the house, running through expansive fields or atop the desk of a steam ship, the women are framed with overt connotations of emancipation, in wide-open spaces denied to Sook-hee in the baby-farm house and denied to Hideko in the Gothic house or the sanatorium. This chapter's next section will further analyse the film's uses of space, introducing the ways in which it engages with the Gothic themes of mirroring and abjection.

From Mirroring to Mimesis

Park includes an erotic bath scene that shares many parallels with the scene in which Hideko and Sook-hee escape with the Count, sailing in a rowboat on a river leading out of the house's estate. Each of the scenes feature water that becomes as important aurally as it is visually in carrying a tone of sexual consciousness in the attention to sensory affect. The gentle sloshing sounds and the blurring cloak afforded by the humidity and vapour in the atmosphere, whether in the steamy bathroom or on the foggy river, the twinned *mise en scène* surrounds the women, its gossamer aesthetic reminiscent of the lesbian sex scene between Miriam and Sarah (Catherine Deneuve and Susan Sarandon) in Tony Scott's *The Hunger* (1983).

Park connects these surroundings to the body and the subjective viewpoints of Hideko and Sook-hee: the camera lingers on extreme close-ups of Hideko's mouth as Sook-hee works a thimble against her sharp tooth; later in the boat the slowing sounds of heavy breathing accompany a slow blinking effect of the camera to create synchronicity between subjectivity and space. The lapping sounds of the water are layered with the sounds of breathing, which could be the diegetic breathing of the Count as he rows, or it could be the breathless panting of Sook-hee or Hideko. The reprisal of images, the literal doubling of scenes from each protagonist's perspective encourages this impulse to parallel other scenes in order to frame a non-chronological narrative of queer attachment and subjectivity formation.

A kind of doubling is present in the context of the film's form to connect scenes and emphasise the tone of intimacy and synchronicity between place and queer female subjectivity, but Park uses doubling most overtly to suggest the entanglement of the two female protagonists' identities as their attraction to each other develops. Doubling emerges as a significant method for exploring the national and colonial identities of these two women. The first striking instance of this occurs in one of the film's early scenes that follows Sook-hee's arrival at the house as the new handmaiden – on Miss Sasaki brusque tour of the house, Sook-hee pauses on the stairs at the sight of an intimidating portrait. The camera follows her gaze as she climbs the stairs and sees the large portrait of Hideko as a child, dressed in traditional Japanese kimono and hamaka, and a change of light as she passes eerily personifies the still image. A smirk appears on the child's face and is accompanied by the extra-diegetic score of pitchy pipe music, which lands on several moments of tension and suspense throughout the film. This short scene is pregnant with symbolic meaning: initial readings would focus on the queer uncanny of this supernatural, precocious image of the child. It stands like a custodian to the next level of the house, a curious symbol of Hideko's infantilised situation of forced stasis in the house and in her inflexible role. However, the coy expression that queers the child and suggests the loss of innocence, which is later revealed in scenes that recall Hideko as rebellious during her training in erotic orating from a very young age. One scene especially captures such a loss of innocence, showing Hideko at the age of about eight or nine, learning words with her aunt: the two recite words associated with genitalia and giggle. Uncle Kouzuki grabs both of their faces with leather-gloved hands and squeezes their mouths in punishment. When released Hideko and her aunt share fearful gasps instead of laughter. The smirking image could also be read as defiant, though to the apprehensive Sook-hee, picking her way through the house by the light of Miss Sasaki's dull lamp, it bespeaks an overwhelming sense of affinity: the little girl in a big portrait and the vast house dwarfing the new handmaiden, interning her. A psychoanalytical reading of this double would draw on Otto Rank, Sigmund Freud and Karl Jung's theories around doppelgängers. Freud's 'Unheimlich' (1919) essay was of course inspired by Rank's work on the subject. In 'The Uncanny' (Unheimlich), Freud describes the double in ancient cultures as signifying an 'insurance against the extinction of the self', which reflected a desire for immortality; 'the primordial narcissism which dominates the mental life of the both the child and primitive man, and when this phase is surmounted, the meaning of the double changes: having once been an assurance of immortality, it becomes the uncanny harbinger of death.'[13] Rank dwelt on the literary representations of the double, drawing on such examples as E. T. A. Hoffmann's 'The Sandman' (1816), Fyodor Mikhailovich Dostoevsky's *The Double* (1846) and Oscar Wilde's *The Picture of Dorian Gray* (1890) to illustrate where the double-motif signalled such diagnoses as the:

> persecution complex . . . not only Freud's concept of the narcistic disposition toward paranoia, but also, in an intuition rarely attained by the mentally ill, they reduce the chief pursuer to the ego itself, the person formerly loved most of all, and now direct their defence against it. This view does not contradict the homosexual etiology of paranoia. We know, as we already mentioned, that the homosexual love object was originally chosen with a narcissistic attitude towards one's own image.[14]

With this outdated, prescriptive pathologising of homosexuality, we are reminded of the historical intimacy shared between psychoanalysis, paranoia, homophobia and the Gothic. So, the uncanny introduction given through the figure of a rather supernaturally precocious Hideko double, immediately situates the film in this paranoid frame, equipping it with rich intertextual Gothicity.

Broadly speaking, the doubling of the same-sex female couple is hardly a Gothic trope on its own, but more of a mainstay in lesbian representation. Bradbury-Rance lists examples of films in which the doubling of women has 'structured narrative drives from '*Metropolis* (Fritz Lang, 1927) to *Sisters* (Brian de Palma, 1973), *That Obscure Object of Desire* (Luis Bunuel, 1977) and *The Double Life of Veronique* (Krzysztof Kieslowski, 1991)'. Drawing on Mulvey's pioneering work on the male gaze, Bradbury-Rance writes that 'woman represents a threat to the coherence of the male ego, the source of both his pleasure and his potential undoing . . . This male ambivalence about women's duplicity is brought into visual form by mirrors, doppelgängers, portraits and disguises.'[15] A true revenge film, Park's *The Handmaiden* presents all of these tropes, though it seems to have an ameliorative objective of holding cinema's long struggle with questions of the male gaze at the forefront of its conscience. Indeed, the explicit sex scenes, as Bradbury-Rance and others have noted, were attended by a female-only cast and crew to avoid claims of pandering to heterosexual male spectatorship. Whether that goal was achieved remains ambiguous.

As their relationship develops and the convoluted plot unravels, Park crafts his two protagonists into doubles and this serves to paradoxically highlight their interchangeability as well as their aptitude to work together and outwit the systems of oppression in which they find themselves. Similar to a scene present in the source text, Park includes a scene that calls attention to the similarities of the two women's appearance. While dressing Hideko, Sook-Hee is told to try some of her Lady's dresses on, the camera focuses on each woman's unblemished skin as they lace up corsets and unbutton petticoats. As each of them turns her back to be laced or undone by the other, matching hair pieces can be picked out resting uniformly in their almost identically styled hair. Significantly, their physical similarities are presented in parallel to their growing desire for each other, which is expressed through dialogue and the voiceover subjective used earlier in the film to present the inner monologues of the character from whose perspective this part of the film follows. Park's choice of camera angle shows Hideko and the reflection of Sook-hee regarding the earrings she has tried on. The use of the physical mirror is highly symbolic, as it is in this moment that Hideko admits true expressions of desire: 'Each night in bed, I think of your face.' Sook-hee replies, 'Don't be silly, miss', though her voiceover thoughts continue as she leaves the mirror to undress her mistress: 'Ladies truly are the dolls of maids, all of these buttons are for my amusement, if I undo the buttons and pull out the cords, then, the sweet things within, those sweet and soft things. . .If I were still a pickpocket I'd slip my hand inside.' As each character reflects the desiring looks and comes to look more like the object of her desire, the use of doubling becomes connotative of queer desire. This mirroring behaviour seems to become more frequent and overt in both subjective viewpoints of Hideko and Sook-hee, presenting each woman as similar but separate subjects, experiencing resonance and reflection which encourages the formation of an independent self. This suggests allusions to the Lacanian process of subjectification through identification. That this narrative shows women 'fall[ing] in love with [her] own image reflected back . . . from the other, outside self',[16] seems, however, to contend with Anneke Smelik's appreciation of the Mirror Stage. Smelik writes that, 'for Lacan the same-sex love between women equals the loss of the boundary between self and other. Self and other are inextricably bound in a bond that will inevitably explode in violence when the "Law of the Father" intervenes and draws the boundaries between the Imaginary and the Symbolic'.[17] The boundary necessary for individual subjectivity is conversely achieved only after the women in *The Handmaiden* discover and experience real queer desire.

This progressive increase in the process of fashioning Hideko and Sook-hee into doubles climaxes in the film's love scenes. The film follows the three-part structure of presenting the narrative through the maid's subjective viewpoint, then the Lady's subjective viewpoint, before mixing perspectives in the final scenes, these parts are indicated by headings that appear at the bottom of the screen alongside the subtitles. This structure thus allows for two different presentations of the same action, much like the narrative construction of the source text. The differences in each woman's subjective account allude to the unreliability of the story's narration; however, these differences also mark each character as independent subjectivities experiencing the same acts slightly differently but with equal pleasure. Park includes a more graphic and acrobatic sex scene in Part Two's extended depiction from Hideko's perspective. It is significant that the chronology of the film, as queerly out of step as it is, places this scene after the revelation of the women's desire for one another. This being established, the highly stylised sex presents as a series of positions in which the characters become mirror images of each other, whether that is in a triumphant holding of hands during tribadi or the 'Yin and Yang' appearance of mutual simultaneous oragenitalism.[18] The use of the Gothic trope of mirroring/doubling, which is a normatively paranoid one in both Gothic fiction and in cinematic representations of same-sex desire, is here presented as essential to the character's development of individual subjectivity and to their queer becoming.

Hideko's process of subjectification is presented to the audience in *The Handmaiden* as a being navigated via her relations to a series of doubles. First, Hideko is doubled with her mother, the paragon of beauty that she and her aunt must aspire to for the pleasure of Uncle Kouzuki and his guests. Second is Hideko's Aunt, the predecessor driven to suicide and the image of Hideko's future if she were to remain in her uncle's possession. Third is the wooden puppet that metaphorically reflects Hideko's dehumanised existence after a life dedicated to simulating desire and sexual titillation for others before accruing her own knowledge and understanding of desire and pleasure. Fourth is Sook-hee, the double that Park presents as truly identifiable, sharing with Hideko expressions of queer love that she had only ever read about in abstraction. A fifth double might be read as the count. When Hideko and Sook-hee escape from the Count's honeymoon hotel and the mental asylum, respectively, they meet to forge new identities that will grant them passage out of the country. As Kouzuki tortures the Count for information, he gloats that he had arranged it to be impossible for two girls travelling together to leave Kobe. Hideko, however, anticipates this and dresses very much like the Count in his imposter-gentleman attire and Park shows how the lovers now play with gendered 'appearance' as a 'negotiation of power'. The final use of cross-dressing bolsters previous appellation of gender and sexual performativity. To follow Butler then, the trajectory of queer subjectification, working through desire and identification, sees performativity as a catalyst in the 'becoming' process. Where before there was the rigidity of binary roles, it is realised that 'there is no gender without this reproduction of norms that risks undoing or redoing the norm in unexpected ways, thus opening up the possibility of a remaking of gendered reality along new lines'.[19] Hideko and Sook-hee board a ferry away from Japan and the tossing of a fake moustache overboard and into the wind conveys the final shedding of a skin meant only for the purpose of circumventing social trappings in order to continue on a queer path.

Subjectivity, Mimesis and Abjection

The double motif, as used in literary and cultural representation, shares many parallels with the theory of mimesis and mimicry. The setting of the stairwell is a particularly poignant one for this first queer encounter with paranoia and with a Gothic double. For Homi Bhabha the stairwell is a 'liminal space [which], in-between the designations of identity, becomes integral to the process of symbolic interaction, the connective tissue that constructs the difference between upper and lower'.[20] The impossibility of 'settling into primordial polarities' is established by the 'hither and thither of the stairwell'; indeed, for Bhabha, the stairwell is a prudent symbol of cultural hybridity, as an 'interstitial passage between fixed identifications' that 'entertains difference without assumed hierarchy' (p. 5). In this way it starts to become clear how *The Handmaiden* begins to draw these two figures together, and with them, the threads of paranoia, queerness and cultural hybridity. The colonial and racial identities presented in *The Handmaiden* are framed via dialogues of class, and of the male character's plans of social ascension and 'passing' as rich Japanese noblemen. With its preoccupation with performance, recitation, pornography and doubles, *The Handmaiden* offers more challenges to the politics of identity and power than Eurocentric New Queer Gothic texts, certainly more than its source text, and this has much to do with the ways in which Gothic doubling also present as examples of mimesis.

Mimesis in *The Handmaiden* frequently teases at the notion of the double. Here, Bhabha describes his contention with mimicry:

> The ambivalence of mimicry – almost but not quite – suggests that the fetishized colonial culture is potentially and strategically an insurgent counter-appeal. What I have called its 'identity-effects' are always crucially *split*. Under cover of camouflage, mimicry, like the fetish, is a part object that radically revalues the normative knowledges of the priority of race, writing and history. For the fetish mimes the forms of authority at *the point at which it deauthorizes them*. Similarly, mimicry rearticulates presence in terms of its 'otherness', that which it disavows. (pp. 129–30)

Hideko and Sook-hee represent such ambivalence, specifically in this narrative, as well as in this period and colonial setting, and the queer sexual relationship they develop is significant to that. Through the instances of doubling, Park crafts the two characters into mirror images of each other. They sit in perfect parallel in the film's final scene, taking turns at warming silver bells in their mouths, sharing identical postures, the couch on which they kneel emphasises the symmetry of their foreplay. As in *Fingersmith*'s narrative, it is eventually revealed that the two protagonists were swapped at birth, one should be a lady and the other a thief/maid; one was brought up believing her high status and Japanese heritage made her superior to low Korean women. Hideko and Sook-hee realise their hybrid identities and twist the plot accordingly. This hybridity that they share, coupled with their rejection of the roles they, especially Hideko, have had to play, and their same-sex desire to be free and to be together, combines to create the perfect postcolonial queer storm, and their hybridity, moreover, reads as something that emboldens their emancipation from categorisation. Bhabha explains why hybridity is so challenging:

> Hybridity is the name of this displacement of value from symbol to sign that causes the dominant discourse to split along the axis of its power to be representative, authoritative. Hybridity represents the ambivalent 'turn' of the discriminated subject into the terrifying, exorbitant object of paranoid classification – a disturbing questioning of the images and presences of authority. (p. 162)

The New Queer Gothic

What hybrid identity does is propose the problem of reversing some of the effects of colonialism and 'colonialist disavowal, so that other 'denied' knowledges enter the deviant discourse and estrange the basis of its authority – 'its rules of recognition' (p. 162). Hideko and Sook-hee deviate from their prescribed roles in more ways than one.

Queer subjectivity is represented in the film as an escape from bondage with a rather utopic trajectory, and this necessarily implicates ideas of subjectivity and mimesis. Ruth Robbins has described 'subjectivity' as a term born out of a melange of philosophy on the nature of 'reality', human consciousness and subjecthood, from Cartesian *cogito* to Lacanian thought. Lacanian psychoanalysis bring with it much theorising on the child, as the child enters into knowledge of language and swaps the imaginary realm for the symbolic and learns, most importantly, the 'no of the father'.[21] 'Writing in patriarchal Western Europe, Lacan posited the impetus to repress comes from the figure of the father, both the child's literal "daddy", and also – metaphorically or symbolically – all those other patriarchal structures which legislate appropriate behaviour in a given culture.' As much a part of Hideko's education as anything else, and accompanying her entry into the symbolic order, is the entry into the knowledge and language of sexuality. Uncle Kouzuki is shown in the film as tyrannical in his objective of raising a perfect orator of erotica. Robbins describes the relationship between the self and reading as an important thematic concern of subjectivity: 'subjectivity produces a necessary illusion of autonomy that is always at odds with the problems of subjection' (p. 16). Park suggests that the problems Hideko has with her subjectivity come largely from the abuse suffered at the hands of her uncle – as a child she watched that abuse turn her aunt, her mentor and predecessor, to suicide. It is in a scene where Hideko performs her reading to her uncle's guests that we really understand her lack of agency and crisis of subjectivity.

Dressed as a finely painted geisha, Hideko reads her uncle's erotica in his fully operational theatre/library. There is a similar scene of Maud Lilly reading to her uncle's guests in *Fingersmith*. However, in this transformation of the narrative, Park adds a life-sized wooden mannequin puppet. This could, of course, be read as a nod to the source text, in suggesting an allusion to the wooden sex toy used in another of Water's historic novels exploring queer sexuality, *Tipping the Velvet* (1999). Because one of the rare erotic tomes from which Hideko reads is missing its woodcut frontispiece, Kouzuki demands Hideko offer an alternative visual demonstration in lieu of an available illustration. Obeying, Hideko mounts a faceless life-size doll, and each are winched into the air; various strings are then manoeuvred, and Hideko and the puppet incline away from one another in an expressionless simulation of a sex position. The climax of Hideko's performance receives gasps from the squirming men in the audience as she hangs suspended, legs parted, leaning back, without holding on, to suggest it is only by the strength of her thighs, or her genitalia, that she may remain suspended. This performance of unreal sex, this simulacrum of sex, provides a metonym of heteronormative sexuality being, rather queerly, totally absent from the 'reality' of the narrative. Although sex permeates the life of Hideko, it is not until she desires Sook-Hee and acts on those desires that she is shown to experience and understand pleasure. This is something pointed out by the Count in the scene immediately following, when he opines misogynistically to Kouzuki that his advances would be wasted on Hideko because she lacks desire. He mocks the Count in suggesting that his efforts to train Hideko as an erotic orator have left her desensitised and passionless, which he can tell from the look in her eye. He warns, 'you should go easy on her training, unless you enjoy making love to a corpse'. This instance of doubling recalls another from earlier in Part Two of the film that recounts Hideko's life with her uncle since being a little girl.[22] This part shows Hideko's relationship with her aunt, the only member of the household to ever show her any kindness. This aunt is Hideko's predecessor, but expresses her feelings of inferiority in comparison to Hideko's beautiful late mother. While being taught to read and perform by her aunt, Hideko also learns the cruelty and brutality of her uncle. Hideko's aunt makes numerous escape attempts but is eventually driven to suicide by the sadist who keeps her captive. As a grown woman, Hideko hangs from the cherry blossom tree where her aunt's body was found hanging. With the image of Hideko suspended in mid-air, limp and dead behind the eyes, as noted by the Count, she is a tableau of auto-erotic asphyxiation, clearly painting her as the double of her suicidal aunt. Doubling, in this way, connects sexuality devoid of desire with death: unreal heterosexual sexuality and non-consensual sex are thus the sites of paranoia in *The Handmaiden* rather than any queer sexuality.

Doubling and abjection oscillate throughout the plot of *The Handmaiden*. 'The subject has to continually play acrobatics in order to guard that boundary. Loss of the boundary between self and other will swallow up the subject.'[23] The image of the swallowed-up woman or girl is a site of deep Gothic anxiety in *The Handmaiden*, compounded by the famous pornographic illustration of the girl and a giant octopus, which appears on-screen on numerous occasions. However, in the South Korean film, it is not the threat of imagined or dreamed cannibalism, but a very real threat encumbered with the magical realism of a side-show attraction or *Bluebeard* fairy tale. In Part Two of the film, Uncle Kouzouki takes Hideko down to his basement beneath his library. The act is set up to frame the hold that he has over his niece, the threat and horror of what dwells down there shown only in the little girl's terrified reaction. Later in the film, we see the Count counterfeiting an illustration for Kouzuki: a monstrous giant octopus devouring the genitals of a woman. The original image used in the film is a piece titled 'Kinoe no Komatsu'. The Edo-period book illustration by Katsushika Hokusai (1814), depicts a Japanese myth about a pearl-diving woman. The image is one of the most famous illustrations in a three-volume book of erotica. The myth depicted involves a character named Fujiwara, which suggests the purposeful use of this particular piece of imagery. The politics of this image connect to the ambiguity of female agency and questions of female desire in the genealogy of Japanese pornography featuring sea creature bestiality. The phallic, grotesque creature, with which Kouzuki has a clear fascination, is only granted a mediated on-screen presence and visibility until the final scenes when Kouzuki puts his torture chamber basement to use against the Count. Here, the phallic creature, a Giant Pacific Octopus, can be observed thrashing its tentacles out of a too-small tank. It comes to represent less of a devouring threat able to consume whole girls, and more a symbol of the hopeless impotence of both Kouzuki and the Count – neither of them achieve securing Hideko as a fully penetrated sexual conquest; each is thwarted by her and Sook-Hee's double-crossing.

Postcolonial Queerness

This chapter, and this books more broadly, is not in the business of discussing men, queer or otherwise. As detailed in my introduction, there exists a wealth of scholarship dedicated to the queer readings of Gothic fiction focused on the experiences of gay or queer men. However, the homosocial relationship between the two male characters central to the narrative of *The Handmaiden* prove to be an interesting point of contrast for the representation of queer desire conveyed by the female protagonist. It is my argument that queerness intersects crucially with colonial identity and is navigated via the postcolonial Gothic.

The postcolonial Gothic is a mode of fiction that Sue Chaplin has identified as engaging with 'themes of Gothicism in order to interrogate the legacies of colonialism, especially its impact upon the subjectivity of individuals who have been displaced by colonial practices'.[24] During Japan's occupation of Korea from 1910 to 1945, Korean people were treated as inferior to the Japanese. Wealthy businessmen, like Kouzuki, would often aspire to a Japanese name in order to move more easily within the circles of high society. The connections that Park draws between colonial and queer identity are uncanny when reading the flourishing romance between the two female protagonists. The identities of the two villainous male characters also mark them as queer, insomuch as their desire for social ascension, for the wealth and status accrued by 'becoming Japanese' means forfeiting the heteronormative sexual lives once possible. Kouzuki's avarice sees him divorce his Korean wife Miss Sasaki (who performs the role of housekeeper but continues to share his bed) in favour of an incestuous union with his heiress niece. Paralleling the way in which his Korean wife becomes his mistress, Japanese Hideko is placed in something of a birdcage, where she is represented as perched precariously between whore and wife status; untouchable and pristine yet wholly kept and objectified. Kouzuki's identity is split colonially, and the reasons offered are presented in his dialogue to expose the crude simplistic racism of his internalised imperialism: 'Because Korea is ugly and Japan is beautiful. Korea is soft, slow, dull, and therefore hopeless.' Not only does this line expose a logic that equates beauty with power, a central theme that Park returns to throughout the film, it also suggests Kouzuki aligns his own identity with that of his work and seems to envelop himself in the value systems that he uses to judge women, whether in life or as they appear in the pornography that he collects, copies and forges.

Dichotomies are created in performances of identity, and this is starkest between how the men and women in the film present themselves via desire. Count Fugiwara reveals that his sexual attachments are based on his lust for affluence. In the first scene when enlisting Sook-hee to be his 'mouse', to spy on the Lady Hideko and convince her to fall in love with him, he describes attaining her wealth as his greatest desire announcing: 'every night in bed I think of her assets'. Hideko later says the words 'every night in bed I think of your face' to Sook-hee, providing a variation on the Count's phrase. This works to establish a dyad of desire in a matrix of deception: the count's desires and objectives are set up to be read as exploitative and avaricious, while Hideko's and Sook-hee's desires turn false declarations into true ones. Sook-hee asks the Count to ease up on his mock courtship of Hideko after seeing him grope her, he pulls her hand to his crotch while describing the arousal of edging ever closer to the heiress's fortune. Sook-hee watches from outside a window as the Count pinches at Hideko's body, appearing as the flirt and lecher. Later, the audience is given this scene again from inside the room. The Count's dialogue is mocking of any assumed sexual interest with the heiress's body: 'If there's one thing I'm after, Miss, it's not your eyes or your hands or your ass, it's money.' After the Count believes that his fortune is won, he returns his attention to the body he had earlier sneered at, now revealing a predilection for rape over consensual sex, which he suggests throughout the narrative as far too easy a conquest. The film builds the insinuation that his confused masochism is, in part, an effect of the pornography that he deals in with Kouzuki. Holding Hideko in place, he tells her, 'It won't hurt. You know from those books. In truth women feel the greatest pleasure when taken by force. Now I'm going to rip your underwear.' The pornographic fantasies bought, copied and sold by the men and orated by Hideko, cross the border from fantasy to reality and show the harmful perpetuation of porn fallacies when women come to be homogenised and turned into the mythic, fictional beings written by men. The Count is rendered unconscious by Hideko's poison moments before the intended rape. In these ways the men in the film are marked as queer by their privileging of money and power over love and sex; thus, the film represents a hyperbolic, almost parodic twin personification of patriarchy as purely economic and sexually impotent. The only heterosexual sex presented in the film exists in pornographic artwork, and the only real intimacy that the film sees the two central male figures experience is with one another in the basement when Kouzuki tortures Fugiwara with antique bookmaking equipment. One by one, appendages (fingers) are lopped off, as the men sit together sweating in open shirts and dressing gowns while a phallic sea creature thrashes around in the background: one man starts to get excited about the other's sexual conquests before they die, almost, but not quite, in each other's arms. Women, or the mythic, fictional, pornographic, representations of women, are merely the medium through which male desire for male ascension is communicated; the asexuality of this process is intensely exploitative and antisocially queer.

This final scene, where Kouzuki can be seen chopping off the Count's fingers, certifies the *Bluebeard*-esque uncle as the character most associated with abjection in *The Handmaiden*. In earlier scenes, his small black spectacles and black ink-stained tongue mark him as serpentine and demonic. Park creates the effect of misophonia by pairing the visuals of Kouzuki licking his pen with special attention given to the over-dubbing of and super-audibility of the mouth sounds.[25] Stephen Brown comments that in horror cinema 'haptic sonority' such as this, 'opens an intensive space where one does not so much hear sounds as one feels them in one's body in ways that are by turns bone-rattling, gut-wrenching, and hair-raising'.[26] The triumphant scenes of Hideko and Sook-hee destroying Kouzuki's library right before they make their escape are placed towards the end of the film and show his precious erotica defaced by the same ink used to counterfeit works, the black ink that stains his tongue, and the black ink produced by his pitiful pet octopus. The tone of retributive abjection is accentuated when Hideko throws red ink onto the pornography and slashes through pages with a letter opener. This scene of literary destruction is paralleled with that of corporeal destruction, as, although out of chronology, Park situates this scene close to that of the Count's torture in the basement. Kristeva describes the process and purpose of corporeal abjection:

> The body's inside . . . shows up in order to compensate for the collapse of the border between inside and outside . . . The abjection of those flows from within suddenly become the sole 'object' of sexual desire – a true 'ab-ject' where man frightened, crosses over the horrors of material bowels and, in an immersion that enable his to avoid coming face to face with another, spares himself the risk of castration.[27]

Following Kristeva, Barbara Creed suggests that the borders of the body reparatively engage with the female subject via the traditionally paranoid Gothic trope of abjection, writing that 'placed on the side of the feminine [and] exists in opposition to the paternal symbolic, which is governed by rules and laws'.[28] Where in *Fingersmith*'s ending Maud teaches the illiterate Sue to read using the inherited collection of pornography, Hideko and Sook-hee destroy the erotica but do carry out some means of reparative reusing of it; the silver bells are used by the couple in the final scene of very stylised symmetrical sex on the journey crossing the sea of Japan. The bells are suggested to be one of the trinkets liberated from Kouzuki and featured in one of his erotic stories. Reframed, reappropriated, they are resignified in the changing of hands; these pieces of erotic paraphernalia become imbued with intensely paranoid and reparative significance. In the possession of free queer women, the bells reflect progression from fetish object to active chiming.

In Park Chan-wook's *The Handmaiden*, an already significant Queer Gothic text is adapted and transformed into a postcolonial Queer Gothic text. What is revealed as performative about these women's identities throughout the narrative not only pertains to essentialist class identity but also colonial, racial and national identity. Park encourages a parallel between the two queer couples in the film, which has the effect of gendering desire and reflects the source text's narrative project towards a queer utopia, a denouement in Water's writing that I discussed in Chapter 1. The feminism of *Fingersmith* is overt: queer women achieve emancipations from patriarchal control and live happily, the economic spoils intact. I argue that *The Handmaiden* elaborates on this notion of a queer emancipation, and it does so by calling attention to the paranoid and reparative gestures of social ascension in colonial Korea. Kouzuki and Count Fugiwara are Korean men who represent internalised racism in their desire to 'become' Japanese. Hideko and Sook-hee represent queer desire for one another overcoming colonial division.

Part III

5

Queering the Cannibal in Raw

ஒ

> *The strong abuse, exploit and meatify the weak, says Sade. They must and will devour their natural prey. The primal condition of man cannot be modified in any way; it is eat or be eaten.*[1]

While the previous chapter dealt with expanding the scope and remit of my project of demonstrating and reading the New Queer Gothic in a postcolonial context, this chapter's key concerns include incorporating other cultures, but with keener analytic attention to questions of female subjectivity as they relate to ideas of queerness, feminism and national identity. This chapter will set up some of the conceptualisation foundational to both this and the final chapter; for example, this chapter will begin to theorise queer subjectivity as it relates ideas of biopolitics and hybridity with its investigations into the implications of girlhood and womanhood in a microcosm patriarchal society, which I argue the institutional veterinary school setting presents in Julia Ducournau's *Raw* (2016). Another key objective is to conceptualise and contextualise the queer cannibal, debating the representation of monstrosity inherent in this. I will be moving away from highlighting paranoid and reparative reading methods here, taking instead an interdisciplinary and multivalent approach to my analysis.

Raw is a film about rites of passage, initiations and ritual hazing; moments that characterise the journey of protagonist Justine

(Garance Marillier) from child to adult, girl to woman, vegetarian to cannibal, all while studying to be a veterinary surgeon. Justin follows in the footstep of her parents (Joana Preiss and Laurent Lucas) and older sister Alexia (Ella Rumpf) in attending veterinary school. The school, with its patriarchal, fraternity-house stylings, provides the setting for Justine's coming-of-age narrative. In this narrative she is initiated into the hierarchy of the school's social order as a 'rookie' and into the trappings of femininity as her older sister dresses, plucks and waxes her, and as her sexuality develops. The carnality of Ducournau's debut feature film interweaves Gothic themes of dehumanisation and cannibalism with themes of sexual awakening and queer female subjectivity. The queerness of the protagonist, Justine, is an aspect that is featured in the narrative, although it can also be read as a rather ambivalent aspect of her identity, pertaining both to her subjecthood and her relationships with others. She is a girl facing the adversity of not fitting in very well with her peers; she is childlike and uninterested in sex and parties, unlike the sexually active, drugged-up teens surrounding her; she is disparaged by the only tutor featured in the film, a male professor who presumes her natural intelligence equates to arrogance and could hinder the progress of his other students; and her body is changing. As the camera follows Justine through the ritual hazing of 'hell week', she finds her only allies are her wayward older sister, and her gay roommate (Rabah Nait Oufella) with whom she develops feelings of affection and of predatory sexual attraction.

Fitting in, mediocrity, and 'passing' as normal, are paramount in the culture of the veterinary school, effectively assuming a status as metonym for a culture that Ducournau seems to decry. Speculatively named after the protagonist of the Marquis de Sade's *Justine*, the narrative in *Raw* and the characterisation of Justine invites many parallels with her supposed namesake; she and her sister, Alexia, are reminiscent of de Sade's Justine and Juliette, for example. De Sade's Justine suffers torture and rape throughout the sequential tragedies that befall her, leading to a life of vice; while Ducournau's Justine undergoes punishing hazing rituals and an unfriendly welcome into school, suffering somewhat shy of the Sadeian. We might appreciate Ducournau's subversion of de Sade's narrative in relation to the sisters' relationship: Alexia is the dark double in this narrative, whereas in de Sade, Justine's sister Juliette finds her way out of a life of vice and achieves a comfortable situation where Justine does not. Taking the film's parallels with de Sade as a starting point highlights the generic form of the film, since de Sade is one of the earliest and most notorious purveyors of French extremity, and, while difficult to categorise, this film certainly belongs to that same family.

Raw can be placed in many genres, movements and trends, and this chapter will begin by exploring some of those contexts. Of all the texts that this study examines, *Raw* is the most likely to be categorised as a horror film. That status should not detract in any way from its shared status as a piece of Gothic cinema. Peter Hutchings notes that these two terms – 'Gothic' and 'horror' – have been theorised differently, as horror has accrued the reputation as 'a vulgarised, exploitative version of the Gothic'.[2] Films like *Raw* exist at the intersection of horror and Gothic, and new modes of reading films that are valuable to Gothic academia. Critical terminology such as Xavier Aldana Reyes's 'body Gothic' can be used to bridge the gap between the imagined high and low cultures of horror and the Gothic. Aldana Reyes notes that while the psychological and uncanny aspects of the Gothic, including their presence in Gothic cinema, are very popular and interesting areas of enquiry, 'the Gothic is also inherently somatic and corporeal'.[3] What makes *Raw* a Gothic horror film is its presentation of the somatic and corporeal. However, because the film also represents the queer Gothic in its themes and narrative, methods for reading it should consider a differentiated approach, which the following analysis will unpick.

Queering Femininity in Raw

Before placing *Raw* in its formal contexts, it is important to identify how its queer themes also situate it within an existing body of work. I would like to claim *Raw* as one of a handful of contemporary films made in Europe and the United States that explore themes of queer kinship and queer families. Mainstream horror films dealing in the disruption of the heteronormative nuclear family include Jaume Collet-Serra's *Orphan* (2009), James Watkins's *The Woman in Black* (2012), James Wan's *The Conjuring* (2013), Andy

Muschietti's *Mama* (2013), Jennifer Kerr's *The Babadook* (2014) and Robert Eggers's *The Witch* (2015). In each of these films, children are at risk from malevolent forces. Failure to protect the children speaks to a failure to uphold conservative values that privilege what Edelman calls 'reproductive futurity'. Other aspects threatening the heteronormative nuclear family include the uncanny Gothic child whose uncanniness or possession by some supernatural force works to deconstruct the image of the fetishised ideal child. Steven Bruhm discusses *Orphan*'s protagonist Esther (a thirty-three-year-old 'psychopath' passing as a nine-year-old adopted orphan bent on seducing and murdering, as a means of dispatching the all-American nuclear family) as an excellent example of the counterfeit Gothic child: 'she performs the Gothic underbelly of American familial sentimentality, which is Gothic precisely because it is sentimental. In doing so, she divests childhood of its empty innocence and figures the child – the counterfeit child – as the performance of sexual knowingness.'[4] Bruhm explains that because Esther performs childhood she simultaneously invokes and destroys our phantasmic ideas about childhood: 'That she is "really" an adult is a sop thrown to us at the film's end to rescue "real" children for innocence, but the game has already been played' (p. 43). There are moments in *Raw* when the viewer is made to worry for the youthfully naïve Justine – for example, at student raves she looks out of place, she gets drunk quickly on her own. There is auteur intention with the casting of Marillier whose child-like appearance works to accentuate her girlishness.

Marillier's status as something of a muse for Ducournau was established when she was cast in the role of protagonist a second time after initially appearing in *Junior* (2011), a thematical precursor to *Raw* in which a thirteen-year-old tomboy, also named Justine (nicknamed Junior), contracts a strange virus with transformative corporeal effects. *Raw* develops much of its characterisation and thematic concerns from Ducournau's twenty-two-minute French-language short. The initially androgynous Junior relishes her disdain for hygiene, revelling in her girlhood grossness. The first scene of the short shows Junior scraping the slimy plaque from her teeth with her finger then sucking it back into her mouth, she lets the shower run to make her mother think she is washing and pulls on layers of baggy clothes; extra diegetic heavy metal music plays throughout, offering anarchist undertones to the girl's mundane ablutions. At school, Junior hangs out with a group of boys, and the very feminine girls – seen wearing their hair loose and long, with lip gloss and various pink accessories – bully her for her tomboy identity. When Junior contracts a mysterious illness, she begins a metamorphosis: her skin becomes almost gelatinous with long strips coming loose and an unknown slime starts to ooze from her, saturating her bed and bedroom carpet. After the illness subsides, Junior returns to school with wolf-whistles from the boys in her class. Her large glasses, acne, greasy pony-tail and baggy clothes have been replaced by a much more conventionally attractive feminine presentation; she wears her (now clean) hair long, framing her neutrally made-up face, while glasses and baggy clothes no longer hide her. The transformation is very similar to the much-satirised shallow makeover featured in the 1999 teen film *She's All That*. One of the bullying girls exhibits similar symptoms when she pulls off a strip of her own skin in the bathroom, compounding the allusion that the illness is an overt metaphor for girlhood puberty. The short won significant acclaim at Cannes (winning the Small Golden Rail Award in 2011). The culture of misogyny internalised by the figure of the tomboy in an institutional setting is a prevailing theme of *Raw*, which works to trouble the project of reading it as a queer feminist piece of Gothic cinema. Such a continuation in theme begs the question of whether internalised anti-feminist feeling is endemic to French culture.

While an assertion connecting the gender and sexual politics of Ducournau's films to France as a nation might be a bold one – and one that can be substantiated only by the anecdotal evidence that follows – such evidence provides at least a limited explanation of the complex attitudes around some aspects of sex and feminism in France. In the very least, this investigation probes at a disturbing zeitgeist. *Junior* was released in 2011, which was also the year that the former French economy minister, Dominique Strauss-Kahn, was accused of rape. This cannot be used to fortify a claim that French people, specifically Ducournau, felt compelled to react. For the BBC Radio 4 documentary, *#metoo, moi non plus*, however, this event was a watershed moment responsible for encouraging conversations about how French people think about sex and feminism. The documentary was made in response to an open letter and worked to explain the culture within which that letter was penned. Written by Catherine Deneuve, with Sarah Chiche (writer and psychoanalyst), Catherine Millet (author and art critic), Catherine Robbe-Grillet (actress and writer), Peggy Sastre (author and journalist) and Abnousse Shalmani (writer and journalist), and signed by 100 other eminent French women, the letter described an aversion to the 2018 #MeToo movement popular in the United Kingdom and the United States. The movement, instigated by US actor Rose McGowan, and endorsed by popular feminist icons and celebrities around the world, implored people to share their experiences of sexual abuse by men using the hashtag as a tool to show the ubiquity of such abuse, to foster solidarity and to mobilise both legal and social action against abusers. Importantly, the movement helped to bring some high-profile cases of abuse to light and men who had hidden behind power and privilege were judged, creating a shift in cultural understandings of sexual abuse and terms such as 'consent' and 'coercion'. In the letter, French women denounce the movement for sometimes equating sexual abuse with more mundane and apparently harmless gestures of seduction or men's awkward attempts to express interest in women, which led to statements defending the 'freedom to pester'[5] women. After sex scandals circulated around a man known for representing a mode of masculinity that boasts powers of seduction as tantamount to success in the worlds of politics and business, denationalised conversations about gender entered popular discussion and the image of French femininity – as much milder than it's 'fem-radical' Anglo-American counterpart – started to change. Part of France's national identity features 'gallantry' as a code of behaviour on which to build notions of heteronormative masculinity and sexual liberation on which to build notions of femininity. In France, as the documentary describes, 'seduction' is a 'French speciality' and instinctive to French people as a game of language necessary for any social processes. What is considered harassment is therefore a contested topic between, for example the United States or the United Kingdom and France, which worryingly suggests a wilful ignorance in French public discourse on the realities of violence against women. What that open letter did was counterintuitive to anyone's version of feminism: it legitimised the beliefs and excuses of abusive men. While this chapter agrees with the documentary's presenter, Catherine Guilyardi, that the imbalance of the power dynamic in the game of seduction undermines whatever perceived benefit to sexual liberation exists in the French psyche, it also appreciates that French films are undeniably a product of, or response to, this sociopolitical climate.

The art of 'seduction' as a marker of masculinity and as a sustaining phenomenon supporting French patriarchy, accepted so unquestioningly as to provoke intelligent French women to defend it publicly, is a heteronormative and misogynistic concept that this chapter argues is challenged by *Raw*. Rather than the highly conventional makeover presented in her *Junior* short, this time Ducournau puts her protagonist in front of a mirror, smearing lipstick wantonly beyond the lines of her lips, kissing her reflection and dancing to a French pop song about female sexual freedom, inclusive of sex, drugs and necrophilia. The song, 'Plus putes que toutes les putes' by ORTIES, begins 'Seduction 101: Be a whore with decorum' and later the song offers a short narrative about devouring a husband on the wedding night: 'Suck ya bones, lap it up honey.' The song deftly reflects the film's aims to parody 'seduction' as integral to French national identity. Furthermore, the way in which the song's lyrics involve a cannibal narrative, directly correlates these two themes. That the song is also diegetic is significant. Justine listens to the song through earphones, dancing and singing along as she seduces her own reflection, enjoying herself in a display that is not masturbatory but is certainly auto-erotic. Significantly, the connective tissue binding identity, sexuality and cannibalism becomes all the more realisable when considering this scene as a precursor to the later sex scene that, crucially, features the autocannibalistic bite accompanying Justine's climax. The queer cannibal emerges as an incredibly antisocial sexual subject.

'What fresh hell is this?': Genre, Mode and Affect in Raw

Sexuality and subjectivity are keenly performed through the somatic and gestures of body horror. Readings of what Justine's strange affliction might signal are more replete in Ducournau's feature-length film than compared to her short. Puberty inducing the societal demand for a normatively feminine gender presentation is, in *Raw*, only one of the many roadblocks that Justine encounters on her queer journey. As in many of the texts that *The New Queer Gothic* examines, queer becomings and subjectivity development are very much played out on the body. The transformations presented in *Jack & Diane* and *Black Swan*, as discussed in Chapter 3, show very physical, corporeal, sometimes wholly phantasmic displays giving visual representation to metamorphoses of sexual subjectivity and desire. In all three of these transformations, a sexual awakening is coupled with blood lust, often leading to literal or fantastical homicide or cannibalism.

The significance and enduring trend for body horror in contemporary Gothic film is confirmed by this French-language, Belgium-set film that should also be situated within the popular movement of New French Extremity (NFE). This term was first coined by the film critic James Quandt and pertains to transgressive art-house and mainstream films made by French directors released from the turn of the twenty-first century to the present. Most well-known NFE films include *Frontière(s)*, ('*Frontier(s)*') (dir. Xavier Gens, France, 2007) and *Martyrs* (dir. Pascal Laugier, France, 2008); those usually associated with the horror subcategory of this trend include films such as *Martyrs*, *Dans ma peau* ('*In My Skin*'), a 2002 NFE film written, directed by and starring Marina de Van, *High Tension* (2003), *Them* (2006) and *Inside* (2007). The titles of these films alone signal their family resemblance in suggesting such a preoccupation with abjection, specifically Kristeva's definition concerning the corporeal border-control of identity, system and order.[6]

To define NFE cinema, Mauro Resmini describes the trend as intrinsically transgressive in its 'exceptionally graphic depictions of sex and violence', which 'generally deploy an aesthetic that privileges the shocking, the horrific, and the abject'.[7] Where popular criticism laments these themes as merely sensational in Ducournau's debut – Nick Pinkerton's review for *Sight and Sound* calls it 'an excruciating curatorial precociousness . . . more showroom than film, its purported depths impossible to see past the glare of the vitrine, or is it a specimen jar?'[8] Film scholars, Resmini writes, are drawn to the NFE for the way that it connects to larger questions about cinematic ontology:

> The promise of touching the real, which buttresses the NFE trend, is ingrained within a specific conception of cinema – namely, the medium's essential striving to attain the invisible in the visible, to grasp the elusive substance that at once grounds and transcends representation.[9]

Resmini describes the dominant critical discourse surrounding NFE as the 'aesthetic practice of deframing', by which he means that all the films share in the preposition that there is such a thing as a true reality and the only way to access that is through sensation: deframing is an act of divesting the film of any mediating mechanisms that separate the audience from the real. Extremity, he continues, is 'the triangulation of authenticity, sensation, and immediacy [which] finds its condensation and actualization' (p. 163). With so many scholars comparing NFE to both the Brechtian theory of alienation and Antonin Artaud's 'Theatre of Cruelty',[10] most comment on the moral ambiguity of films that, by and large, do not easily illustrate a 'meaning'. Jerome Schaefer describes this as 'a good thing', because without the aid of 'symbolic bottlenecks and the auteur's intentions', there can be no doubt that a 'differentiated approach is needed and that these films cannot be explained as mere representations. Instead, all these film scholars attempt to get a grip on the strange material-semiotic qualities of these movies' (p. 97). A differentiated approach should then be employed, investigating things such as aesthetics and affect as well as semantics.

In *Raw*, moments of sexual awakening and cannibalistic epiphanies are punctuated by rattlingly disruptive chimes of Gothic church organs or extra-diegetic Euro-Synth house music, to reflect life oscillating on a spectrum between normative student debauchery and strange, monstrous, queer becoming. Justine – whose name alludes to the heroine of one of the first purveyors of French extremity, the Marquis de Sade – is thrown into a world wholly different from her domestic situation with strict vegetarian parents and an overbearing mother. Veterinary school's 'hell week' sees her join other freshers and new students in various dehumanising exercises: being made to crawl like a chattel to gain access to the freshers' party, having their mattresses and belongings thrown out of windows, and being forced to eat rabbit kidneys. At one point Justine fails to fulfil the 'nightclub' dress code and ends up having to borrow a dress from her sister so as to not have to wear a nappy to class again. The emotional stresses of being pushed so far out of her comfort zone are paralleled by the physical manifestation of a horrific rash that makes Justine writhe at her blistered, peeling skin in the middle of the night. Self-destructive body horror is the most defining characteristic of other NFE films like *In My Skin*, where the protagonist becomes obsessed with removing her own skin and mutilating herself further after sustaining an injury to her leg. *Raw* bears further similarities to *In My Skin* in its featuring of auto-cannibalism; Justine's tooth falls out in the shower, and she eats it. Of course, body horror is just one example of the types of extremity that these films explore.

Raw illustrates queerness and extremity as operating on the same level when scenes crafted to create tension and horror in the film also connote non-normativity, monstrosity and the violent rejection of heteronormative systems: (hetero)normative ideas of the family, kinship and sex are all disturbed at this juncture. Two scenes in particular flavour the connective tissue that the film builds between queerness and extremity: one begins with sisterly bonding and ends in Justine devouring Alexia's severed finger; the other is a violent yet tender sex scene with Adrien, ending in the aforementioned auto-cannibalistic event of Justine biting her own arm. Each of these scenes allude to existing thresholds. An initiation into feminine beauty ideals – 'At your age I already gave myself Brazilians' – sees Alexia attempt to wax Justine into a conventional shape. However, Justine's body, as if refusing this particular ritual, holds onto its pubic hair and the wax is unyielding. Alexia must resort to scissors, prompting a poignant 'It's my pussy!' scream from Justine as she kicks out. Alexia holds up her bloodied four-digit hand and passes out. Justine scrambles to call for help, finds the severed finger but realises that there is no ice to preserve it. Soft harpsichord music becomes layered with the long bass notes of a Gothic organ, as Justine collects blood in her palm and her round childish face lights up. Eyes wide, mouth industriously nibbling, the non-diegetic portion of the soundtrack by Jim Williams embosses moments of extremity like this with traditionally Gothic gravitas, thick with allusions to old, kitschy Hammer horror and 'Dracularity'.[11] This scene and others fit snugly Resmini's remit for NFE:

> Extremity, transgression, marginality, and liminality are recurring terms in the discourses of critics and directors alike. In this sense, the films associated with the NFE reveal an obsession with limits. The normative experience – understood socially as conformism or habit and stylistically as convention or constraint – becomes the target for furious audiovisual assaults that attempt to break boundaries open. But instead of giving in to a celebration of this liberating gesture, we ought to remember that it is only in the clash with the limit that any transgressive impulse can come into existence.[12]

Here, Resmini discusses the necessary depiction of limits to delineate boundaries and make transgression possible. He describes any and all transgression as dependent on two distinctions: 'it is an act of trespassing that is at the same time a confirmation and recognition of the limit' (p. 169). Although he does not cite him, Resmini's theories clearly draw on Michel Foucault's *The History of Sexuality*, where Foucault discusses the shock value of sexual discourse as contingent on the role of the 'repressive hypothesis' – psychological and social repression of sexual discourse gives it transgressive power and the knowledge of such a transgression produces pleasure.[13] It is due to the role played by the constraints that qualify broken boundaries as sites of transgression that leads Resmini to claim that these films 'know more than their critics (and sometimes even the directors themselves) about the aesthetic and conceptual fallacy of the simplistic claim to immediacy and authenticity on the part of the transgressive operation of form'.[14] While the personification of the film as self-reflective entity is a dubious proposition, *Raw*'s critical attention certainly reflects this notion. Pinkerton describes Ducournau's use of her thematic hook as 'a charm bracelet to dangle fetish images from', comparing it to the way that Nicolas Winding Refn portrays fame in *The Neon Demon* (2016), with critic Margaret Barton-Fumo noting that the film nods to the hallmarks of the NFE 'but stops short of a faithful replication'.[15] As a film that connects art-house and horror in its exploration of female subjectivity through the Gothic lens, and that focuses so much on the body, violence and sexuality as vehicles for challenging sociopolitical conventions, *Raw* might not be a totally faithful example of the NFE, but it certainly deserves more critical attention than reviews that undermine its uses of extremity as sensational fetish images.

Films associated with NFE implicitly demonstrate 'that there is such a thing as an authentic reality and that we can experience it only sensuously'.[16] This connects to the theories of horror film and affect. In 1990, Noël Carroll's *The Philosophy of Horror: Or, Paradoxes of the Heart* became one of the first academic monographs dedicated to analysing aesthetic experience and negative affect in horror. This ground-breaking work induced a renaissance in horror studies with a new focus on form and structure rather than on predominantly psychoanalytical and representational readings. This methodology has since been taken up by many horror scholars, not least Xavier Aldana Reyes whose work seeks to develop an understanding of the sociocultural and corporeal significance in post-millennial horror exacts through affect theory. Interviewed twenty-five years after the publication of his pivotal book, Carroll speaks about it coming out of a love for horror film and an opposition to the dominance of Lacanian and Althusserian frameworks:

> I often thought that Freudian analysis especially is not very strong on giving specific analyses of specific emotional states. I began to study the philosophy and the psychology of emotions, to deal with what I thought of as the lack of specificity in the ruling approaches to the emotions. I felt that trying to offer alternatives to the ruling views of psychoanalysis made it imperative for me to look toward a more cognitively oriented psychology and a more cognitively oriented philosophical position, which provides resources that would enable us to determine important variables in the elicitation of horror.[17]

Aldana Reyes calls Carroll's book 'the most important of the cognitivist interventions in the field of horror', and explains that his own desire to explore horror with these theoretical frameworks also comes from a similar feeling of malaise with over-prescribed psychoanalytical theory. He mentions Barbara Creed as one leading voice reliant on psychoanalysis to associate horror with instances of attack on the symbolic body, 'which is coupled with a certain regression to a prelapsarian state of substance and unity with the mother' (p. 246). Aldana Reyes's contention is that this builds a set of codes around experiencing horror:

> In this respect, psychoanalysis can be seen, not as the ultimate meta-discourse, but instead as an additional source of affect for the viewer. Inasmuch as it is productive to read the process of viewing horror as a 'pleasure in perversity'[18] its final inscription within the realms of the symbolic and the repressed lead to an analytic cul-de-sac.[19]

Rather than ponder the symbolism and the inner working of an 'unknown real', the power of body horror (sometimes referred to as 'corporeal horror') lies in its capacity to affect the viewer physically, to make them wince, to make them feel something. It does this by making the fictional on-screen body 'a virtuality, a potential body-in-suffering that can be consumed. Alignment with the on-screen body is therefore crucial for affect to occur' (p. 253). So, when Justine retches up fistfuls of what appears to be her own hair after a scene showing her chew on it nervously, the spectator retches with her. The camera is tight on Marillier's face as she pulls and pulls knots of hair from her throat. Following the thinking of Steven Shaviro, Aldana Reyes aims to analyse films, and he has looked at films predominantly in the body horror and torture horror genres, via how they might seem to amplify corporeal sensation and subjectivity:

> Rather than drive us away from reality and into a world of simulacra and hyperreality conducive to the waning of affect . . . these images put us in direct contact with the fibre of life. They show us how the body 'mutates into new forms, and is pushed to new thresholds of intense, masochistic sensation',[20] . . . Modern body horror films thus become affect machines that exalt, enthral, 'manufactur[e] and articulat[e] lived experience'. Instead of erasing the body or subjugating it to a kingdom of flattened images, they engage the body in novel procedures invested in intensity, excitation, and excess.[21]

Aldana Reyes describes this understanding of post-millennial horror as particular timely and significant in terms of its turn of the twenty-first-century context because of its emphasis on the realism of mutilated bodies framed with 'spectorial affect' (p. 253). He clarifies that what is lost in this understanding is not the body or sensation itself but everything else that might get in the way: the immaterial and the socially constructed.

I argue that a differentiated approach to reading cinema, encompassing old and new methods, is more effective than one that is completely dismissive or hostile to existing popular frameworks. Shaviro has since described *The Cinematic Body* as such an aggressive polemic that it embarrasses him. In it he wrote that 'the psychoanalytic theorist's need for control, his or her fear of giving way to the insidious blandishments of visual fascination, and his or her consequent construction of a theoretical edifice as a defense against a threatening pleasure'.[22] Fifteen years later he remarked on the hypocrisy of this, amending that deconstructive analysis and cinephilia necessarily interweave, and he concedes that the anti-theory backlash he was enveloped in the 1990s, and which has extended throughout the humanities over the past decade, 'is far more pernicious than psychoanalysis ever was'.[23] Calling the cognitive turn in film theory 'deplorable', Shaviro laments not having included the arguments of William James 'that cognized emotions are the effects of bodily states, so that I am afraid because I tremble, rather than trembling because I am afraid' (p. 53). But he had not read James before writing his book. Significantly, and I believe that Aldana Reyes advocates for this too, Shaviro calls for a differentiated look at films read through theories of affect. These should be inclusive of political, representational, psychoanalytic and embodied readings, as it is 'only because thought is embodied, because it is grounded in feeling, that it makes sense to think abstractly, or theoretically, at all' (p. 54). Taking this differentiated approach to reading *Raw* should consider its other contexts: its status as a cannibal narrative and its potential to pass political comment on French queer politics.

'What do you eat?': Queers, Animals and Cannibals

What Justine eats drives the narrative of the whole film and the clear transition in her dietary tastes makes visual the trauma of other transitions. Justine's parents are strict vegetarians, which is made clear in an early scene of the film where Justine's spits out a meatball hidden in her mashed potato to the horror of her mother. On discovering her sister has not kept up the family vegetarianism while away from home, it soon becomes apparent that their diet had been imposed on them and was not an individual ethical decision. However, Justine discovers eating flesh of any kind awakens a ravenous appetite for meat found further up the food chain. A pickled rabbit kidney is the gateway drug forced on Justine as part of her hell week hazing, from here she is tempted by cooked meat, raw chicken, human corpse and finally living human flesh. Justine's submersion in the intensely sexist and heteronormative patriarchal culture of the veterinary school that causes her to abandon her vegetarianism could read as a didactic tale advocating vegetarian feminism, a school of thought proffered by thinkers such as Carol J. Adams. Adams's pioneering *The Sexual Politics of Meat* (1990) draws significant parallels between the mythos of meat-eating with the mythos of masculinity and manliness and makes the persuasive argument that animals, women and sexual minorities have been historically objectified by patriarchal culture in similar ways. She uses the notion of the 'absent referent' to describe the ways in which violence against women and animals is hidden in discourse.

The figure of the cannibal is ubiquitous, it cannot exist in a fiction literally without it also existing as a metaphor. As a figure that straddles the intersection between fairy tale, folklore and real biopolitical enquiry, the cannibal has become an archetype of human monstrosity. For this reason, the Hannibal Lecter franchise endured well into 2015, beginning with Thomas Harris's novel *The Silence of the Lambs* in 1988 and continued with further novels, film and television adaptations. Gothic narratives that involve children and growing up often draw on the figure of the bogeyman . Marina Warner's comprehensive study of this figure describes the bogey as defined by appetite, stating that 'much of this lurid cannibalistic material acts as a metaphorical disguise for issues of authority, procreation, and intergenerational rivalry: it relates ways of confronting the foundations of the sense of identity and the self and of the self's historical and social place'.[24] From this we can appreciate that the cannibal's symbolic meanings stretch widely across human ontology.

However, as a queer Gothic character, this figure can also be appreciated as standing for a very niche set of values. Warner goes on to describe how the monsters, ogres and beastly people of cannibal narratives and folklore 'dramatize the complexity of the issue: they variously represent abominations against society, civilisation and family, yet are vehicles for expressing ideas of proper behaviour and due order' (pp. 11–12). As I will demonstrate in this chapter, there is queer activism at work in *Raw*'s depiction of cannibalism, but to begin unravelling that, this section must first develop how Ducournau's film defines the human.

Before any cannibalistic activity takes place in the film, Ducournau sets the scene by building a nexus of attitudes around the relationships between animals and humans. This implicates sexuality and food as well, which can be paralleled with Justine's unknown affliction. Scenes that work to introduce this nexus of ideas and attitudes about the distinctions between animal and human, subject and meat, include those that feature living and dead animals, instances where characters eat meat, and a cafeteria discussion about HIV, a virus that exists on the discursive intersection of sexuality, animal exploitation and biopolitics. Audiences are introduced to the complicated picture that Ducournau paints of the complex relationship between humans and animals in the film's opening scenes showing Justine with her vegetarian parents, on a journey away from the family home, accompanied by her dog. The dog acts as a loaded symbol for Justine's queer girlhood – she rejects its slobbering affection, suggesting her desire to move away from adolescence. Kathryn Bond Stockton argues that novels of the 1930s that she describes as sapphic use the dog as a metaphor for the queer girl's delay. Describing delay as 'the notion that children should approach all things adult with caution and in ways that guarantee their distance from adulthood',[25] Stockton uses this idea to support her thesis about queer children growing up sideways. Identifying the dog as 'a living, growing metaphor for the child itself . . . and for the child's own propensities to stray by making the most of its sideways growth' (p. 90), Stockton argues that the dog can provide a vehicle for the queer child's 'strangeness', in the way that it acted as an enabling totem or substitute love object in lieu of relationships with a heterosexual, marital and procreative trajectory.

Indeed, the culture of the veterinary school marks an entry into both adulthood and patriarchal society, socio-temporal states that Justine balks at. Rather than grow up laterally, Justine is subsumed in a culture so hostile that her sexuality and subjectivity seem to be induced unnaturally, and the pressures of this influence her ethics. The dogs in the film are the first indicator of this. Quicky, Alex's dog, lives with her at the school, sitting patiently by her side or in the corner, even during the nightly student raves, like a witch's familiar. Justine's dog can be seen lavishing unrequited kisses all over her face on the drive to school. However, each dog is treated with a kind of cold apathy, especially when Justine's finger-eating gets blamed on Quicky – the girls' father states the dog must be destroyed, since 'an animal that has tasted human flesh isn't safe', and the only response to this is a text from Alex to Justine later in the film reading, 'Mom says they put Quicky down. She's so sad. LOL #waytoocute'. The transition in Justine's ethical view of animals and humans is compounded by the dehumanising hazing rituals. However, as Ducournau explains in an interview for *Film Comment*, the metaphor extends to a notion of queering normativity and social convention:

> I think it's dark magic. It's really scary. So the fact that I took part in it makes me question myself. I also heard stories about hazing, because my parents are doctors and there is a lot of hazing in med school. But I chose hazing not because of memories, but because of society and the idea that we still have to fit in a box today. It hurts me profoundly. I don't think it's fair to everyone, and I wanted the cannibalism to become a punk gesture against this patriarchy, against the establishment that is hazing, and against the sheep-like movement of everyone doing the same thing.[26]

The deconstructionist aims, however, become obfuscated by an emerging ethics that errs on the essentialist gestures of some eco-feminism, by which I mean an overdetermined association between women and nature. Early in the film, a cafeteria scene sees a student articulating a theory that the AIDS virus originated with someone having sex with a monkey. He wonders whether, if a man wanted commit bestiality with a monkey, he should wear a condom. Adrien, a mixed-race gay man retorts, 'What do I care? Cuz I fuck monkeys or have AIDS?' addressing the homophobic and racist connotations of the student's question. These connotations are founded on the media coverage and oral speculation around the virus originating in African apes. Observing the moment that HIV became known as a zoonosis, Megan Glick tracks the moral panic around the virus's transmission, appreciating the racial and homophobic assumptions accrued there which impacted on speculation about its origin. After these speculations erred more towards the consumption of 'bush-meat' rather than bestiality, the narrative changed from one of 'sexual impropriety to a narrative of dietary impropriety'.[27] Glick describes this shift as having taken shape around 'a particular politics of literal and figurative dehumanisation' (p. 267), which builds on historical imperialist imaginings of non-white and non-Western people as subhuman, more specifically imagining West African people as bestial or cannibalistic. Imperialist dehumanisation works first to feminise the subject, which 'always results in profound forms of biopolitical disenfranchisement, precisely because it links certain subjects to the animal world, marks them as less than human, and brings them under the broader rubrics of gendered and ethno-racial prejudice' (p. 267). It is my argument that what emerges from the ignorant comment and the subsequent conversation, set significantly in the dining area of the cafeteria, reveals the culture of the school as an existential quagmire for students like Adrien and Justine.

Justine's retort to the other student's question is, 'I bet a raped monkey suffers like a woman'. This prompts a girl sitting at the end of the table to question her and look offended. Interestingly, Ducournau explains this scene as 'a way of showing that Justine is not an adult woman yet'.[28] Ducournau's personal ethics surrounding the development of female subjectivity occludes the larger point in the film, that humans exploit each other just as much as they exploit animals. Ducournau reasons that Justine 'thinks that her body is the same as that of an animal, which means she hasn't become aware of her femininity. Even though, of course, she's correct in saying animals have rights, essentially what she's implying in that conversation is that she doesn't have free will' (p. 53). So, Ducournau's appreciation of subjectivity development is proving free will via a series of ethical impasses where choice and volition are exercised. To access this, then, Ducournau shows Justine's growth as a constant fight to overcome animality, in the process making some problematic yet provocative associations between non-humanity or inhumanity and queerness.

On the axis of queerness and cannibalism lies Justine and Adrien's relationship, which is perhaps the best example of exposing a cultural paradigm in its observation of queer kinship as both a source of support and affinity but also an exercise in predatory human behaviour and exploitation. *Raw* can be read initially as a queer film in a similar way to how Darren Elliott-Smith reads Brian de Palmer's 1976 cult horror film *Carrie*. In his book, *Queer Horror Film and Television*, Elliott-Smith offers *Carrie* in a cogent argument that connects the horror film to queer spectatorship. Both *Raw* and *Carrie* feature a scene in which the female protagonist (an outsider in both texts) is doused in pig's blood. The initial moment at which the audience are given the opportunity to pity the wide-eyed, petite-framed girl is set up as a point of contract for the later revelation of her subversive violent potential; Justine is doused in blood for the class picture that fresher students must pose for as part of their hazing ritual. In *Raw*, as in *Carrie*, abject scenes like this can be appreciated to invite queer spectatorship. Elliott-Smith writes that '[g]iven Carrie's simultaneous status as victim and monster, alongside the narrative concerning her burgeoning attraction to boys, she is situated as a powerful figure of identification for the gay male spectator'.[29] Elliott-Smith develops this via an analysis of the mechanisms of cross-gender identification at play:

> The gay man is forced to take up contradictory patriarchal and heteronormative ideals of masculinity that he both identifies with and rejects, making his attempts at identification with masculinity particularly prolonged and uneasy. Horror film, and particularly *Carrie*, offers gay spectators the (un)pleasurable and transformative experience of cross gender identification which serves to underline the fragility of masculine identity, particularly in relation to sexual, political and power structures. (p. 32)

This chapter neither subscribes to nor challenges ideas of cross-gender identification, where gay men, as suggested by Elliott-Smith's argument, narcissistically align themselves with exaggerated presentations of femininity. However, *Raw* can, like *Carrie*, 'be read by gay male subjects (which I would amend to all queer subjects) allegorically as a variation on the "coming out" tale, both sexually and socially' (p. 23). The 'coming out' tale is something that cements this chapter's reading of Justine as a queer character in her own right. Justine's 'coming out' event occurs in the one and only sex scene of the film, immediately after Justine experiences a subversion of the *Carrie* moment. Justine stumbles into a paint party where she's doused in blue paint rather than blood. She is thrown by her peers into a room with a man who is painted yellow and they are told to not come out until they are both green. Dashing all expectations, Justine remains mostly blue and bites off part of the man's lip. Interestingly, at the 2017 'Horror in the Eyes of Women' symposium, film critic Cerise Howard remarked that this scene marked heteronormativity as the site of monstrosity in the film: 'This whole hazing business – get a boy, get a girl, put them in a room together and don't let them out until they've merged in some way – it's rape culture writ large and is truly monstrous.'[30] To be clear, the scene does not show Justine being forced to have sex, but it powerfully evokes the culture of socio-sexual pressures towards heterosexual conformity. It provided the viewer with the suggestion that her cannibal impulses might be induced by sexual contact, which is confirmed in the next scene when Justine 'comes out' to Adrien.

Returning from the shower, Justine is invited by Adrien to have a drag of his joint. She lies on his bed with his arm around her, and he asks whether the guy that she had bitten had forced her to do anything but she laughs it off, embarrassed. He asks whether the guy 'turned her on', and whether she is still turned on. Justine is incredulous about his curiosity – he tells her that he is just trying to see how she works, venturing to ask whether she might like 'S&M shit or worse'. Justine gets up to go to bed and Adrien returns to the gay porn that he is midway through watching, he masturbates and continues smoking. Justine returns, interrupts, telling him 'it's worse', and they have sex. Energetic from the start, each appears as eager as the other. They fall off the bed, kissing and embracing throughout the intercourse, but Justine's kisses soon turn into fervent licking and gnashing. She bites at Adrien's neck, and he tells her to stop but does not put an end to the sex, instead holding her head away from his neck. Justine climaxes and finally sinks her teeth into the flesh of her own arm. Adrien holds her head as she bites down, stroking her hair. The scene is expertly choreographed to be presented as violent yet consensual, but the precarious control that Justine shows is troubling. That it ends in such a display of tenderness says less about sexual desire than it does about the significance of queer kinship as a source of support and belonging. Ducournau elaborates on this idea:

> Sexual identity is fluid, and you may be different things at different stages in your life. It was interesting to show a young woman who is not scared, or worried she may have made the wrong decision. This kind of representation of young girls' sexuality is too common, the idea that it is like losing something. Quite the opposite: Justine gains an identity and a unique relationship that cannot be pigeonholed, and she is triumphant. I've had enough of seeing sexuality represented as something that's difficult for girls.[31]

As empowering as this representation of sex and 'deflowering' (as it is misogynistically referred to in the film) is, it risks a problematic recasting of another player into the role of exploited, used body. Later, when Justine questions Adrien's relationship with her sister, he shouts: 'I'm gay, OK? If I spent twenty years hiding, it's not to fuck girls now, OK?' The predatory nature of Justine's developing sexuality builds from earlier scenes where she leers at Adrien's neck while helping him to fasten his overalls, or her scopophilic watching as he plays football shirtless – in this instance, the lusting after his body appears to cause her nose to bleed. These bloodletting episodes suggesting a climax of desire connected to fetishized carnality – discussed in an earlier chapter in my analysis of *Jack & Diane* – seem to parody the 'money shot' hallmark of most heterosexual porn, offering a Gothic reinterpretation of male ejaculation. This theme in contemporary film dealing with female sexuality and subjectivity has become a clichéd metaphor that quite harmfully associates menstruation with active sexual desire and problematically suggests that when women are aroused, a physiological loss of control must also provide a reminder of their leaking bodies.

Not only does the representation of the Gothic body and the queer cannibal draw on misogynistic tropes, but the film also implicates colonial and racist mores. A pivotal scene to my argument, that the parallels that *Raw* encourages between cannibalism and queer sexuality problematically implicate a wilful ignorance of the undeniable colonial roots of cannibal fiction, comes immediately after Adrien's 'I'm Gay!' outburst. Opening on another party, Justine blends seamlessly into the background as a couple practice oculolinctus in the foreground. The camera passes by the couple with the cold apathy that Justine has now swapped for a lustful stare. She sits behind the spectacle, legs wide open, staring from under her dark brows, and licks her lips, watching a white woman licking the eyeball of a Black man. The woman and the man go uncredited in the film and do not appear again. This might not be such an issue if there were other Black faces in the cast, but the only other non-white actor is the intensely erotised Rabah Nait Oufella who ends up dead and mostly eaten. In this way, *Raw* can be easily read as part of an enduring history of Western culture capitalising on its own colonial hypocrisy of appropriating and fetishising the very phenomenon used to justify the 'civilisation' of Othered cultures. It matters that Justine lusts over a white woman licking and tasting the eyeball of a Black man; it matters that the person who most falls victim to cannibalism is a non-white gay man. The punk gestures towards developing queer female subjectivity that Ducournau presents either grossly overlook cornerstones of knowledge within cannibal criticism or seem to intentionally substitute one hierarchy for another: cannibalism no longer exists as something to separate normative humanity and sub-human figures and animals. It is at one and the same time a means of rethinking mastery and a means of justifying a fear of the queer, revelling in queer theory's anti-relational modes and its antisociality.

Joan Smith discusses the neutral term that anthropologists prefer to use, 'anthropophagy', a portmanteau of the Greek words *anthropos* ('human being') and *phagein* ('to eat'). Cannibalism, she writes, 'associates the practice with a racial group', referring to Europeans who landed on the West Indian islands in 1492, and who regarded the people that they found there 'as a bunch of painted savages'.[32] This being the case, Smith summarises that these 'European invaders felt little compunction in forcing them to change their customs by converting them to Christianity or wiping them out, using highly coloured accounts of human sacrifice and flesh-eating as a justification' (p. 216). Since these accounts, cannibalism has become one of the most significant topics in cultural criticism because of its ability to pierce the heart of crucial conversations on identity and difference across time, space and discipline. So, 'cannibal criticism', a term that I use to apply to the raft of work available on the figure and symbol of the cannibal, is wide and multifarious, often associating cannibalism to the cultural logic of late capitalism (see Crystal Bartolovich and Rosalind Morris), while thinkers such as bell hooks refer to the incorporation or appropriation of different cultures as 'eating the other'.[33] C. Richard King comments on the hypocrisy of the colonising West whose contemporary society consumes cannibal culture out of context, dislocating it to places like museums to make it more palatable and digestible. King is 'terribly sympathetic with these perspectives, particularly their political commitments and theoretical creativity'; however, he also comments that he is 'disturbed by the practices and effects that animate them'.[34] For King, problems lie less in the way that these criticisms defamiliarise ideas of consumption and cultural production, and more in the way that they do nothing to develop understandings of them; never mind underscoring any effective methods to challenge them. Instead, these institutions and individuals risk committing the same kinds of appropriation or exploitation, and binaries become reified (p. 108). This significantly mirrors what I have argued takes place in *Raw*.

Regardless of whether Ducournau intended Justine's cannibalism to read as a 'punk gesture', like all other cultural artefacts it does not and cannot exist in a representational vacuum. As the most overt metaphor for difference, the Othering that takes place is inherently problematic, calling for more markers of boundaries and binaries than for the radical deconstruction or destabilisation of such. King qualifies: 'The presence of cannibalism, real or imagined, demands that social orders and subjectivities be remade in the image of the West' (p. 109). It cannot, in contemporary culture, even in the guise of a Gothic metaphor, jettison its associations with domination and exploitation as they relate to alterity and identity. Shirley Lindenbaum phrases it differently, however:

Going beyond the narrow view of anthropophagy merely as human consumption, cannibal metaphors are said to speak about different social, cultural, and religious realities. The creativity of the metaphor establishes connections among objects in different contexts: between eating human flesh and relations of kinship and alliance, as well as notions of identity and difference, savagery, animality, the excessive use of power, and the operations of the law. The figure of the cannibal allows authors in different epochs to think reflectively about other ways of life and different ways of being human.[35]

Metaphorically, then, *Raw* has undeniable value. The way in which the film uses cannibalism as a metaphor for sexuality is the most interesting aspect, something that this chapter appreciates. However, I argue that uneasiness remains around the implications of queering the cannibal that is particular to this film. To develop why that is, this chapter will now turn to addressing the fraught relationship between an Anglo-American set of beliefs around sex, gender and queerness, and, crucially, what the French commonly believe.

Chéri Je Suis Rentré: *Queering the French Cannibal*

The aesthetics and general shape of queer theory, ethics and ontology as it exists today are very much informed by American thinkers such as Eve Kosofsky Sedgwick and Judith Butler; however, while most UK-based work on homosexuality and social constructivism (see Mary McIntosh, 1968) is passed over in favour of Foucault's *Will to Knowledge*, much of the founding theory comes from French thinkers. As Claire Boyle notes, it is significant that Butler is influenced by Foucault and Irigaray; that both Bersani and Sedgwick develop their epistemologies through their readings of Proust; that Fuss builds her queer theories of identification from the work of Lacan and Fanon. It is fair to say, then, as Boyle concludes, 'that American queer theory is deeply rooted in European, and specifically French thought'.[36] However, as is evidenced by the comprehensive special issue of *Paragraph* journal, 'Queer theory's Return to France', collated by Oliver Davis and Hector Kollias, queer theory may have been born in France, but it certainly does not maintain an easy relationship with its parentage. Much of that difficult relationship, which is threaded throughout this book as its main contention, implicates identity politics. Boyle takes this contention and calls for a turn towards the concept of 'post-queer', reasoning that:

> Ultimately, the notion that the deconstructive logic of 'queer' could be seen as an intellectual powerhouse able to unlock and scramble systems of meaning, and also function as a politically potent force able to effect material change to the benefit of sexual minorities, comes to be very considerably weakened in Anglo American academic and activist circles alike. (pp. 166–7)

Doubting queer theory's potential as a productive mode of thinking that is capable of effecting real change, Boyle situates this rift just after the millennium, stating that the loss of faith is felt within and beyond the academy. Like Justine, queer theory has quite a different world view to its parents – contemporary queer theory is similar to the foundational theory from which it was developed; however, it thinks about difference differently and this leads to opposing ethical values. It is this precise reason that blocks any straightforward queering of the cannibal in *Raw*. The thinking that stimulated the advent of queer theory circulated around radical anti-humanism through deconstruction; in its Anglo-American appellations, Kollias argues that metaphysics was swapped for sexuality. Significantly, French queer theory, specifically Foucauldian, laid out the idea that the body is connected directly to deployments of power but that 'the biological and the historical are not consecutive to one another'.[37] Foucault states that forms of power produce specific kinds of pleasure and bodies, and it is wrongheaded to assume the inverse: that historically observable manifestations of sexuality, gender and the body follow on naturally or neutrally from purely biological realities. The biological and the social exist in temporal and situational contingency, their meanings being fixed according to the constellations of power and knowledge in operation at different moments.[38]

Kollias goes on to lament the encroachment of identity politics into queer theory, imagining Foucault's own similar disdain with contemporary accoutrements of 'self-report' and representation via identification. He takes 'these 'axiomatic' pronouncements to be emblematic if not definitional of queer theory precisely in that they seek to put the 'science of differ(e/a)nce' in the service of particular differences, thereby seeking not to interrogate but to shore up the practical and theoretical intelligibility of any, and that means all, sexual differences.[39] There are problems with difference and social constructivism, and there are problems emanating from disquiet in the canon:

> It steps aside from theories and practices of understanding which it cannot possess as specifically queer in a move which is, in effect, a regression from the same 'French Theory' that motivated and haunts the canon as it has adopted. The Manichaean duo of saint-*intraitable* Foucault and the villain Lacan occludes the unevenness and contradictoriness of queer thinking's coming into visibility, the delicate balance between the polymorphous and the entropic, which hangs on a capacity not to flinch, for instance, in the passage between the Scylla of rectum-grave in Bersani and the Charybdis of Kristeva's concept of the feminine as an instantiation of the disabused subject.[40]

While Kollias suggests an anxiety about identity and identification diluting politics and activism, it is important to note that not all fields as broad as queer theory contain groups and factions that maintain overwhelming consensus. Founding father, Foucault, remains a potent figure for queer criticism, yet, as Hélène Bourcier reminds us, he was never interested in the 'gender-fucking' that has become so central to Anglo-American queer thinking. She describes his avoidance of gender as his most problematic limitation: 'everything happens as if, for him, there were only one gender: homoerotic masculinity'.[41] Although it is discussed in more detail elsewhere in this book, it bears repeating that some contemporary branches of queer theory continue structural misogyny well into the present decade.

Conclusion

In *Raw*, cannibalism could well be read as a punk gesture, railing against patriarchy, the limitations of contemporary beauty ideals and heteronormativity. The film shows humans doing horrible things to each other, and this is reflected neatly in the physical fight that Justine and Alexia have towards the film's conclusion. Their animal brutality sees each taking actual chunks of flesh from the other. Alexia manages her cannibal impulses by causing road accidents near the veterinary school, so that she can feed on the dead or dying car-crash victims. When this method of managing her hunger fails, she commits the ultimate crime of murdering and eating Adrien, Justine's protected choice cut of meat. Justine wakes up next to Adrien, horrified to find him dead and terrified that she may have attacked him. She then finds her sister slumped against the fridge with a PlayStation controller in her hands, much like the domesticated zombie ending of *Shaun of the Dead* (2004), a tongue-in-cheek allusion to a loss of humanity, with a mindless and tragic impulse to maintain kinship. Justine undresses and fastidiously washes her sister in the shower, rinsing her of Adrien's blood. The next scene shows the family visiting Alexia in prison. On departing, each shows the other their injuries through the glass, lasting reminders of their shared potential for harm and violence, as well as of love and forgiveness. Justine returns home and is told by her father that Alexia is the way she is because she was spoilt as a child and has too headstrong a personality not to 'be herself'. He begins to tell his daughter about the way her mother managed her affliction, as he tells the story of their first kiss, he grazes his scared lip with his fingers. Unbuttoning his shirt, he shows Justine the horrific scars and lesions decorating his torso. Apparently, Justine's only options are her sister's unsustainable method of premeditated murder, lapping up the flesh and blood of freshly made corpses, or her mother's method of strict vegetarianism and restrained cannibal practice within a monogamous relationship with a consenting donor. This heteroglossic message to Justine is that her sexuality and identity are bound up with violence, and that the best way to manage her humanity is to replicate her parents' pretence of heteronormativity. *Raw* is interesting in the way that it relates sexuality to questions of humanity and monstrosity and the ways in which it exploits the symbol of the real and metaphoric cannibal, loaded as that is with gendered, postcolonial and psychoanalytical meaning. The cannibal in *Raw*, as elsewhere, is both an extremely marginal and antisocial identity category that refuses normativity, yet also emphasises difference and binary thinking.

6

'She would never fall, because her friend was flying with her': Gothic Hybridity, Queer Girls and Exceptional States in The Icarus Girl *and* The Girl with all the Gifts

⁂

This chapter returns attention to New Queer Gothic fiction in an investigation of how representations of girlhood in two examples of New Queer Gothic literature provoke important questions about hybridity, exceptionality and the broader relationship of Gothic and queer representations of subjectivity to the lived realities and power structures on which many aspects of subjectivity depend. This chapter argues that in reading New Queer Gothic girlhood each of these novels becomes positioned ambivalently on the spectrum of regressive/progressive representation, yet each effectively represents the formation of hybrid subjectivity as a challenge to real systems of power.

The Icarus Girl's Jessamy Harris is British and of mixed British and Nigerian descent; during her first visit to Nigeria, Jess makes a friend in Titiola and gives her the nickname TillyTilly. Through the course of the novel, TillyTilly's supernatural abilities and malevolence are revealed, as it become clear that she aims to possess Jess and steal her place in the world. Jessamy's hybridity is presented as a trauma and a conflict, an internal civil war in which she is conscripted to harm others. Her body and her subjecthood are under threat from becoming possessed by TillyTilly and, in themselves, figure as the abstract site of exception. The heterotopic space that Jessamy occupies during her war with TillyTilly, and the place that she fears becoming trapped in is conveyed as a place without sovereignty or the possibility of subjectivity. There is no utopic outcome to her sacrifice, and importantly Oyeyemi leaves unclear as to whether Jessamy prevails in her battle or loses. In *The Girl with all the Gifts*, Melanie, a half human, half hungry (an infected human, much like a zombie) is the top of her class on an army-base compound where military scientists test her capacity for human learning and emotion. When their base is overrun by 'hungries', those who have been colonised by the Ophiocordyceps fungus and subsequently lost most semblance of humanity, Melanie helps a group of human civilians traverse an apocalyptic wasteland and encounters other children like her. Melanie's biologically hybrid status places her and her fellow 'hungry' children on the apex of Earth's new food chain. Carey's plot sees Melanie become a 'bioweapon',[1] as villainous Scientist Dr Caldwell predicted, and her role as such serves to wipe out humanity so that a new order might thrive.

Both novels represent Gothic girlhood intersecting with tropes and motifs already demonstrated as endemic to the New Queer Gothic genre; these include, but are not limited to, the presence of the Gothic child, Gothic doubling, mirroring, the monstrous feminine, abjection, and the use of Gothic space and place. Analysing the presence of some of these motifs will provide a springboard from which to launch an argument that the New Queer Gothic girl in contemporary fiction provides a valuable symbol for hybrid identity and provokes readers to think about identity, ontology, queer ethics and biopolitics. This chapter will begin its analysis by situating each text within existing criticism, paying special attention to how the child figures in contemporary Gothic fiction. Hybridity will be the next topic of discussion, framed through a discussion of how each novel envelops and appropriates the Greek myths referred to in their titles. Comparing and contrasting the presentation of postcolonial hybridity in *The Icarus Girl* with biological hybridity in *Gifts*, this chapter will argue that each novel suggests a critique of similar real-world power structures. This chapter will then discuss each text's construction of queerness to argue that each uses it very differently. Drawing on the work of Giorgio Agamben, and Achille Mbembe, this chapter will assemble its reading of these New Queer Gothic novels around the broader concepts of postcolonial queerness and biopolitics, working towards the argument that these readings evidence the undeniable value of Gothic fiction as a tool for understanding how power structures affect individual and social identities.

Jessamy and Melanie, as protagonists, figure as examples of the pre-pubescent queer Gothic girl introduced and analysed in Chapter 2 of this book. This chapter aims to explain how their similar presentations of queer Gothic girlhood situate each of these novels in an ambivalent position on the spectrum of regressive/progressive representation, while arguing that they have a representational value in their complex presentations of subjectivity and political literary value in presenting critiques of existing power structures.

Subjectivity and the Gothic Child

Jessamy is eight years old and Melanie is around ten years old, they are the youngest characters to be considered by my investigations into the phenomenon of the New Queer Gothic. Building on the analyses embarked on in Chapters 2 and 5, which respectively considered queer Gothic girlhood in *Florence and Giles* (2010) and Gothic adolescence and queer cannibalism in *Raw* (2016), this chapter extends its reading of this figure to address broader questions of hybrid identity and biopolitics. Like the previously considered queer girls in this thesis, Melanie and Jessamy are uncanny, but they are not malevolent, supernaturally precocious or sinister; they are not children who murder (like Florence), but they are presented as having the potential to harm others. Out of all the queer girl protagonists explored, Melanie is perhaps most similar to *Raw*'s Justine in her struggle to manage her bloodlust. The inherent gothicity of the child is something that critics have long pondered. Sue Walsh draws together some of these ideas, citing David Punter's psychoanalytic readings of the child character signifying the 'locked door of the unconscious'[2] and provoking depth metaphors, while Steven Bruhm regards the contemporary construction of the child character in the Gothic as a paradox, representing both 'fully-fledged and developed' as well as 'an infinitely malleable, formable being who can turn out right if only the proper strategies are employed'.[3] This contradiction is made visible in the Gothic, where children are constantly constructed within a paradox of fetishised innocence and corruptibility. Walsh proffers that '[t]hough these comments register different constructions of childhood, they also point to a desire to attain a stable answer to an implicit question: 'What is the child really?'[4] As Chapter 2 discussed and as Walsh develops in her essay on 'Gothic Children', more interesting conclusions might be drawn by swapping an ontological question for a representational one to ask: 'What are the implications of writing the child?' (p. 184).

The form used by the novels analysed in this chapter is significant to my overall argument that the value of New Queer Gothic fiction lies in its ability to engage in complex representational politics. Following Walsh, my aim is not to speculate 'about child readers and their responses, but [to read] closely the wider implications of the relationship . . . between "the child" and the Gothic' (p. 184). This chapter will provide evidence that the representational significance and intrigue of the New Queer Gothic exists across literary and mainstream or popular fiction texts. Chloé Germaine Buckley describes the growing prevalence of discourse within Gothic scholarship to question the readership, value and validity of contemporary forms of Gothic fiction when introducing her book *Twenty-First-Century Children's Gothic*. While Oyeyemi's novel is literary fiction read predominantly by adults, Carey's novel falls into the category of genre fiction, specifically contemporary science fiction, and is popular with child and adult readers alike. The paratextual signifiers of *Gifts* draw attention to its appeal to younger readers: in the 2014 Orbit edition there is, for example, a list of book-club questions included, as well as an informal interview with the author. Carey's graphic novels already claim a large young-adult readership, particularly his work on the DC *X-Men* comic franchise and the *Lucifer* series, a spin-off of Neil Gaiman's earlier series, *The Sandman*. Of these graphic novels, similar dark themes associated with contemporary Gothic fiction are noticeable, particularly in the narrative structure of young protagonists overcoming adversity via supernatural ability, and a narrative concern with notions of morality and ethics that navigate or embrace alterity, monstrosity and Otherness. It follows, then, that fans of his other works would likely be attracted to his fiction. Buckley writes that Gothic studies 'dismisses "mainstream" cultural production according to the logic of subcultural capital', arguing against Fred Botting and Maria Beville, whom, in their lamenting over the consumerism inherent in franchised contemporary Gothic texts marketed at children and young people, overlook many rich texts for little reason. Buckley offers her book as a tonic against 'such elitist evaluations with a reminder that the Gothic has its roots in popular culture, in consumption and in fakery'.[5] Buckley uses the critical framework of nomadic subjectivity 'to extricate the image of the child from an ethical dilemma that plagues children's literature criticism. This criticism paradoxically constructs children as passive even as it seeks to read them as active'. Buckley contends that:

> The child must submit to the pedagogy of the text in order to be produced as active. Echoes of this paradox appear in some Gothic criticism, particularly in discussions that dismiss 'trashy' Gothic texts, such as *Twilight*, because of the negative messages they transmit to a child reader (imagined as gullible, naïve and, usually, female). (p. 11)

Moving away from child subjectivity being framed by questions of pedagogy and consistently situated on a sliding scale of activity and passivity, Buckley opts to read children's Gothic texts through the theoretical framework of nomadism. Reasoning that this framework is ideally suited to analysing the diegetic child's relationship to the child reader, Buckley writes that nomadic subjectivities that are 'constructed within texts and cultures may be passive, or restricted in some way, but that space exists nonetheless within such locations for agency and empowerment' (p. 11). Buckley's methodology calls attention to the alternative lenses through which we can observe the Gothic child, crucial to a field so saturated with psychoanalytical and pathologising readings of fictive and real queer children.

This chapter, methodologically, works towards similar aims to that of Buckley in casting a wide net of critical frameworks to appreciate the child figure and to consider the wider representational impact of Gothic fiction. While Buckley uses nomadic subjectivity to analyse children's Gothic in twenty-first century texts, this chapter will later consider it to establish connections between two texts that are similar in their presentations of gothicity and queerness yet diverging in their presentations of Gothic hybridity. Rosi Braidotti describes the formation of subjectivity as 'rather like pitching a musical tone',[6] describing the subjects as 'collective assemblages . . . dynamic but framed: fields of forces that aim at duration and affirmative self-realization'. Needing to be drawn together along a line of composition, blocks of becoming inclusive of 'Others', Braidotti prescribes to the Deleuzian line of overcoming the self/other, same/different dualisms in order to appreciate the subject as a series of becomings and as an assemblage (p. 173). Braidotti describes a 'yearning for in-depth transformation' in the nomadic subject. It is a transformative force that propels multiple, heterogeneous 'becomings' of the subject (p. 174). The next section of this chapter will discuss the ways in which each text presents Gothic hybridity as indicative of a strained, laboured, difficult subjectivity formation, arguing that the dualism it conveys suggests each of the girl protagonists have an inherent ambivalence to their identity that they must overcome. To argue this, I will first discuss how hybridity is deployed by the Greek myths suggested in each novel's title, then I will argue that each hybrid girl is framed as having their sexual and racial identities informed by their subjective hybridity.

Gothic Hybridity

Hybrid identity is central to the characterisation of the girl protagonists in *The Icarus Girl* and *Gifts*. Each novel implicates sexual and racial subjectivity in its construction of hybridity and, while two very different readings are prompted by the novels' uses of hybridity, *The Icarus Girl* and *Gifts* similarly provide readers with opportunities to engage with questions of subjectivity formation. In both novels there is a little girl who is figured as queer and Gothic in her search for who or what she is, and both girls consistently prompt the reader to understand this figure as a symbol of the conflicting, ambivalent, fragmented image that our contemporary neoliberal society has of the human citizen and its future. Where in *The Icarus Girl* the signification of hybrid excess, palimpsest assimilation and disjointed belonging builds a sobering image of postcolonial, biracial identity coloured by psychic trauma, *Gifts* illustrates hybrid identity as new, exceptional and revolutionary, as it draws not only on postcolonial discourse but on ideas of post-humanism in a trajectory towards a queer utopia.

Helen Oyeyemi's novels often represent an interplay between gendered, sexual and postcolonial identity using Gothic motifs and narrative devices. Her first novel, *The Icarus Girl*, presents a young female protagonist who experiences a supernatural invasion on her sense of identity via queer and Gothic interactions with a morally darker double – TillyTilly is a dark-skinned Nigerian girl who appears to Jessamy to be around the same age as her. We learn that TillyTilly is not a little girl, however, but a folkloric Yoruba spirit with malevolent intentions. Similar Gothic plot dynamics are explored in Oyeyemi's later novel, *White is for Witching* (2009), which, as with *The Opposite House* (2007), describes sexuality more overtly and so lends itself more readily to readings appropriative of queer politics. *The Icarus Girl* has been described as a Gothic Bildungsroman (Ilott and Buckley, 2017) – the reader follows Jessamy, a mixed-race girl on her journey to her mother's home in Nigeria where she picks up a peculiar new friend, Titiola (TillyTilly), a manifestation only Jessy can see and communicate with. TillyTilly has been read as a Gothic double[7] embodying the fissures and fragmentation of mixed race, postcolonial and diasporic identity; however, she has never been read as a queer Gothic figure.

Sarah Ilott and Buckley's reading of *The Icarus Girl* foregrounds its framing of hybridity as negative and disturbingly Gothic. They argue that although there is an impulse, following such texts as Homi Bhabha's *The Location of Culture* (1994), to read hybrid spaces and hybrid peoples in a 'utopian light':

> Oyeyemi adopts the Bildungsroman form deliberately to subvert it, as not only does the protagonist become increasingly divided as the novel proceeds (both physically and psychologically), but

any transformation of national space is rendered threatening as the protagonist is effectively displaced, slipping between worlds.[8]

Highlighting the Bildungsroman form of the novel, Buckley and Ilott make the case that traditional narratives of hybridity are 'assumed to embody transformative potential' (p. 405), which can be noted in other critics' readings of the novel, particularly with respect to its ambiguous ending. Oyeyemi makes it clear that TillyTilly wants to possess Jessamy and usurp her position in the living world, so that they would swap places and Jessamy would be confined to the spirit world. After presenting this battle for subjectivity, Oyeyemi writes a scene of violent corporeal assimilation of the Gothic Other:

> TillyTilly pleaded in a scream that rang in Jess's ears, but Jess ran at her with the wind and an invisible current of fast-moving air behind her, taking her feet nearly off the slippery ground (she didn't hear the silent sister-girl telling her that it wasn't the right way, not the right way at all) and *hop, skip, jumped* into Tilly's unyielding flesh as she clawed at Jess's presence (*it hurt them both burningly*) back into herself. Jessamy Harrison woke up and up and up and up.[9]

Among those critics who read this ending as utopic, Diana Adesola Mafe argues that it suggests the ending of the novel as an 'awakening' that proves 'symbolic, hinting at a broader awakening in her new millennial postcolonial landscape, and perhaps ours as well'. Mafe reads *The Icarus Girl* as an 'adaptation and subversion of traditionally androcentric narrative' (p. 22). Noting that feminist interventions in Gothic studies gained traction in academia during the 1970s and 1980s 'in tandem with postcolonial criticism', Mafe contextualises Oyeyemi's novel and its re-gendering of a hero from Greek mythology (as suggested by the novel's title) as part of an ongoing impulse that began in 1976 when Ellen Moers coined the term 'female Gothic fiction', to reclaim 'female-authored and female-centred Gothic fiction, as narratives that indict patriarchy, critique the "othering" of women, and represent the suppressed Feminine' (p. 22). The compulsion to view Jessamy as a utopic figure with a reparative ending is understandable, though it certainly undermines the significance of choosing the particular Greek myth of Icarus. Aligning 'up and up and up' with being 'awoken' (or, as has entered the popular lexicon, being politically, socially or culturally 'woke', signalling a conscious concern with inequality) rather than the fabled narrative import of flying too close to the sun and falling, suggests an incongruence with the narrative. The Icarus myth did not speak to ascension as the goal, as Mafe seems to have it, but to flying neither too close to the sea nor to the sun. To me, the ending links to the titular myth in describing the precarious balancing act that Jessamy has had to perform throughout the course of the novel, struggling to reconcile the constituent parts of her hybrid identity.

Carey's protagonist in *The Girl with all the Gifts* is also introduced to the reader via her association with Greek mythology. This time the novel's title refers to the Greek heroine Pandora. Where one novel uses its titular myth to highlight the ambivalence involved in hybridity as it relates to Jess's mixed-race identity, *Gifts* appropriates the story of Pandora more literally. Melanie's narrative trajectory towards unleashing all sorts of disease and horror and catalysing the end of humanity and the beginning of a new age is tied to her hybrid identity. The duality of Pandora hinges on her status as a goddess and bringer of life, as well as her status as the first human woman, made by Hephaestus, and bringer of death.

Carey's *The Girl with all the Gifts* is an apocalyptic science fiction, fantasy novel, following Melanie, an intelligent 'hungry' child tasked with proving her capacity for human intelligence and emotion at the collapse of the human world. Initially held on a military base and subject to experimentation for the research of Dr Caroline Caldwell, Melanie develops an infatuation for her teacher, Miss Justineau. Her burgeoning love inspires her to lead a tribe of other non-human children and the role-reversal ending sees Justineau incarcerated (or preserved) in a research pod so that she can continue her work as a teacher. The plot, in the vein of Mary Shelley's *Frankenstein* (1818) or Richard Matheson's *I Am Legend* (1954), spins dystopic apocalypse into a tale of post-human utopia, provoking readers to wonder who the real monsters are, between the humans remaining on earth and the new species set to inherit it. Melanie's hybrid identity is marked by her ability to pass as human, in her ability to look and act like a normative human child, while also proving capable of the super-sensory abilities and the animalistic attacks that define the full hungries, or first-generation hungries that appear in the narrative: these are subjects who are no longer human, thought to be devoid of intelligence and emotion, and driven wholly by their hunger for flesh. Much of what indicates monstrosity in Carey's novel has to do with senses and sensory ability, revolving around controlled and uncontrolled desire. Melanie's hybrid identity sees her accepted into the company of human characters, as well as able to pass as a hungry and operate within close proximity to otherwise dangerous monstrous characters. When Caldwell discovers that Melanie's hybridity is a result of being born to an infected mother, born with the Ophiocordyceps fungus rather than having her body colonised by it, Melanie and other children like her are described as 'second generation' hungries. The children's 'second generation' status allegorises postcolonial identity in paralleling discourses around diasporic or migrant communities in neoliberal multicultural Britain.

Where Oyeyemi specifically re-genders her Icarus, appropriating the male myth for her girl protagonist – something Mafe recognises as paralleling her re-gendering of the traditionally male bush tale protagonist of West African folklore – Carey shows Melanie to appropriate the icon of Pandora reimagined as an androgyne, embodying the curiosity and thirst for knowledge in the mythic feminine archetype, as well as incorporating attributes of the traditionally male Titan figures. Gods, Titans and the myth of Pandora feature in the lessons that Miss Justineau gives to Melanie's class. In one of the many instances where Carey shows Melanie repressing her love for her teacher, she expresses her desire to perform mythic hero traits in order to preserve their relationship: 'Melanie wants to call her back, wants to say something to make her stay: *I love you, Miss Justineau, I'll be a god or a titan for you, and save you*'[10] (italics in original). Melanie's hybridity is always already bound up with her queer desire to love and protect her teacher and to help build a new world. Comparing herself to Aeneas setting out to found Rome, she 'seriously doubts now that the princes she once imagined fighting for her exist anywhere in this world, which is so beautiful but so full of old and broken things' (p. 292). Towards the end of the novel, her hybrid identity proves crucial to looking forward to the creation of a new society, and this foreshadowing of her grief at the death of man and his archetypical patriarchal heroism works to emphasis her role as a path-carving queer Gothic girl.

Hybridity and Racial Identity

'Her name is Melanie', begins *Gifts*, 'It means "the black girl", from an Ancient Greek word, but her skin is actually very fair so she thinks maybe it's not such a good name for her' (p. 1). With his introductory sentence, Carey ushers in the first of his novel's problematic incursions into queer and racial representation.[11] For example, Melanie's hero-worshipping infatuation with her teacher certainly evokes fetishisation of her skin colour:

> Nobody gets bored on Miss Justineau days. It's a thrill for Melanie even to look at her. She likes to guess what Miss Justineau will be wearing, and whether her hair will be up or down. It's usually down, and it's long and black and really crinkly so it looks like a waterfall. But sometimes she ties it up in a knot on the back of her head, really tight, and that's good too, because it makes her face sort of stand out more, almost like she's a statue on the side of a temple, holding up the ceiling. A caryatid. Although Miss Justineau's face stands out anyway because it's such a wonderful colour, it's dark brown, like the wood of the trees in Melanie's rain forest picture whose seeds only grow out of the ashes of a bushfire . . . it's as dark as Melanie's is light. (pp. 11–12)

While the language is positive and complimentary, this novel's dynamic of a young white girl, described as beautiful and blonde, the archetypal image of innocence, speaks not only to the 'white saviour' trope, or 'white saviour industrial complex', but also to representations of childhood innocence engaged with via whiteness.

The 'white saviour' is a trope described by many critics of representational politics as having an enduring history in visual and popular culture narratives that see a white protagonist gaining a virtuous or heroic status after coming to the aid or assistance of a Black figure or community. While there is no overtly recognisable project to align whiteness with morality in the racialising of characters in *Gifts*, it does serve in Carey's novel to set Melanie and her love interest apart. The fetishising of Miss Justineau's skin, the impulse to preserve her, which ends in Melanie keeping her as a live specimen in the research pod (much like a display case) after all life on Earth has been purged, conjures the 'white saviour' trope as one aspect of the naïve and problematic presentation of a queer post-human utopia suggested by the end of the novel.

Another factor crucial to explaining the problems of this 'utopic' ending concerns Melanie's saviour status as contingent on her status as a child – the connotations of 'innocence' are compounded by her whiteness; however, her status as child also has the cultural cache of moral purity attached firmly to it. Via her relationship with Miss Justineau, and the impression she makes upon her adult love-object, Melanie's hybrid status is revealed to revolve around the paradox of the Gothic child as expounded by Bruhm: of innocence and monstrosity. The construction of her hybridity is presented through the initial mistrust and revulsion with which Justineau perceives her:

> It's like she dug a pit trap, nice and deep, squared off the edges, wiped her hands. Then walked right into it. Except that it was test subject number one, really, who dug the pit. Melanie. It was her desperate, obvious hero-worshipping crush that tripped Justineau up, or at least threw her enough off balance that tripping became inevitable. Those big, trusting eyes, in that bone-white face. Death and the maiden, all wrapped up in one tiny package.[12]

Here, Carey shows Justineau self-consciously assessing the emotional toll that her job is taking, testing the second-generation hungry children and their capacity to present as human. Later in the novel, her hybrid status as both a human child and a zombie creature is accepted, and the mistrust and disgust are swapped for something more like awe:

> She's out in the world now, her education accelerating from a standing start to some dangerous, unguessable velocity. She thinks of

an old painting. *And When Did You Last See Your Father?* Because Melanie's stance is exactly the same as the way the kid stands in that picture. For Melanie, though, that would be a completely meaningless question. (pp. 260–1)

Remarking her curious orphan status, this quotation emphasises a new appreciation for Melanie as post-human. Moreover, the quotation suggests Melanie as a postmodern image of childhood, as it pertains to its genealogy since nineteenth-century Western society's invention of the category and of its general obsession with the figure of the child, owing, as Catherine Robson describes, to the various strains of Victorian Christianity that 'found themselves variously in contention and agreement with Romanticism's view of the child as pure and innocent'.[13] The painting discussed, 'And When Did You Last See Your Father?' (1878) by William Frederick Yeames, depicts a fictional scene set in a royalist manor house during the English civil war showing a boy being questioned by parliamentarians about the whereabouts of his father. The child figure stands out as the central point of light in the composition, his pale skin, blond hair and light-blue suit contrast starkly with the dark and muted figures littered around the periphery, giving him an angelic aura.

The effect of using the Yeames painting is that it relates the action in the novel to a nineteenth-century image of the innocent child at an instance in which he is called on to do the morally 'right thing'. Significantly, however, the painting's scene used for this comparison depicts a fictional event. The reader's assessment of Melanie is therefore mediated through this Black character's gaze, mediated again through nineteenth-century representations of child-as-innocent remarked by her comparison with the painting. This treatment of the child figure works to situate her within the paranoid tropes of the Gothic, which this thesis has continually demonstrated throughout its analysis and that it has found more reparative methods of reading. What is more interesting, however, in the way Melanie becomes situated in a genealogy of white, innocent, heroic children, is the fact that this description is accessed via a painting of a *fictional* scene set in the English Civil War. It does not depict real people, or a real event but serves to strike a tableau of the innocent and truthful child responsible for the fate of his family in the context of wartime violence. This returns us to the overarching argument of this chapter: New Queer Gothic fiction can and should be used to address the effects of real structures of power and mechanisms of violence.

Where Melanie's hybridity hinges on her embodiment of the monster/saviour, zombie/child dichotomies, Jessamy's hybridity is crucially postcolonial. Oyeyemi's *The Icarus Girl* is similar to *Gifts* in that it also explores the hybridity of its girl protagonist via a maternal relationship. Jessamy meets her friend Titiola, who she nicknames TillyTilly in the abandoned boys' quarters on her grandfather's compound in Nigeria, her mother's home. The two connect initially over a book. When Jessamy fears that she might not get to see her friend any more, Oyeyemi italicises her thoughts: '*Please, please, please. Let me keep her. She is my only friend; I have no on else. She gave me a book, my mother's book. I have no one else.*'[14] Coupled with the 'stain of thick, wrong-flowing biro ink' (p. 4) that Jess smells on her mother in the novel's opening passage, the connections between TillyTilly's arrival into her life and Jess's relationship with her mother are bound up with the notion of writing the self and articulations of identity.

Oyeyemi's focus on the complexity of representing female subjectivity is central to the many insightful readings that exist on how this text represents postcolonial identity through its gothic lens:

> Oyeyemi's fiction joins the Platonic analogue of the mirror-as-art to the motifs of mirroring and doubling that are so central to conceptualisations of race and anticolonial, postcolonial and modernist writing. The reflections, twins, dolls, portraits, and mannequins in the novels are crucial to her engagement with issues of race and nation, the problems of mimetic representation for raced bodies, the blurring of lines between fictive and 'real' bodies, and the difficulties of writing more broadly. These doubles, in turn, offer the best interpretive guide to Oyeyemi's novels, enabling us to tease at the frameworks through which it has been read (or refracted).[15]

Emphasising the problematic potential of representing raced bodies through mimesis and doubling, Natalya Din-Kariuki comments on the importance of Oyeyemi's fiction to questions of postcolonial narrative as it relates to subjectivity. Jess's relationship with her mother is implicitly conflated with her relationship with her Nigerian roots and heritage. Oyeyemi shows her child protagonist as resistant to the idea of embracing that part of her identity: 'Jess blinked. It was incredible that her mother could really believe that a mother's dreams, a mother's fears, were the same as her child's, as if these things could be passed on in the same way as her frizzy hair had been, or the shape of her nose.'[16] While travelling, Jess notices a woman watching her, she keeps 'her eyes on the woman, caught by her gaze, gradually growing frightened, as if somehow she could not look away or let this woman out of her sight. Would that be dangerous, to *not* look while being looked at? . . . Nigeria felt ugly. Nye. Jeer. Reeee. Ah' (p. 9). The implication is that Jess internalises how she appears much in the same way as Frantz Fanon describes in *Black Skin, White Masks* where he encounters the gaze of a little boy on a train: 'My body was given back to me sprawled out, distorted, recolored, clad in mourning in that white winter day. The Negro is an animal, the Negro is bad, the Negro is mean, the Negro is ugly.'[17] Oyeyemi inverts this scenario by placing the child's gaze, complete with the internalisation of the corporeal and epidermal schema Fanon describes still, horribly, as the sight of innocence, where the child is too frightened to break the gaze for fear of what looking at her induces.

Fanon describes being not only hyper-self-conscious, but also aware of his body in the third person: 'in a triple person. In the train I was given not one but two, three places. . . . I existed triply: I occupied space. I moved toward the other . . . and the evanescent other, hostile but not opaque, transparent, not there, disappeared' (p. 84). Oyeyemi's novel echoes Fanon's metaphor; she actualises it for Jessamy, who over the course of the novel finds herself at once bifurcated then soon sliced into three subjects: her human self; her sister-girl twin, Fern, who alternates in appearance as a baby or a tall silent woman with long limbs; and TillyTilly. Jess's mother realises that this as a culturally, racially specific phenomenon affecting her child: 'Three worlds! Jess lives in three worlds. She lives in this world, she lives in the spirit world, and she lives in the Bush. She's abiku, she always would have known! The spirits tell her things. Fern tells her things.'[18] Oyeyemi's inclusion of a parent character who subscribes to this seemingly fantastical situation frog-marches the story out of the realms of childhood imaginary: with adult validation, the threat on Jessamy's life is emphasised and what Oyeyemi achieves is a moment in which the reader is encouraged to feel guilt or complicity in not wholly accepting the veracity of the child's subjective account. This returns us to the paranoia with which children are traditionally read in Gothic fiction, as discussed in Chapter 2; but, importantly, it also complicates the construction of reality in the novel. Until this point, TillyTilly would most likely read as an imaginary friend. Now that her status as a metaphor or symbol is questioned, Oyeyemi imbues her with more tangibility as a Gothic threat. What this revelation also does is supplement this chapter's overall argument that Gothic fiction of this kind synthesises the factual and the imaginary to construct representations of real structural conflicts and problems, like the many forms of racism rife in our society, but more specifically the hostilities faced by mixed-race people in British society.

Hybrid Identity and Queerness

As noted elsewhere in this book, Gothic spaces are used with similar effect throughout New Queer Gothic fiction and film. The trope sees the proclivity of queer female subjectivity to be framed within claustrophobic spaces connotative of the constricted self and a sense of closeting, which, as discussed in Chapter 3, draws intertextually on such classic examples of female Gothic as *Jane Eyre* and *Wuthering Heights*. At the start of Oyeyemi's and Carey's novels, we find the girl protagonists each in their own closet spaces. Jess sits tucked away in the airing cupboard; Melanie in her small cell at the army base. Each is shown in the very first lines of their respective novels to be contemplating their identity from within those closet spaces: For Jess, 'sitting in the cupboard, the sound of her name was strange, wobbly, misformed, as if she were inside a bottle, or a glass cube, maybe, and Mum was outside it, tapping' (p. 3). Immediately, Oyeyemi establishes her strained relationship with her mother, which implicates her biracial identity, and this is followed by Jessamy's whispered affirmation to herself: 'I am in the cupboard . . . My name is Jessamy.

I am eight years old' (p. 3). This functions as exposition but also suggests an insecurity with her identity.

Oyeyemi and Carey present queerness in their girl protagonist differently but both suggest same-sex attachments and narratives that speak to notions of self-discovery rather than any over 'coming out' tale. Melanie is certainly more self-assured than Jessamy. The present-tense omnipotent narration that Carey uses allows Melanie's feelings of love for her teacher to be conveyed explicitly to the reader as moments of desire, as in the pivotal scene where Miss Justineau breaks the strict protocol prohibiting staff from physical contact with the dangerous children and caresses Melanie's hair: 'lights are dancing behind Melanie's eyes, and she can't get her breath, and she can't speak or hear or think'.[19] This focus on desiring touch is returned to throughout the novel; when Justineau stops Dr Caldwell from dissecting Melanie, there is a tonal shift from expressions of desiring maternal embrace to more libidinal same-sex desire: 'she raises her arms in an instinct too strong to resist. She wants Miss Justineau to lift her up. She wants to hold her and be held by her and be touching her not just with her hair but with her hands and her face and her whole body' (p. 70). There is an urgent desire conveyed here, which is overtly sexual.

Rather than present as a correlated effect of her queerness, as it so often figures, historically, in queer Gothic fictions, Melanie's monstrous or fiendish impulse is something she is able to overcome because of her queer desire for human Miss Justineau. After Sergeant Parks's demonstration of the hungry children's capacity for harm, rubbing off the e-blocker that masks the scent of human skin and sending one child into a frenzy of biting and snapping, Melanie's restraint in controlling her hunger is indicated to be a feat contingent on her protective feelings for her human companion. Desire to maintain close proximity to Miss Justineau, to overcome her aggressive, hungry impulse to attack when detecting human scent, confirms her desire for a relationship based on physical affection. The reader is invited to believe that Melanie has the capacity to privilege her sexual and romantic attachments over other kinds of desire and impulse.

While others have interpreted TillyTilly's possession of Jessamy psychoanalytically, as with Din-Kariuki's reading, which posits the return of the dead twin as 'a phantom other of the living, a spectacular substitution, which extends and develops the Lacanian mirror stage' (p. 27), a more multivalent approach can best appreciate the multiplicity of such a symbolically loaded figure. There has been no criticism to date that embraces the queer potential of this Gothic text. As in *Gifts*, *The Icarus Girl* accesses queer desire through descriptions of touch. Recalling this book's analysis in Chapter 1 of the pivotal queer scene in Shirley Jackson's *The Haunting of Hill House*, touch, and particularly hand holding, can be appreciated as an enduring trend in representations of female queerness in the Gothic mode. Just as Eleanor grasped Theodora's hand in Jackson's novel and the 1964 Robert Wise film adaptation, TillyTilly draws Jess into the darkness, 'and she wasn't at all afraid because someone was holding her hand'.[20] Touch establishes desire and alters the dynamic between the girls from an affinity contingent on mimesis, to an abject transgression, an invitation of corporeal intimacy and involvement.

While their first meeting is amiable, TillyTilly presents as little else but a 'veritable Jessamy-echo' (p. 45) in the copycat game, it soon becomes apparent that this urge to mimic betrays a broader desire to possess Jessamy, to bring her 'down' (p. 150) so that Titiola might possess and animate her body. This is the project Oyeyemi suggests with Titiola's subsequent gaslighting behaviour.

Where queer attachment in *Gifts* enabled Melanie to control the harmful and dangerous part of her hybrid identity, it functions to bind Melanie closer to the malevolent Titiola in *The Icarus Girl*. Lovelorn and lost without her new companion, Jessamy's reaction to being separated from Titiola is written as a corporeal, physical trauma that she does not, herself, understand: Jess stares, forlorn, out of the window, sails 'eagerly towards the front door whenever there was a knock or the doorbell rang . . . Then, after this period of absorption (with . . . what, exactly? Friendship bracelets? Expectancy? Impossible to tell) came the inevitable fever' (p. 80). Much in the vein of James's *The Turn of the Screw*, the child is seduced by the corruptible spirit: TillyTilly, in her developing malevolence, methodically manipulates then seduces Jessamy through alternating presentations of supernatural prowess and vulnerability. Threatening to snatch away the friendship that Jessamy has come to rely on,

TillyTilly uses mimetic performance again to re-present a version of the love-sick episode that Jessamy had experienced:

> Her head was flopping listlessly to one side and her limbs were spread limply, looking more as if they surrounded her than belonged to her. Jess, embarrassed, tried not to look at her pink knickers. After the initial throb of panic at seeing Tilly, Jess stared for a second longer when Tilly didn't get up but continued to gaze impassively at the ceiling. (p. 233)

Here Jess sees her love object, for the first time, as a vulnerable object. However, the performance of vulnerability is clearly a parody of Jess's internalised insecurities surrounding her fragmented sense of self, where limbs appear disarticulated from the body. What this quotation further indicates is the objectification of the disarticulated body in its availability to an eroticised gaze. Oyeyemi suggests that Jess is making connections between her queer self as Other and her queer self as desiring, with the pink knickers providing a crux to this anxious and complex image.

Titiola represents an intensely malevolent form of desubjectivation. Her primary aim, Oyeyemi stresses throughout the novel, is to rob Jessamy of her subjectivity by putting her in the place she inhabits, where only half-girls, dead sister-girls and formless spirits live. While there is no clear seduction in her manipulation, the queer subtext of TillyTilly's manipulation of Jess is overt. Once her manipulations take root, Oyeyemi builds TillyTilly's aggression, which conveys as possessive jealousy driven as it is by vengeful impulses to 'get' anyone who threatens to come between her and Jess. TillyTilly's powers to project through time and space parallel her ability to possess and puppeteer living people. Her method for this is described in one of the novel's most horrifying passages:

> The voice came from above her, a high, lilting, sing-song voice that sounded younger than TillyTilly's normal voice. 'Just a little girl. Nothing more. Do you find it hard to believe? I thought you wanted to be like me? That's your problem! You always want to know where you belong, but you don't need to belong. Do you? Do you?' . . . Then something began to drip slowly on to Jess's back, so slowly that she almost didn't feel it until she felt the cloth of her pyjamas cling

and stick to her back. She nearly put her fingers to the wet patch, but, with enormous effort, lay still, her eyes wide and watchful. She felt as if her mind was slipping away from her, soaring so high that she would not be able to reclaim it.[21]

The language here is connotative of a sexual assault, where a young girl is paralysed by fear as she feels an interloper in her bed at night. The 'dripping' of hateful ideas that Titiola impresses on Jessamy quickly manifest physically into real liquid, a 'wet patch' that she feels through her pyjamas, a wetness that makes her clothing and skin stick together. While Oyeyemi leaves it ambiguous as to what this liquid might be, the inference that it could represent saliva is supported by Sarah Ilott's argument about female subjectivity and genesis often playing 'through the mouth' in Oyeyemi's fiction:

> Not only does the genesis of Oyeyemi's female characters 'go through the mouth' as a form of individual and cultural knowledge gained through acts of consumption and voice, but characters also come to identify through erotic desires – often constructed as transgressive – that focus on the mouth. There are many moments of erotic pleasure in Oyeyemi's novel, between women, and between women and men, yet all references to sexual desire and fulfilment are described orally (though kissing, biting, and the contemplation of cunnilingus), without a single reference to the penis or penetrative sex. (pp. 137–8)

TillyTilly's method of possessing Jess via the drip-feeding of corruption is, however, penetrative and connotes a malevolent sexual transgression devoid of consent. Oyeyemi shows Jess as only realising this behaviour as aberrant when she witnesses her friend and Tilly's rival, Siobhan, undergo the same abuse:

> It was some fearsome, grotesque dance: Siobhan tiptoeing and then dragging across the floor . . . while TillyTilly, partially elevated in the dim light, was somehow *operating* her, although Jess couldn't see quite how: her hands were at Siobhan's back (*in her? Above her? Oh, don't be in her, don't let TillyTilly have her hands jammed into my friend's body*).[22]

Siobhan is the antithesis of Titiola: when she and Jess meet, Oyeyemi tells the reader how Jess 'didn't think she knew anyone as . . . solid, as *there*, as this girl' (p. 127). For Titiola to transform such a solid girl into a Gothic marionette speaks to the overwhelming power that she, a spirit girl, has. Sovereignty is contested in *The Icarus Girl*, identity is fractured beyond metaphor, postcolonial representation is explored beyond mimesis, and this is affected through TillyTilly who symbolises Gothic excess, trauma and above all death. In the next section these ideas will be developed under new frameworks pertaining to biopolitics and exceptionality to conceptualise *The Icarus Girl* and *Gifts* in relation to themes of affect and precarity.

Biopolitics: Mbembe, Puar and Agamben

Achille Mbembe's 2003 article on 'Necropolitics' is an essential piece to the project of understanding biopolitics and applying that understanding to a critical reading of New Queer Gothic fiction. In the article, Mbembe discusses the relationship between politics and death within systems that might only function under what Giorgio Agamben would call a 'state of emergency'.[23] Mbembe develops his thesis from Foucault's theory that biopower functions by presupposing the distribution and division of the human species into different groups, the 'establishment of a biological caesura between the ones and the others . . . racism'.[24] This is one of the mechanisms through which biopower, according to Foucault, 'divides people into those who must live and those who must die' (pp. 16–17). The murderous capabilities of the state are contingent on the economic functions that racism provides. Mbembe builds on these ideas to put forward the notion of necropower and necropolitics, which he describes as having to do with the creation of 'death worlds' where a living-dead status is conferred on whole populations by the threat and deployment of weapons of mass destruction. He explains that 'the lines between resistance and suicide, sacrifice and redemption, martyrdom and freedom are blurred' (p. 40) under the conditions of necropower. Considering the global violence that causes such states of liminal, precarious existence leaves other theorists, such as Judith Butler, preoccupied with the questions, 'Who counts as human? Whose lives count as lives? And, finally, what *makes for a grievable life?*'[25] Mbembe, in proferring the term 'necropolitics' asks, 'is the notion of biopower sufficient to account for the contemporary ways in which the political, under the guise of war, of resistance, or of the fight against terror, makes the murder of its enemy its primary and absolute objective?'[26] Jasbir K. Puar remarks that for Foucault massacres are 'literary events', whereas Mbembe's foregrounding of death serves to evidence 'the brutality of biopower's incitement to life'[27] and proposes her own questions: 'How do queers reproduce life and Which queers are folded into life? How is life weighted, disciplined into subjecthood, narrated into population, and fostered for living? Does this securitization of queerness entail deferred dead or dying for others, and if so, for whom?' (p. 36). Puar's applications of biopolitics in queer theory led her to her thesis of homonationalism,[28] which is tangential to this chapter's argument; however, the research questions employed in her methodology above remain useful to this project of understanding the significance of biopolitical enquiry in New Queer Gothic texts. How are the girls of New Queer Gothic fiction folded into life? While Melanie can certainly be read as narrated into a population, and as I will demonstrate, she can be understood as surviving in a state of exception, embroiled in genocide, Jessamy's battle for subjecthood is individual and specific, extending signification to the gothicity of postcolonial or anti-colonial hybridity.

In *Gifts*, the group arrive at a residential area that was overrun by hungries and firebombed: '*We couldn't kill the hungries, so we killed ourselves* . . . An adult and a child, arms thrown up as though they were caught in the middle of an aerobics workout. Fascinated, the hungry kid measures herself against the smaller shape. It fits pretty well.'[29] Melanie's lessons continue outside the classroom and onto the apocalyptic wasteland that used to be England, no longer learning about ancient Greek myths, Melanie begins learning about biopolitics.

Agamben describes his work on the state of exception as an investigation 'into the "no-man's land" between public law and political fact, and between juridical order and life'.[30] Agamben's theories on the states of exception are interesting because they comment on a paradox: when emergency laws suspend the usual rule of law in any state, they also suspend the juridical powers and sovereignty of that state and thrown into a similar state of suspension are the rights and identities of citizens. The Third Reich is often used as primary example of the state of exception. Oher situations that provide examples often circulate around the circumstances of civil war and places such as concentration camps, prisoner-of-war camps and detention centres. Zones devoid of law, where identity is suspended and there is a dissolution between public and private life have, historically, been and continue to be a lived reality for some in many different contexts. In *Gifts*, Britain has been overrun by humans infected with a fungal virus called Ophiocordyceps, an organism that has colonised most of the planet and transformed the population into zombie creatures called 'hungries'. Most of the action takes place in an army base and research facility controlled initially by 'Beacon', but now a strong-hold for the last of human society. Dr Caldwell (Glenn Close) and her staff, inclusive of teachers, research assistants and military personnel, carry out an experimental educational programme. Melanie belongs to a group of 'second-generation hungries', the programme's test subjects and students, whose human behaviour and mental capacity for reason is believed, by Caldwell, to hold the key to a cure for the Ophiocordyceps scourge. Throughout the novel, the mystery of these children's ability to pass for human is revealed to be a result of having been born (and eaten their way out of) their infected mothers. Tribes of children like them are discovered to thrive in the wasteland, as an organised intelligent society. When all communication ends with Beacon and the base is overrun, the reader is left to believe that the small company of humans, Caldwell, Miss Justineau and Sergeant Parks are the last survivors of their species. Melanie's situation on the base was as a student and specimen, her existence contingent on her level of demonstrable intelligence. Once Caldwell has enough data on a student's academic performance, she desires their brains in a parodic inversion of the zombie trope where cannibalism is swapped for dissection. Literary examples of states of exception usually present contexts of civil war; this example is more reflective of detention centres where laws and rights are suspended and where subjects are controlled by unaccountable military force.

While the plot and setting of *Gifts* fit Agamben's definition of the state of exception precisely, Oyeyemi's novel relates to this notion less directly. Christopher Ouma reads the diasporic abiku motif (tied to the notions of the restless spirit of a deceased twin and 'ghost children') in *The Icarus Girl* as endemic of African literary aesthetic and a key symbol found in much fiction focusing on African, specifically Nigerian and Yoruba, tradition. 'These representations', he writes, 'sought to find narrative interpretability in the modern African world as it was emerging from colonial occupation'.[31] Ouma describes the complications proposed in the novel as stemming from 'postmodernist aesthetic strategies' plotted against 'diasporic subjectivity'. When the abiku narrative is displaced, crosses the Atlantic, 'Jess's biological and mythical heritages clash because the notion of race is complicated by the politics of heritage, myth, and legend' (p. 202). In TillyTilly, this personification of a mythical spirit child carries an overload of signification, which intentionally overwhelms the reader. However, the glibness with which Jess's mixed race, hybridised, identity could figure in racist public discourse is something that Oyeyemi explores via school bullies; 'Maybe Jessamy has all these "attacks" because she can't make up her mind whether she's black or white!'[32] This works to reflect Jess's internalised racism and confirms her superego anxiety around the notion that there are two version of herself and she must decide on one before she loses her mind. This idea of an undecided self is refracted in her relationships with other characters too. Jessamy's own mother cannot fathom her: 'I don't *know* what I'm scared of! That's why it doesn't make sense, it's stupid! I . . . I just feel like . . . like I should know her, but I don't know anything. She's not like me at all. I don't think she's like you, either. I can't even tell who this girl is' (p. 204). She is essentially unknowable: 'Dr. McKenzie thought that he knew what TillyTilly meant, but he was wrong. Nobody knew what Tilly meant, and nobody knew what Jess meant either' (p. 278). What *The Icarus Girl* suggests, as well as the battle for sovereignty over one's own identity, body and life, is individual specific trauma of a kind that is not wholly representable or relatable: hybridity signals a total rejection of heterogeneity. Jessamy exists in a metaphoric state of exception because she cannot recognise a whole singular identity in the dualism of her mixed-raced self. When TillyTilly enters the narrative, she wants to possess Jessamy's body and swap places with her so that she would enter a physical state of exception, an otherworldly place without laws, rights or subjecthood.

The kind of heritage shown to be being passed on in *Gifts* raises broader question of what didactive import humanity offers those who inherit the Earth – the children build their understanding of ethics through Greek myth and ancient world history, and these topics seem preferred over the telling of recent events. Carey includes little to no information of events immediately preceding and explaining the collapse of society via the bio-disaster of the outbreak, so the reader is left to presume that this is a dystopic near-future with political, juridical and social structures like our own, existing in a state of exception since the outbreak, or certainly existing in a state of exception since losing contact with Beacon. This suggests the novel as a critique of existing power structures, specific to Britain and specific to life for people struggling to be appreciated fully as citizens and humans – which returns us to the reading that the hungries metaphorically represent the diasporic migrant population in Britain. More specifically, and in keeping with Oyeyemi's political concern throughout her novels, this metaphor is particular to refugees and asylum seekers incarcerated in detention centres.

Jordan Stouck argues that the concept of hybridity can be little understood without 'full recognition of conflict [,] loss and disjunction'.[33] Stouck argues that 'only when the fraught foundations of hybridity are recognized and validated can reparation for characters like Jess and TillyTilly truly begin' (p. 109). The central idea in each of the texts corresponds to this notion of necessary conflict and loss, although in *Gifts* there is a much more simplistic reconciliation of Melanie's human and hungry identities. A dying Sergeant Parks asks Melanie why she takes the decision to ignite the fungal growths, sprouting from the spent and decaying corpses of first-generation hungries, catalysing the sexual phase of Ophiocordyceps and releasing the spores that will secure the eradication of all other life:

> Because of the war, Melanie tells him. And because of the children. The children like her – the second generation. There's no cure for the hungry plague, but in the end the plague becomes its own cure. It's terribly, terribly sad for the people who get it first, but their

children will be okay and they'll be the ones who love and grow up and have children of their own and make a new world.[34]

Here, Melanie predicts that the state of exception will be temporary and that things will get better for the next generation who will not have had to confront the establishment of a new race in the wake of biological genocide.

The Abiku myth, personified in TillyTilly, is a figure who straddles the barrier between the realms of living and the dead, conjuring in abstract the 'deathworlds' that Mbembe discussed in 'Necropolitics'. Like Melanie, TillyTilly is not bound by juridical law, but neither is she bound by the laws of time and space: she can move through walls, floors and ceilings; she can appear in another country, on another continent, without explanation. The world that TillyTilly inhabits, sometimes referred to as the 'spirit world', the 'bush' or the 'wilderness of the mind', is a heterotopic place that has psychic dominion over Jess's identity so mimics a state of exception. Oyeyemi shows these spaces to form and shape Jess's mind: 'Memories were burdens that took Jessamy through three worlds of hurt, and three worlds that only twins inhabit, and she was only half a twin. Yet even as she fell asleep, Jess was aware on some level that her memories were being moulded so that they were all different' (p. 293). These spaces – the dystopic wasteland and the spirit world – become the sites where queer girls experience conflict, trauma and loss bound up with each of their hybrid identities. Carey's protagonist expresses her queer heroism in burning down the world, whereas Oyeyemi's queer girl fights to maintain her own sovereignty and subjecthood: both novels show the power of intersectional queer feminist politics in survival as an individual and as a community.

Conclusion
Queering Gender and Queers of Colour in the New Queer Gothic

༄

The project on which this book is based has been written with the overall aim of calling attention to a new genre of fiction and film, as well as establishing an associated critical mode of reading that fiction and film. I have proposed the New Queer Gothic as a body of works published or produced in the past fifteen years that is demonstrated by a wealth of films and fiction texts exploring the intersections of queerness and Gothicity. In this work, I have argued that there is a great need to focus on the representations of girls and women so that they are not neglected among the many pieces of queer criticism surrounding masculine identities and gay men. In proposing a new genre and field of study, this book has taken such action to explore new perspectives, broaden the scope and shift focus from topics found in existing fields of study such as the queer Gothic. In the Introduction I highlighted the oversights and omissions of this field, highlighting its lack of nuanced engagement with queer women and privileging of white homosexual cis men. I also highlighted the limitations of other relevant branches of Gothic studies, arguing that the female Gothic is an ineffective lens through which to read queer women's relation to the Gothic because it fundamentally relies on an essentialist account of gender in its expressions of feminist politics. I accounted for the pivotal movement of New Queer Cinema, arguing that it made important headway in cultures of representation and towards developing discourse on studying and critiquing queer representation in film. However, through recognising this as another area in which queer male voices, lives, concerns and narratives are privileged over those of queer women, the rationale for new research focusing on girls and women was bolstered.[1] Thankfully, we are seeing academic interest in ideas around queer spectatorship becoming more inclusive. In the process of readying this book for publication, the University of Wales Press Horror Studies series released Heather O. Petrocelli's monograph *Queer for Fear: Horror Film and the Queer Spectator* (2023), which is a perfect companion piece to this book in offering the first empirical study into the special and dynamic relationship that queer people share with horror cinema. Petrocelli also describes a field of study dominated by gay male perspective in her persuasive and rigorous arguments that all horror cinema has demonstrable value to all kinds of queer people. This follows on from Harry M. Benshoff, Vito Russo and Alexander Dotty, as Petrocelli describes that while 'explicit queerness, coded queerness, and the queerness of filmmakers matter, the queer gaze ultimately sets its sights beyond the singular film'.[2] I think this is true of other media too, certainly the novels and other pieces of fiction explored in this study.

Another aim of this book, which weaves through its chapters, was a call to celebrate the value of the Gothic, particularly to justify the future study of the New Queer Gothic and to encourage more texts to be recognised and added to its canon. The representational value of reading the New Queer Gothic for real queer girls became an emerging theme of my thesis in this book. Fiction of any kind that aims to unpack difficult real-life problems via the fantastical or something as cluttered with paranoid tropes the Gothic is often met with derision. However, I would use the chapters in *The New Queer Gothic* as evidence to the contrary, along with its shelf-fellows in this Gothic Literary Series. The fictions explored here do immensely important work in helping us navigate the slippery, ever-shifting world of sexuality; more specifically, they address the relevant evolutions in queer and feminist theories so that we might consider more carefully the relationships between girlhood, queerness, subjectivity, alterity, exceptionality and hybridity. These are themes that concern contemporary intersectional identity politics as much as they concern contemporary post-structural appreciations of queerness.

This book has argued that the Gothic provides very productive ground for the study of sexuality; however, existing studies have often focused on the shared discourses between Gothic fiction and nineteenth-century sexology and psychoanalysis. The New Queer Gothic, as a genre and a mode, should be used as a tool to read texts in a more variegated and provocative way because it does not rely on stale reading methods and critical frameworks. It should also consider queerness as an expansive umbrella term under which all LGBTQQIA+ identities find themselves represented. Many of the characterisations explored in this book are of child characters and young people still figuring out where to place themselves on gender and sexuality spectrums, which has resulted in a lack of distinct and specific attention paid to trans and non-binary subjectivities. This is a limitation of the book that might have been avoided had I arrived sooner at the horror films of Alice Maio Mackay, a young trans horror director from Australia, who I had the pleasure of interviewing for the 2023 *Fear 2000* 'Horror: Uncaged' Conference. Mackay's films *So Vam* (2021), *Bad Girl Boogey* (2022) and *T Blockers* (2023) use an ensemble cast of queer creatives and performers to deliver DIY queer horror films that comment on contemporary youth culture and the digital world of viral hate speech and violence that our young queer people must contend with. As dark as the subject matter may sound, these films are also very much about trans joy and queer community overcoming patriarchal hegemony.

It is perhaps little wonder then that Gothic media continues to be one of the few places where queer and trans narratives are told, where queer figures take up space on our screens as well as behind productions. There has been a notable increase in queer characterisations in Gothic media, with active, central figures identifying as trans, non-binary, bisexual and other less represented LGBTQQIA+ identities. These are largely confined to television, but many of these contemporary series are adapted from literary fiction in the form of contemporary Gothic novels and graphic novels. Of the latter comes *The Chilling Adventures of Sabrina* (2018–20), based on Roberto Aguirre-Sacasa's *Archie Horror* comic book series of the same name, which began in 2014. The show features Theo, a transgender boy who was named Susie at birth, played by the non-binary, pansexual actor Lachlan Watson. Theo's transitioning occurs in the series alongside the exploits of pansexual witch cliques, and an attic-bound eccentric Black bisexual Spellman cousin (Chance Perdomo). *Lovecraft Country* (2020) is another example, adapted from and continuing the narrative of Matt Ruff's 2016 novel of the same name, which offers interesting and dynamic sexual politics, particularly in relation to sexual identity, racial politics, temporality, and the skin as schema. The relationship between Ruby Baptiste and Christina Braithwhite is especially intriguing from a New Queer Gothic perspective.

Ruby, played by Nigerian-born English actor Wunmi Mosaku, develops a sexual relationship with Braithwhite's lover and hench-man, William (Jordan Patrick Smith), only to learn that William's sister Christina has used her magic to take William's form and seduce her. Ruby continues the relationship after this is revealed and uses Christina's potion to temporarily transform her own form into that of a Nell (Jamie Neumann), inventing the alias of Hilary Davenport, a middle-class white woman, which allows her to pursue employment as a manager at a department store. Ruby describes the gory and torturous shapeshifting process as 'being unmade' and Christina reassures her that it is less painful each time – and we are privy to this when Ruby returns to her original form mid-coitus. The relationship is doomed from the start, since Christina is the series villain and assumes Ruby's form to mislead other characters; however, it is presented as more complex rather than straightforward exploitation of other bodies in that the jouissance of an ambitious and passionate African American woman is explored, unbound by the limitations of her racial identity in 'Jim Crow' era America. It is also one of the few shows to present well-coordinated intimacy between Black and white bodies, as well as fuller shaped bodies, thanks to intimacy coordinator Teniece Divya Johnson. Elsewhere in the show are fully developed and equally desiring queer Black characters, like Montrose Freeman (Michael Kenneth Williams)[3] who is in a committed, semi-closeted, homosexual relationship. The horror of *Lovecraft Country* challenges notions of monstrosity and inhumanity levelled at African Americans in 1950s 'white America', where white 'power' is hyperbolised as supernatural magic and Lovecraftian monsters pale in comparison to the racist ethics of white supremacy. The premise involves time travel that allows for an anachronistic engagement with identity politics as well as the denouement of the adaptation's literary origins. Episodes 'I Am.' and 'Jig-a-Bobo' establish that the *Lovecraft Country* novel and source text exists in the continuity of the series as a novel written by George Freeman II and retrieved from the future by his father Atticus Freeman to try to change the story's narrative conclusion. There is a notable continuation between the Gothic elements of twentieth-century literary fiction and what some call 'Black Horror' and others call 'African American Gothic' or 'Black Gothic'.

Another television text to (tele)visually develop what Black-authored literature of the twentieth century began textually, would be the horror drama series *Them* (2021). Like *Lovecraft Country*, *Them* is also set in Jim Crow era America. The series follows a family who have moved South during the second wave of the great migration. Their new home is in an all-white neighbourhood, and they experience violent persecution from their neighbours as well as from the supernatural entities haunting the plot of land sold to them, voiding a centuries-old covenant that aimed to 'protect' the land from ever falling into Black ownership. Maisha Wester here describes the significance of migration narratives in the Black Gothic mode:

> The failures of Reconstruction, the strife of post-Reconstruction, and the disappointment of Northern migration in addition to the drive to assimilate into American society gave birth to a new era of black Gothic in the twentieth century. In particular, writers in the Jim Crow era sought to negotiate the drive to re-member their Southern origins and pressures to progress beyond the violent racialisms inherent in that heritage becoming something 'new'. Notably, the gothic trope of the descent below ground into darkness, and its associations with living burial, proves recurrent in this period as authors such as Jean Toomer and Ralph Ellison sent their protagonists down South, figuratively and literally, to unearth the meaning and horrors of their Southern origins and Northern sacrifices.[4]

Them often reads as a pastiche of Ralph Ellison's novel *Invisible Man* (1952). However, the narrative is particularly interesting from a New Queer Gothic perspective as well as from a Black Gothic perspective, because rather than presenting a single male subject as something socially supernatural, *Them* assigns a malignant spirit to each member of the central Emory family. The following is a short close textual analysis appraisal of how these personal hauntings speak to literary legacies significant to the New Queer Gothic.

Miss Vera is seen by youngest daughter, Gracie (Melody Hurd), and also by her mother, Lucky (Deborah Ayorinde). She pollutes Gracie's mind via a disturbing and instructive children's book and teaches Gracie the song that her baby brother's murderers sang while her mother was gang-raped by white Southerners. The hellish chanting by a seemingly possessed little girl re-traumatises Lucky, who had moved her family out of the South in effort to escape further trauma. Miss Vera presents as a very sharp-faced governess and represents assimilationist politics in the vein of Booker T. Washington's racial uplift through education, and the debates around elitism and exceptionalism in 'Race Men'. Gracie's chanting of the racist song 'Old Black Joe' and the phrase 'cat in a bag' function to remind her mother of the problems of inescapable trauma, particularly in the transition from concepts of the 'old negro' to the 'new negro'. Henry Louis Gates explains that the 'success of the New Negro paradoxically depended upon self-negation, a turning away from the "Old Negro" and the labyrinthine memory of black enslavement', and Gracie's demonic performance functions as a Gothic redeployment of deference to white authority.

Ruby Lee (Shahadi Wright Joseph), the teenage Emory, invites us to think about the New Queer Gothic aspects of the series after she, lonely as the only Black kid in school, befriends Doris. The two secret themselves away and become very close – Ruby hardly winces when Doris applies her make up and tell her she's pretty 'for a black girl'. They share a kiss, and it soon becomes clear that blue-eyed, blonde-haired Doris is a demonic manifestation of white beauty ideals. She convinces Ruby to go for cheerleading try-outs doused in white paint. Much of this recalls the internalised racism and colourism of African American novels such as Nella Larsen's *Passing* (1929) and Toni Morrison's *The Bluest Eye* (1970);

the former in the context of queer desire intersecting with what Patricia Hill Collins calls the 'fear-admiration dichotomy',[5] and the latter in the context of white ideals of beauty and femininity.

Lucky Emory is the family matriarch. She is established as the Gothic heroine of *Them* by taking sole responsibility for investigating the real and supernatural torment that her family suffers. Everyone's trauma is hers and her traumas are reflective of the double oppression suffered historically by African American women on the basis of their race and gender identity. Significantly, this makes Lucky an especially sympathetic figure for queer audiences who may face double oppression for two or more of their identities. Unsurprisingly, she suffers the most, and this is emphasised in the show as Lucky is also the only character to be haunted by the black hat man (devested of any other guise). The black hat man's manifestations cause violence and harm and show him trying to dupe her into murdering her children. It is overt that this dynamic functions as a continuation more than as a challenge to the ways in which African American women have been represented in the African American literary tradition and in the Anglo-American Gothic tradition. In flashback scenes we see the man behind the ghost, Hiram Epps, whose fair religious mind welcomes Black people into his land (an early settlement town), until a mysterious young boy named Miles poisons his mind. In this way the root of 'evil', and the root of the trauma, is displaced from the historic root of colonialism and slavery and set at the feet of white Gothic literary tradition with the reference to Henry James's influential queer Gothic child, Miles. I would argue that it places the root of 'evil' at the feet of white Christianity, particularly in its arbitrary definitions of the good/evil dichotomy and the notion that it is worth suffering in life for eternal satisfaction in the afterlife. Epps's mission to make Lucky kill her children implicates the nuances of the monstrous-mother motif explored by Morrison in *Beloved*, which developed and novelised the true story of Margaret Garner who murdered her children to keep them from the slavers who came to claim them.

Finally, we come to Henry Emory: Henry is approached by a group of white men while fixing the roof antenna for their new television set. The men of the neighbourhood confront him at the behest of their wives after Lucky is seen chasing a boy for urinating on her drying laundry. Because of Henry's position on the roof, the three men back off and decide against an altercation, calling him King Kong. Bestial comparison is just one example of the ways in which white hegemonic power dehumanises Black men, something that was perpetuated by 1930s cinema – what the mockumentary exploitation film *Ingagi* (1930) said of African women's sexual mores, *King Kong* (1933) extended 'to metaphorically implicate Black men through the imagery of the big black ape in pursuit of a White woman'.[6] Henry is feared as much as he is despised, and his supernatural abuser is no white pioneer settler, instead, what accosts him is a camp queer double, much like Titiola in *The Icarus Girl*.

The appropriation of Black bodies and Black culture for use by white subjects is explored via Gothic-inflected contemporary horror cinema such as Jordan Peele's *Get Out* (2017) and *Us* (2019). Peele is an executive producer for *Them*, which perhaps explains the critical similarities. In *Them*, representations reflecting a warped, white-made perspective of Blackness are the sites of Henry's anxiety, which speaks to W. E. B. Du Bois's theory of 'double consciousness'.[7] Da Tap Dance Man is a terrorising minstrel and tellingly appears to Henry more frequently after he purchases the family's first television set, mocking Henry's attempts to succeed at work, ridiculing his post-traumatic stress disorder after he was a test subject for mustard gas experiments, and taunting his powerlessness to stop his wife's rape or his infant son's murder. Da Tap Dance man embodies the horror of double consciousness by reiterating as absurd any possibility for a Black man to live free in a racist society. His queerness is highly paranoid, carnivalesque and uncanny, and completes the narrative symbolism of the queer hyperreality with which Western culture represents African American experience. So, while the arguments of my explorations in the main body of this book have focused on fiction and film, this conclusion serves to explore how ideas central to the New Queer Gothic transcend my own research scope and can be found in television and other media texts.

It is crucial that future critical work in the arena of the New Queer Gothic continues to experiment with varied reading methods. Equally important is the continuation of scholarly interest in the representation of girls and women. As Melanie's affinity

Conclusion

with Pandora and Jessamy's relation to Icarus describe old systems of existence and ontology, so should we move away from outdated reading methods, the privileging of white male subjectivity in queer studies, and totalising concepts of sexual and gendered identities. My final thoughts on this subject can be expressed by the following quotations taken from *The Girl with all the Gifts* and Heather Love's article, 'Truth and Consequences: On Paranoid and Reparative Reading'. Melanie, the New Queer Gothic girl in the state of exception at humanity's last gasp, advises that we take a leaf from Pandora's book: 'opening the great big box of the world and not being afraid, not even caring whether what's inside is good or bad. Because it's always both. But you have to open it to find that out.'[8] Love similarly appeals to us to remember Sedgwick's teachings, not only on how to analyse in a paranoid reparative mode, but her 'call to acknowledge the negativity and the aggression at the heart of psychic life and to recognize that thinking is impossible without this kind of aggression'.[9] Queer girls and young women are powerful figures, capable of unleashing all kinds of spectacular knowledge into the world.

Notes

Introduction

1. Eve Kosofsky Sedgwick, *The Coherence of Gothic Conventions* (London: Methuen, 1986 [1980]), p. 12.
2. Catherine Spooner, *Fashioning Gothic Bodies* (Manchester: Manchester University Press, 2004), p. 5.
3. George E. Haggerty, *Queer Gothic* (Chicago IL: University of Illinois Press, 2006), p. 107.
4. William Hughes and Andrew Smith, *Queering the Gothic* (Manchester: Manchester University Press, 2009), p. 1.
5. Misha Kavka, 'The Gothic on screen', in Jerrold E. Hogle (ed.), *The Cambridge Companion to Gothic Fiction* (Cambridge: Cambridge University Press, 2002), p. 211.
6. Dale Townshend, 'Love in a Convent: Or, Gothic and the Perverse Father of Queer Enjoyment', in Hughes and Smith (eds), *Queering the Gothic*, p. 11.
7. Mair Rigby, '"Do you share my madness?": Frankenstein's queer Gothic', in Hughes and Smith (eds), *Queering the Gothic*, p. 51.
8. Robin Wood, 'The American Nightmare: Horror in the 1970s', in Mark Jancovich, *Horror, The Film Reader* (London: Routledge, 2002), p. 28.
9. Andrew Owens, 'Queer Gothic', in Maisha Wester and Xavier Aldana Reyes (eds), *Twenty-First-Century Gothic: An Edinburgh Companion* (Edinburgh: Edinburgh University Press, 2019), p. 35.
10. Haggerty, *Queer Gothic*, p. 28.

Notes

11 Owens, 'Queer Gothic', p. 44.
12 Harry M. Benshoff and Sean Griffin, *Queer Images: A History of Gay and Lesbian Film in America* (Lanham MD: Rowman and Littlefield, 2006), p. 232.
13 B. Ruby Rich, 'New Queer Cinema', in Michele Aaron (ed.), *New Queer Cinema: A Critical Reader* (Edinburgh: Edinburgh University Press, 2004), p. 16.
14 Elizabeth Guzik, 'The Queer Sort of Fandom or Heavenly Creatures: The Closeted Indigene, Lesbian Islands, and New Zealand National Cinema', in John C. Hawley (ed.), *Postcolonial Queer Theories: Intersections and Essays* (London: Greenwood Press, 2001), p. 48.
15 For a definition of 'killer queers', see Harry M. Benshoff, *Monsters in the Closet: Homosexuality and the Horror Film* (Manchester: Manchester University Press, 1997), p. 232.
16 Daniel T. Contreras, 'New Queer Cinema: Spectacle, Race, Utopia', in Aaron (ed.), *New Queer Cinema*, p. 126.
17 Judith Butler, *Bodies that Matter: On the Discursive Limits of 'Sex'* (New York: Routledge, 1993), p. 85.
18 Alison Tate, 'Christine Vachon on Queer Cinema and the Legacy of *Carol*', *Advocate* (18 May 2017), www.advocate.com/arts-entertainment/2017/5/18/christine-vachon-queer-cinema-and-legacy-carol (last accessed 31 October 2023).
19 Anneke Smelik, 'Art Cinema and Murderous Lesbians', in Aaron (ed.), *New Queer Cinema*, p. 68.
20 I am referring to Patricia Highsmith who was gay but famously struggled reconciling this with the dominant ideology at the time, which appreciated homosexuality as a mental illness or defect, and to Daphne du Maurier, who was bisexual and genderqueer; the latter is reflected in her diaries, where she describes her innermost spirit as male: 'with a boy's mind and a boy's heart'. By marrying a military man and bearing his three children, she effectively 'passed' where it counted.
21 Alex Davidson, '10 great gay and lesbian horror films', BFI (7 November 2013), www.bfi.org.uk/news-opinion/news-bfi/lists/10-great-gay-horror-films (accessed 1 November 2023).
22 Mary Shelley, *Frankenstein* (Cambridge: Wilson and Son, 1869 [1818]), p. 43.
23 Kavka, 'The Gothic on screen', pp. 209–10
24 Xavier Aldana Reyes's work on affect theory in film is influenced by that of Linda Williams, particularly her article 'Film: Gender, Genre, and Excess', *Film Quarterly*, 44/4 (1991), 2–13.

Notes

25 Xavier Aldana Reyes, 'Beyond psychoanalysis: Post-millennial horror film and affect theory', *Horror Studies*, 3/2 (2012), 251–2.
26 Darren Elliott-Smith, *Queer Horror Film and Television: Sexuality and Masculinity at the Margins* (London: I. B. Tauris, 2016), p. 168.
27 Ellen Moers, *Literary Women* (London: The Women's Press Ltd., 1986 [1976]), p. 90.
28 Susanne Becker, *Gothic Forms of Feminine Fictions* (Manchester: Manchester University Press, 1999), p. 44.
29 Claire Kahane, 'The Gothic Mirror', in Shirley Nelson Gardener, Claire Kahane and Madelon Sprengnether (eds), *The (M)other Tongue* (Ithaca NY: Cornell University Press, 1985), pp. 335–6.
30 See Helene Meyers, *Femicidal Fears: Narratives of the Female Gothic Experience* Albany NY: State University of New York Press, 2001).
31 Sue Chaplin, 'Female Gothic and the Law', in Avril Horner and Sue Zlosnik (eds), *Women and the Gothic* (Edinburgh: Edinburgh University Press, 2017), p. 147.
32 Marie Mulvey Roberts, 'The Female Gothic Body', in Horner and Zlosnik (eds), *Women and the Gothic*, p. 107.
33 Stephenie Meyer, *Twilight*; *New Moon*; *Eclipse*; *Breaking Dawn*; *Life and Death: Twilight Reimagined*; *Midnight Sun* (Boston MA: Little, Brown and Company, 2005–20).
34 Chaplin, 'Female Gothic and the Law', p. 145.
35 Bella is sixteen years old in the first book of the series, and frozen at the age of eighteen after being made a vampire towards the saga's end.
36 Lucie Armitt, 'The Gothic Girl Child', in Horner and Zlosnik (eds), *Women and the Gothic*, p. 72.
37 Annamarie Jagose, 'Feminism's Queer Theory', *Feminism and Psychology*, 19/2 (2009), 157.
38 Jagose, 'Feminism's Queer Theory', 159–60.
39 Iris Marion Young, 'Gender as Seriality: Thinking about Women as a Social Collective', *Signs*, 19/3 (1994), 737.
40 Jagose, 'Feminism's Queer Theory', 162–3.
41 Steve Bruhm, 'Contemporary Gothic: why we need it', in Hogle (ed.), *The Cambridge Companion to Gothic Fiction*, pp. 264–5.
42 Bruhm, 'Contemporary Gothic', p. 274.
43 Elizabeth Freeman, 'Queer Temporalities', *GLQ: A Journal of Lesbian and Gay Studies*, 13/2–3 (2007), 162.
44 Freeman, 'Queer Temporalities', 168.
45 Catherine Spooner, *Contemporary Gothic* (London: Reaktion, 2006), pp. 24–5.

46 Spooner, *Contemporary Gothic*, pp. 24–5.
47 Chloé Germaine Buckley, *Twenty-First-Century Children's Gothic* (Edinburgh: Edinburgh University Press, 2019), p. 6.
48 Buckley, *Twenty-First-Century Children's Gothic*, p. 33.
49 Michael Löwy, 'The Current of Critical Irrealism: "A moonlit enchanted night"', in Matthew Beaumont (ed.), *Adventures in Realism* (Carlton VIC: Blackwell, 2007), p. 206.
50 Sarah Ilott, 'Postcolonial Gothic', in Wester and Aldana Reyes (eds), *Twenty-First-Century Gothic*, p. 19.
51 Ilott 'Postcolonial Gothic', p. 30.
52 WReC, Sharae Deckard, Nicholas Lawrence, Neil Lazarus, Graeme Macdonald, Upamanyu Pablo Mukherjee, Benita Parry and Stephen Shapiro, *Combined and Uneven Development Towards a New Theory of World-Literature* (Liverpool: Liverpool University Press, 2015), p. 70.
53 Löwy, 'The Current of Critical Irrealism', p. 193.
54 Eve Kosofsky Sedgwick, *Between Men: English Literature and Male Homosocial Desire* (New York: Columbia University Press, 1985), p. 11.
55 This book understands the term 'radical feminism' to signal a set of politics that call for a reordering of society, an end to patriarchal control and an end to the oppression of women. These politics were gaining traction in the early twentieth century and theorised and popularised in such texts as Shulamith Firestone's *The Dialectic of Sex: The Case for Feminist Revolution* (New York: William Marrow, 1970).
56 Sedgwick, *Between Men*, pp. 12–13.
57 Sheila Jeffreys, *Unpacking Queer Politics* (Malden: Blackwell, 2003), pp. 35–6.
58 Jeffreys, *Unpacking Queer Politics*, pp. 35–6.
59 Patricia White, *Uninvited: Classical Hollywood Cinema and Lesbian Representability* (Bloomington IN: Indiana University Press, 1999), p. 16.
60 Elliott-Smith, *Queer Horror Film and Television*, p. 3.
61 Clara Bradbury-Rance, *Lesbian Cinema after Queer Theory* (Edinburgh: Edinburgh University Press, 2019), p. 4.
62 Eve Kosofsky Sedgwick, *Epistemology of the Closet* (Berkeley CA: University of California Press, 1990), pp. 32–3.
63 Lee Edelman, 'Unnamed: Eve's Epistemology', *Criticism*, 52/2 (2010), 186–7.
64 Jagose, 'Feminism's Queer Theory', 172.
65 Lee Edelman, *No Future: Queer Theory and the Death Drive* (Durham NC: Duke University Press, 2004), p. 27.

Notes

[66] Lee Edelman, 'Learning Nothing: *Bad Education*', *Differences*, 28/1 (2017), 125.
[67] Edelman, *No Future*, p. 24.
[68] Edelman, 'Learning Nothing', 139.
[69] Edelman, *No Future*, pp. 24–25.
[70] Freeman, 'Queer Temporalities', 167.

Chapter 1

[1] Angela Carter, 'The Lady of the House of Love', in Angela Carter, *The Bloody Chamber, and Other Stories* (London: Vintage, 2006 [1979]), p. 119.
[2] Anne Williams, 'The Horror, the Horror: Recent Studies in Gothic Fiction', *Modern Fiction Studies*, 46/3 (2000), 793.
[3] Michelle Massé, 'Gothic Repetition: Husbands, Horror and Things that go Bump in the Night', *Signs*, 15/4 (1990), 680.
[4] Steven Bruhm, 'Gothic Sexualities', in Andrew Smith and Anna Powell (eds), *Teaching the Gothic* (Basingstoke: Palgrave, 2006), p. 93.
[5] Bruhm, 'Gothic Sexualities', in Smith and Powell (eds), *Teaching the Gothic*, pp. 97–8.
[6] Angela Hague, '"A Faithful Anatomy of our Times": Reassessing Shirley Jackson', *Frontiers*, 26/2 (2005), 90–1.
[7] Darryl Hattenhauer, *Shirley Jackson's American Gothic* (New York: State University of New York Press, 2003), p. 2.
[8] Michael T. Wilson, '"Absolute Reality" and the Role of the Ineffable in Shirley Jackson's *The Haunting of Hill House*', *Journal of Popular Culture*, 48/1 (2015), 121–2.
[9] Hattenhauer, *Shirley Jackson*, p. 2.
[10] Eric Savoy, 'Between as if and is: On Shirley Jackson', *Women's Studies*, 46/8 (2017), 838.
[11] Betty Friedan, *The Feminine Mystique* (London: Penguin, 1963), p. 40.
[12] Hague, 'A Faithful Anatomy of our Times', 76.
[13] Rebecca Munford, 'Spectral Femininity', in Avril Horner and Sue Zlosnik (eds), *Women and the Gothic* (Edinburgh: Edinburgh University Press, 2017), p. 125.
[14] Hague, 'A Faithful Anatomy of our Times', 74.
[15] George E. Haggerty, *Queer Gothic* (Chicago IL: University of Illinois Press, 2006), p. 149.

16. Mary Ann Doane, *The Desire to Desire: The Woman's Films of the 1940s* (London: Macmillan, 1988), p. 13.
17. Haggerty, *Queer Gothic*, p. 149.
18. Michael Koresky notes that the Warner Brothers DVD audio commentary reveals that the original script by Nelson Gidding featured an early breakup scene that established Theodora's sexuality more explicitly. Before first setting out for Hill House, she would have been seen writing 'I HATE YOU' in lipstick on her bedroom mirror before yelling out of her window at a departing woman. Michael Koresky, 'Queer & Now & Then: 1963', *Film Comment*, www.filmcomment.com/blog/queer-now-1963/ (last accessed 28 February 2019).
19. Patricia White, *Uninvited: Classical Hollywood Cinema and Lesbian Representability* (Bloomington IN: Indiana University Press, 1999), p. 84.
20. See White's caption, *Uninvited*, p. 84.
21. Haggerty, *Queer Gothic*, p. 148.
22. White, *Uninvited*, p. 61.
23. Laura Mulvey, 'The Visual Pleasure of Narrative Cinema', *Screen* 16/3 (1975).
24. White, *Uninvited*, p. 63.
25. Doane, *The Desire to Desire*, p. 13.
26. White, *Uninvited*, p. 73.
27. Haggerty, *Queer Gothic*, p. 141.
28. Koresky, 'Queer & Now & Then'.
29. The Netflix series is only loosely based on the novel, it is an anthology series following two timelines based around the Crain family who live in Hill House as children and revisit it as adults. One of the central characters is named Shirley and the children's mother is an architect. Jackson has been quoted widely explaining that architecture was her family's business for generations and building homes for millionaire Californians was the source of her family's wealth.
30. Koresky, 'Queer & Now & Then'.
31. Shirley Jackson, *The Haunting of Hill House* (London: Penguin, 1959), p. 162.
32. Munford, 'Spectral Femininity', p. 127.
33. White, *Uninvited*, p. 93.
34. Munford, 'Spectral Femininity', p. 129.
35. Angela Carter, 'Afterword' to *Fireworks: Collected Short Stories* (London: Vintage, 1996), p. 460.

36 Fred Botting, 'Aftergothic: consumption, machines and black holes', in Jerrold E. Hogle (ed.), *The Cambridge Companion to Gothic Fiction* (Cambridge: Cambridge University Press, 2002), p. 285.
37 Rebecca Munford, *Decadent Daughters and Monstrous Mothers: Angela Carter and European Gothic* (Manchester: Manchester University Press, 2013), p. 52.
38 Sally Keenan, 'Angela Carter's *The Sadeian Woman*: Feminism as Treason', in Joseph Bristow and Trev Lynn Broughton (eds), *The Infernal Desires of Angela Carter: Fiction, Femininity, Feminism* (London: Longman, 1997), p. 133–49.
39 Margaret Atwood, 'Running with the Tigers', in Lorna Sage (ed.), *Flesh and the Mirror, Essays of the Art of Angela Carter* (London: Virago, 1994), p. 121.
40 Sage, *Flesh and the Mirror*, p. 16.
41 Sarah Gamble, *Angela Carter: Writing from the Front Line* (Edinburgh: Edinburgh University Press, 1997), p. 4.
42 Merja Makinen, 'Sexual and textual aggression in *The Sadeian Woman* and *The Passion of New Eve*', in Bristow and Broughton (eds), *The Infernal Desires of Angela Carter*, p. 163.
43 Gamble, *Angela Carter*, p. 133.
44 Laura Mulvey, 'Cinema Magic and Old Monsters', in Sage (ed.), *Flesh and the Mirror*, p. 241.
45 Maggie Anwell, 'Lolita Meets the Werewolf: The Company of Wolves', in Lorraine Gamman and Margaret Marshment (eds), *The Female Gaze: Women as Viewers of Popular Culture* (London: The Women's Press, 1988), p. 81.
46 Kim Snowden, 'Fairy Tale, Film and the Classroom: Feminist Cultural Pedagogy, Angela Carter and Neil Jordan's *The Company of Wolves*', in Pauline Greenhill and Sidney Eve Matrix (eds), *Fairy Tale Films: Visions of Ambiguity* (Logan UT: Utah University Press, 2010), p. 176.
47 Rebecca Wolff, 'Maryse Condé', BOMB, 68 (1999), *https://web.archive.org/web/20161101132353/http://bombmagazine.org/article/2248* (accessed 5 February 2020).
48 Maha Marouan, *Witches, Goddesses, and Angry Spirits: The Politics of Spiritual Liberation in African Diaspora Women's Fiction* (Columbus OH: Ohio State University Press, 2003), p. 105.
49 Lizabeth Paravisini-Gebert, *Literature of the Caribbean* (Westport CT: Greenwood, 2008), p. 62.
50 Sandra Tomc, 'Dieting and Damnation: Anne Rice's *Interview with the Vampire*', in Joan Gordon and Veronica Hollinger (eds), *Blood Read:*

The Vampire as Metaphor in Contemporary Culture (Philadelphia PA: University of Pennsylvania Press, 1997), p. 108.
51 Gail Abbott Zimmerman, 'The World of the Vampire: Rice's Contribution', in Katherine Ramsland (ed.), *The Anne Rice Reader* (New York: Ballentine Books, 1997), p. 109.
52 Candace R. Benefiel, 'Blood Relations: The Gothic Perversions of the Nuclear Family in Anne Rice's *Interview with the Vampire*', *Journal of Popular Culture*, 38/2 (2004), 263.
53 Haggerty, *Queer Gothic*, p. 199.
54 William Hughes, '"As much a family as anyone could be, anywhere ever": Revisioning the family in Poppy Z. Brite's *Lost Souls*' in Agnes Andeweg, and Sue Zlosnik, (eds.), *Gothic Kinship* (Manchester: Manchester University Press: 2013) p. 178.
55 Haggerty, *Queer Gothic*, p. 185
56 Maria Holmgren Troy, Elizabeth Kella and Helena Wahlström, *Making Home: Orphanhood, Kinship, and Cultural Memory in Contemporary American Novels* (Manchester: Manchester University Press, 2014), p. 172.
57 Christopher S. Lewis, 'Queering Personhood in the Neo-Slave Narrative: Jewelle Gomez's *The Gilda Stories*', *African American Review*, 47/4 (2014), 447.
58 Jewelle Gomez, *The Gilda Stories* (San Francisco CA: City Lights, 2016 [1991]), p. 11
59 Orlando Patterson, *Slavery and Social Death: A Comparative Study* (Cambridge MA: Harvard University Press, 1982), p. 336.
60 For a contemporary meditation on this dynamic in the context of South African Apartheid, explored via Gothic themes, see the 2021 film *Good Madam*, directed by Jenna Bass.
61 Sarah Kent, '"The Bloody Transaction": Black Vampires and the Afterlives of Slavery in *Blacula* and *The Gilda Stories*', *The Journal of Popular Culture*, 53/3 (2020), 730.
62 Gomez, 'Afterword', in *The Gilda Stories*, p. 257
63 Lewis, 'Queering Personhood in the Neo-Slave Narrative', 447.
64 Sarah Parker, '"The Darkness is the Closer in which Your Lover Roosts Her Heart": Lesbians, Desire and the Gothic Genre', *Journal of International Women's Studies*, 9/2 (2008), abstract.
65 See Patricia Smith, *Lesbian Panic: Homoeroticism in Modern British Women's Fiction* (New York: Columbia University Press, 1997).
66 See Gayle Rubin, 'The Traffic in Women: Notes on the "Political Economy" of Sex', in Julie Rivkin and Michael Ryan (eds), *Literary Theory: An Anthology* (Oxford: Blackwell, 1998), pp. 533–60.

Notes

67 Parker, 'The Darkness', p. 6.
68 Stefania Ciocia, '"Queer and Verdant": The Textual Politics of Sarah Waters's Neo-Victorian Novels', *Literary London: Interdisciplinary Studies in the Representation of London*, 5/2 (2007), unpaginated.
69 Rachel Carroll, 'Rethinking Generational History: Queer Histories of Sexuality in Neo-Victorian Feminist Fiction', *Studies in the Literary Imagination*, 39/2 (2006), 136.
70 Marie-Luise Kohlke, 'Into history through the back door: The "past historic" in *Nights at the Circus* and *Affinity*', *Women: A Cultural Review*, 15/2 (2004), 155.
71 Helen Davies, *Gender and Ventriloquism in Victorian and Neo-Victorian fiction: Passionate Puppets* (London: Palgrave Macmillan, 2012), p. 116.
72 Carroll 'Rethinking Generational History', 140.
73 Davies, *Gender and Ventriloquism*, p. 134.
74 Ann Heilmann and Mark Llewellyn, *Neo-Victorianism: The Victorians in the twenty-first century, 1999–2009* (Basingstoke: Palgrave Macmillan, 2010), p. 243.
75 Davies, *Gender and Ventriloquism*, p. 162.
76 Paulina Palmer, *The Queer Uncanny: New Perspectives on the Gothic* (Cardiff: University of Wales Press, 2012), p. 86.
77 Cora Kaplan, *Victoriana: Histories, Fictions, Criticism* (Edinburgh: Edinburgh University Press, 2007) p. 111.

Chapter 2

1 Lynne Huffer, *Are the Lips a Grave: A Queer Feminist on the Ethics of Sex* (New York: Columbia University Press, 2003), p. 43.
2 Ellis Hanson, 'Screwing with Children in Henry James', *GLQ: A Journal of Lesbian and Gay Studies*, 9/3 (2003), 367.
3 The children in the original text and its film adaptation have their sexual identities scrutinised by the paranoid adult governess, which has the effect of queering them.
4 Huffer, *Are the Lips a Grave*, p. 14.
5 Louisa Yates, 'The Figure of the Child in Neo-Victorian Queer Families', in Marie-Luise Kohlke and Christian Gutleben (eds), *Neo-Victorian Families: Gender, Sexual and Cultural Politics* (Amsterdam: Rodopi, 2011), pp. 94–5.
6 Ellen Moers, *Literary Women* (London: The Women's Press Ltd., 1986), p. 90.

7. John Harding, *Florence and Giles* (London: Blue Door, 2010), p. 14.
8. For more a more detailed account of the connections between apparitional subjectivity and queer identity, see Terry Castle, *The Apparitional Lesbian: Female Homosexuality and Modern Culture* (New York: Columbia University Press, 1993).
9. Steven Bruhm, 'Nightmare on Sesame Street: Or, The Self-Possessed Child', *Gothic Studies*, 8/2 (2006), 104.
10. Harding, *Florence and Giles*, p. 46.
11. Sue Walsh, 'Gothic Children', in Catherine Spooner and Emma McEvoy (eds), *The Routledge Companion to the Gothic* (London: Routledge, 2007), p. 183.
12. Virginia Blum, *Hide and Seek: The Child Between Literature and Psychoanalysis* (Chicago IL: University of Illinois Press, 1995), p. 23.
13. Harding, *Florence and Giles*, p. 14.
14. Catherine Robson, *Men in Wonderland: The Lost Girlhood of the Victorian Gentleman* (Oxford: Princeton University Press, 2001), p. 10.
15. James Kincaid, *Child-Loving: The Erotic Child and Victorian Culture* (London: Routledge, 1992), p. 365.
16. Robson, *Men in Wonderland*, p. 3.
17. Kincaid, *Child-Loving*, p. 70.
18. Carol Mavor, *Becoming: The Photography of Clementina, Viscountess Hawarden* (Durham NC: Duke University Press, 1999), p. xxxii.
19. Claire Kahane, 'The Gothic Mirror', in Shirley Nelson Gardener, Claire Kahane and Madelon Sprengnether (eds), *The (M)other Tongue* (Ithaca NY: Cornell University Press, 1985), p. 337.
20. Abigail Bray, 'Governing the Gaze: Child sexual abuse moral panics and the post-feminist blindspot', *Feminist Media Studies*, 9/2 (2009), 177. (See James Kincaid, *Erotic Innocence: The Culture of Child Molesting* (Durham NC: Duke University Press, 1998).)
21. Rachel Carroll, *Rereading Heterosexuality: Queer Theory and Contemporary Fiction* (Edinburgh: Edinburgh University Press, 2012), p. 83.
22. Henry James, *The Turn of the Screw* (London: Penguin, 2017 [1898]), p. 108.
23. Hanson, 'Screwing with Children in Henry James', 381.
24. Kathryn Bond Stockton, *The Queer Child, or Growing Up Sideways in the Twentieth Century* (Durham NC: Duke University Press, 2009), p. 64.
25. Bray, 'Governing the Gaze', 177.
26. Clifford T. Rosky, 'Fear of the Queer Child', *Buffalo Law Review*, 61/3 (2013), 610–21.

[27] Rosky notes that this belief continues in the public imagination into the 1970s, where discourse simply changed from phrases like 'seduction' to 'role-modelling', with the effect of making more palatable the myth that queerness is a form of indoctrination for America's youth. In UK legislation, this myth is evidenced in the roll out of Section 28 (1988), which prohibited councils from intentionally promoting homosexuality through the dissemination of any educational publications pertaining to homosexual issues.
[28] Harding, *Florence and Giles*, p. 37.
[29] Mair Rigby, '"Do you share my madness": Frankenstein's queer Gothic', in William Hughes and Andrew Smith (eds), *Queering the Gothic* (Manchester: Manchester University Press 2009), p. 39.
[30] Harding, *Florence and Giles*, p. 13
[31] 'The New Woman' has been analysed extensively by Sally Ledger in her book *The New Woman: Fiction and Feminism at the* Fin de Siècle (Manchester: Manchester University Press, 1997).
[32] Harding, *Florence and Giles*, p. 71.
[33] See Shoshana Felman, 'Turning the Screw of Interpretation', *Yale French Studies (Literature and Psychoanalysis. The Question of Reading: Otherwise)*, 55/56 (1977), 94–207.
[34] Eric Savoy, 'Theory *a Tergo* in *The Turn of the Screw*', in Steven Bruhm and Natasha Hurley (eds), *Curiouser: On the Queerness of Children* (Minneapolis MN: University of Minnesota Press, 2004), p. 257.
[35] Harding, *Florence and Giles*, p. 44.
[36] Michel Foucault, *The History of Sexuality 1: The Will to Knowledge* (London: Penguin, 1998 [1976]), p. 109.
[37] Harding, *Florence and Giles*, p. 76.
[38] Harding, *Florence and Giles*, p. 46.
[39] Robson, *Men in Wonderland*, pp. 4–5.
[40] Harding, *Florence and Giles*, p. 91.
[41] Barbara Creed, 'Horror and The Monstrous-Feminine: An Imaginary Abjection', in Barry Keith Grant (ed.), *Dread of Difference: Gender and the Horror Film* (Austin TX: University of Texas Press, 2015), p. 46.
[42] Marie Mulvey Roberts, 'The Female Gothic Body', in Avril Horner and Sue Zlosnik (eds), *Women and the Gothic* (Edinburgh: Edinburgh University Press, 2017), p. 107.
[43] See Peter Stallybrass and Allon White, *The Politics and Poetics of Transgression* (Ithaca NY: Cornell University Press, 1986).
[44] Leo Bersani, 'Is the Rectum a Grave?', *AIDS: Cultural Analysis/Cultural Activism*, 43 (1987), 222.

Notes

45 Huffer, *Are the Lips a Grave*, p. 36.
46 Mikko Tuhkanen, *Leo Bersani: Queer Theory and Beyond* (New York: State University of New York Press, 2014), p. 13.
47 Huffer, *Are the Lips a Grave*, p. 43.
48 Harding, *Florence and Giles*, p. 8.

Chapter 3

1 Katharina Lindner, *Film Bodies: Queer Feminist Encounters with Gender and Sexuality in Cinema* (London: I. B. Tauris, 2018), p. 22.
2 Richard Dyer, *Pastiche* (London: Routledge, 2006), p. 2.
3 See, for instance, the scene in which Nina's mother (Barbara Hershey) thrusts a finger of pink birthday-cake icing at her.
4 Dyer, *Pastiche*, p. 179.
5 This is perhaps most prevalent in *Requiem for a Dream* (2000), where characters struggling with addiction conflate cultures of consumption with jouissance; and in *mother!* (2017), where the creation story, flavoured by paranoid, carnage and hysteria, is told through the metonym of a heterosexual relationship.
6 Julia Kristeva, *Powers of Horror: An Essay in Abjection* (New York: Columbia University Press, 1982), p. 4.
7 The notion of Freddy Krueger symbolising latent homosexuality was explored during a special screening of *Nightmare on Elm Street 2: Freddy's Revenge* for pride month June 2019 at the Queer Fears Symposium held by the University of Hertfordshire at the Odyssey Cinema in St Albans. The screening was accompanied by a short video introduction by the film's star Mark Patton. *Scream, Queen! My Nightmare on Elm Street* (February 2019) is a documentary film exploring the homosexual subtext of the film as it related to the actor's experience of his own closeted sexual identity.
8 Linda Williams, 'When the Woman Looks', in Barry Keith Grant (ed.), *The Dread of Difference: Gender and the Horror Film* (Austin TX: University of Texas Press, 2015), p. 23.
9 Paulina Palmer, *The Queer Uncanny: New Perspectives on the Gothic* (Cardiff: University of Wales Press, 2012), pp. 121–2.
10 *Basic Instinct*, dir. Paul Verhoeven, United States, 1992.
11 Mark Fisher and Amber Jacobs, 'Debating *Black Swan*: Gender and Horror – Mark Fisher and Amber Jacobs disagree about Darren Aronofsky's film', *Film Quarterly*, 65/1 (2011), 60.

Notes

[12] *Ginger Snaps*, dir. John Fawcett, United States, 2001.
[13] Clara Bradbury-Rance, *Lesbian Cinema after Queer Theory* (Edinburgh: Edinburgh University Press, 2019), p. 33.
[14] Sakshi Dogra, 'Lacan, "The Mirror Stage" and Subjectivity: A Psychoanalytic Reading of *Black Swan*', *New Man International Journal of Multidisciplinary Studies*, 2/6 (2015), 62–8.
[15] Fisher and Jacobs, 'Debating *Black Swan*', 58.
[16] Judith Butler, *Bodies that Matter: On the Discursive Limits of 'Sex'* (New York: Routledge, 1993), p. 22.
[17] Barbara Creed, *The Monstrous-Feminine: Film, Feminism, Psychoanalysis* (London: Routledge, 2003) p. 42.
[18] Lindner, *Film Bodies*, p. 118.
[19] Fisher and Jacobs, 'Debating *Black Swan*', 60.
[20] Bradbury-Rance, *Lesbian Cinema after Queer Theory*, p. 25
[21] Fisher and Jacobs, 'Debating *Black Swan*', 60.
[22] Ellis Hanson, 'Queer Gothic', in Catherine Spooner and Emma McEvoy (eds), *The Routledge Companion to The Gothic* (London: Routledge, 2007), p. 175.
[23] Heather Love, 'Truth and Consequences: On Paranoid Reading and Reparative Reading', *Criticism: A Quarterly for Literature and the Arts*, 52/2 (2010), 238–9.
[24] Hanson, 'Queer Gothic', p. 176.
[25] Eve Kosofsky Sedgwick, 'Paranoid Reading and Reparative Reading, or, You're so Paranoid, You Probably Think This Essay is About You', in Eve Kosofsky Sedgwick, *Touching Feeling: Affect, Pedagogy, Performativity* (Durham NC: Duke University Press, 2003), p. 126.
[26] Equally paranoid is the scene in which Nina masturbates and the camera cuts to Barbara Hershey's sleeping face as Nina realises that her mother has sat vigil over her for the duration.
[27] Lindner, *Film Bodies*, p. 125.
[28] Tania Modleski, *The Women Who Knew Too Much* (London: Routledge, 1988), p. 26.
[29] Julia Kristeva, *Strangers to Ourselves* (New York: Columbia University Press, 1988), p. 192.
[30] Annamarie Jagose, 'Queer Theory', *Australian Humanities Review*, 4 (1996), unpaginated, para 13, *https://australianhumanitiesreview.org/1996/12/01/queer-theory/* (accessed 18 September 2019).
[31] Lindner, *Film Bodies*, p. 27.
[32] See Vito Russo, *The Celluloid Closet: Homosexuality in the Movies* (New York: Harper and Row, 1985).

33   Hanson, 'Screwing with Children in Henry James', 176

Chapter 4

1. Clara Bradbury-Rance, *Lesbian Cinema after Queer Theory* (Edinburgh: Edinburgh University Press, 2019), p. 15.
2. Park Chan-wook's revenge trilogy includes *Sympathy for Mr Vengeance* (2002), *Oldboy* (2003) and *Lady Vengeance* (2005).
3. Terry Castle, *The Apparitional Lesbian: Female Homosexuality and Modern Culture* (New York: Columbia University Press, 1993), p. 12.
4. Castle, *The Apparitional Lesbian*, p. 13.
5. Julian Daniel Gutierrez Albilla, 'Reframing *My Dearest Señorita* (1971): Queer embodiment and Subjectivity through the poetics of cinema', *Studies in Spanish and Latin American Cinema*, 12/1 (2015), 29.
6. Annamarie Jagose, *Inconsequence: Lesbian Representation and the Logic of Sexual Sequence* (New York: Cornell University Press, 2002), pp. 3–4.
7. Eunah Lee, 'Trauma, Excess, and the Aesthetics of Effect: The Extreme Cinemas of Chan-wook Park', *Postscript: Essays in Film and the Humanities*, 34/2 (2014), non-paginated.
8. Benjamin Harvey, 'Contemporary Horror Cinema', in Catherine Spooner and Emma McEvoy (eds), *The Routledge Companion to the Gothic* (London: Routledge, 2007), p. 237.
9. Harvey, 'Contemporary Horror Cinema', p. 237.
10. Eunah Lee writes that 'for Korean audiences, the extreme cinema of Park delivers the otherwise unrepresentable trauma of the modernizing process that South Korea has undergone'. Lee's analysis takes Park's Revenge Trilogy as its focus, and she foregrounds the Asian Extreme style of Park's films as a complex method of representing historic and contemporary national trauma of modernisation and such other events as the Asian economic crisis.
11. Homi K. Bhabha, *The Location of Culture* (London: Routledge, 1994), p. 15.
12. Interestingly, another postcolonial Gothic text, Arundhati Roy's novel, *The God of Small Things*, features a house referred to as the 'History House' by the child characters in the novel. Sarah Ilott has written about this house as illustrative of a Keralan colonial past haunting the present action in the narrative: she describes the novel as 'concerned with the familial guilt following a sequence of traumatic events centred on the family of twins Rahel and Esthappen, personal narratives are

Notes

largely dictated by the howling "Big God" of national history, who demands "obeisance" and overshadows personal turmoil' (2004: p. 19). Ilott goes on to liken the way that the house is figured in the novel as bearing an 'uncanny resemblance to the mansions of English Gothic', compounded by the family Anglophilic turn: 'The implication is that Anglophilia amounts to a colonisation of the mind that displaces their sense of native Indian history; they have been possessed by an "English" manner of thinking.' See Sarah Ilott, 'Postcolonial Gothic', in Maisha Wester and Xavier Aldana Reyes (eds), *Twenty-First-Century Gothic: An Edinburgh Companion* (Edinburgh: Edinburgh University Press, 2019), p. 21.

[13] Sigmund Freud, *The Uncanny* (London: Penguin, 2003 [1919]), p. 142.

[14] Otto Rank, *The Double: A Psychoanalytic Study*, trans. by Harry Tucker Jr (Chapel Hill NC: North Carolina Press, 1971 [1914]), p. 75.

[15] Bradbury-Rance, *Lesbian Cinema after Queer Theory*, p. 24.

[16] Rosalind Minsky, *Psychoanalysis and Gender: An Introductory Reader* (London: Routledge, 1996), p. 145.

[17] Anneke Smelik, 'Art Cinema and Murderous Lesbians', in Michele Aaron (ed.), *New Queer Cinema: A Critical Reader* (Edinburgh: Edinburgh University Press, 2004), p. 74.

[18] This is the posh academic word for '69ing', for those interested.

[19] Judith Butler, 'Performativity, Precarity and Sexual Politics', *AIBR: Revista de Antropología Iberoamericana*, 4/3 (2009), 1.

[20] Bhabha, *The Location of Culture*, p. 5.

[21] Ruth Robbins, *Subjectivity* (Basingstoke: Palgrave, 2005), p. 16.

[22] Breaks between the film's three acts are indicated by intertitles reading Part One, Part Two and Part Three.

[23] Smelik, 'Art Cinema and Murderous Lesbians', p. 74.

[24] Sue Chaplin, *Gothic Literature: Texts, Contexts, Connections* (York: York Press, 2011), p. 279.

[25] This technique is akin to autonomous sensory meridian response and is used elsewhere in the film, when Hideko and Sook-Hee kiss, for example.

[26] Steven T. Brown, 'Ambient Horror: From Sonic Palimpsests to Haptic Sonority in the cinema of Kurosawa Kiyoshi', *Horror Studies*, 7/2 (2016), 271.

[27] Julie Kristeva, *The Powers of Horror: An Essay on Abjection* (New York: Columbia University Press, 1982), p. 53.

[28] Barbara Creed, 'Horror and The Monstrous-Feminine: An Imaginary Abjection', in Barry Keith Grant (ed.), *Dread of Difference: Gender and the Horror Film* (Austin TX: University of Texas Press, 2015), p. 37.

Notes

Chapter 5

1. Angela Carter, *The Sadeian Woman: An Exercise in Cultural History* (London: Virago, 1979), p. 140.
2. Peter Hutchings, 'Tearing your soul apart: Horror's New Monsters', in Victor Sage and Allan Lloyd Smith (eds), *Modern Gothic: A Reader* (Manchester: Manchester University Press, 1996), p. 89.
3. Xavier Aldana Reyes, *Body Gothic: Corporeal Transgression in Contemporary Literature and Horror Film* (Cardiff: University of Wales Press, 2014), p. 2.
4. Steven Bruhm, 'The Counterfeit Child', *English Studies in Canada*, 38/3 (2012), 42.
5. Translation of Deneuve's 'Open Letter', www.liberation.fr/debats/2018/01/15/metoo-controversy-read-catherine-deneuve-s-letter-published-in-liberation_1622561/ (accessed 7 November 2023).
6. Julia Kristeva, *Powers of Horror: An Essay in Abjection* (New York: Columbia University Press, 1982), p. 4.
7. Mauro Resmini, 'Reframing the New French Extremity: Cinema, Theory, Mediation', *Camera Obscura*, 90 (2015), 162.
8. Nick Pinkerton, '*Raw* Review', *Sight and Sound*, 27/5 (May 2017), 88.
9. Resmini, 'Reframing the New French Extremity', 162.
10. Jerome Schaefer, *An Edgy Realism: Film Theoretical Encounters with Dogma* (Cambridge: Cambridge Scholars publishing, 2015), p. 96.
11. My own phrasing, meaning comparable in tone to the cultural afterlife of Bram Stoker's *Dracula* (1897).
12. Resmini, 'Reframing the New French Extremity', 169.
13. Michel Foucault, *The History of Sexuality, vol. 1*, trans. by Robert Hurley (New York: Pantheon Books, 1978), p. 11.
14. Resmini, 'Reframing the New French Extremity', 169.
15. Margaret Barton-Fumo, 'Pleasures of the Flesh', *Film Comment*, 53/2 (2017), 44.
16. Resmini, 'Reframing the New French Extremity', 162.
17. Noël Carroll, 'Paradoxes of the Heart: The Philosophy of Horror Twenty-Five Years Later: An Interview by Caetlin Benson-Allott', *Journal of Visual Culture*, 14/3 (2015), 338.
18. Barbara Creed, 'Horror and the Monstrous-Feminine: An Imaginary Abjection', *Screen*, 1 (1986), 44.
19. Xavier Aldana Reyes, 'Beyond psychoanalysis: Post-millennial horror film and affect theory', *Horror Studies*, 3/2 (2012), 246.

[20] Steven Shaviro, *The Cinematic Body* (London: Minneapolis University Press, 1993), pp. 138–9.
[21] Steven Shaviro, '*The Cinematic Body* REDUX', *Parallax*, 14/1 (2008), 50.
[22] Shaviro, *The Cinematic Body*, p. 13.
[23] Shaviro, '*The Cinematic Body* REDUX', 50.
[24] Marina Warner, *No Go the Bogeyman: Scaring, Lulling and Making Mock* (London: Virago, 2000), p. 10.
[25] Kathryn Bond Stockton, *The Queer Child, or Growing up Sideways in the Twentieth Century* (Durham NC: Duke University Press, 2009), p. 90.
[26] Julia Ducournau interviewed by Nicolas Rapold, in 'Pleasures of the Flesh', *Film Comment*, 53/2 (2017), 45.
[27] Megan H. Glick, 'Of Sodomy and Cannibalism: Dehumanisation, Embodiment and the Rhetorics of Same-Sex and Cross-Species Contagion', *Gender and History*, 23/3 (2011), 267.
[28] Julia Ducournau in interview, Virginie Sélavy, 'Fresh Meat', in *Sight and Sound*, 27/5 (May 2017), 53.
[29] Darren Elliott-Smith, *Queer Horror Film and Television: Sexuality and Masculinity at the Margins* (London: I. B. Tauris, 2016), p. 22.
[30] Cerise Howard, '*Raw* (2017): Horror in the Eyes of Women', *Diabolique*, https://diaboliquemagazine.com/raw-2017-horror-eyes-women/ (accessed 3 January 2019).
[31] Ducournau in Sélavy, 'Fresh Meat', 53.
[32] Joan Smith, *Hungry for You: From Cannibalism to Seduction – A Book of Food* (London: Vintage, 1997), p. 216.
[33] See bell hooks, 'Eating the Other: Desire and Resistance', in bell hooks, *Black Looks: Race and Representation* (London: Routledge, 2015), pp. 21–41.
[34] C. Richard King, 'The (Mis)Uses of Cannibalism in Contemporary Cultural Critique', *Diacritics*, 30/1 (2000), 108.
[35] Shirley Lindenbaum, 'Thinking About Cannibalism', *Annual Review of Anthropology*, 33 (2004).
[36] Claire Boyle, 'Post-Queer: (Un)made in France', *Paragraph: Queer Theory's Return to France*, 35/2 (2012), 260.
[37] Foucault, *The History of Sexuality*, (1978), p. 152.
[38] Lisa Downing, 'Interdisciplinarity, Cultural Studies, Queer: Historical Contexts and Contemporary Contentions in France', *Paragraph: Queer Theory's Return to France*, 35/2 (2012), 223–4.
[39] Hector Kollias, 'Queering it Right, Getting it Wrong', *Paragraph: Queer Theory's Return to France*, 35/2 (2012), 151.

Notes

40 Adrian Rifkin, 'Does Gay Sex Need Queer Theory?', *Paragraph: Queer Theory's Return to France*, 35/2 (2012), 203.
41 Hélène Bourcier, *Queer Zones*, trans. by Lisa Downing (Paris: Balland, 2001), p. 229.

Chapter 6

1 M. R. Carey, *The Girl with All the Gifts* (London: Orbit, 2014), p. 125
2 David Punter, *The Literature of Terror: A History of Gothic Fictions from 1765 to the Present Day*, vol. 2: *The Modern Gothic* (Harlow: Pearson Education, 1996), p. 48.
3 Steven Bruhm, 'Work in Progress: The Gothic Child', *http://faculty.msvu.ca/sbruhm/gothchild.htm* (accessed 7 October 2019).
4 Sue Walsh, 'Gothic Children', in Catherine Spooner and Emma McEvoy (eds), *The Routledge Companion to the Gothic* (New York: Routledge, 2007), p. 183.
5 Chloé Germaine Buckley, *Twenty-first-century Children's Gothic* (Edinburgh: Edinburgh University Press, 2018), p. 5.
6 Rosi Braidotti, 'Writing as a Nomadic Subject', *Comparative Critical Studies*, 11/2–3 (2014), 173.
7 See, for example, Sarah Ilott and Chloé Buckley, '"Fragmenting and Becoming Double": Supplementary Twins and Abject Bodies in Helen Oyeyemi's *The Icarus Girl*', *Journal of Commonwealth Literature*, 51/3 (2016).
8 Ilott and Buckley, 'Fragmenting and Becoming Double', 405.
9 Helen Oyeyemi, *The Icarus Girl* (London: Bloomsbury, 2005), p. 322.
10 Carey, *The Girl with All the Gifts*, p. 28.
11 The film adaptation, which is incredibly faithful to the plot and action of the novel – a virtue of each being written at the same time – swaps the racial identity of its two leading female characters, casting a Black actor, Sennia Nenua (who was twelve years old at the time), as Melanie, and the white actor, Gemma Arterton, as Miss Justineau. While this might seem a trivial decision to some, and while Carey himself has hedged that the casting decision was 'as neutral as we could make it, but with the explicit aim of ending up with a racially diverse line-up', it proves a divisive choice, provoking audiences to wonder about the ongoing white-washing of Hollywood adaptations, as well as the implications of 'race-bending'. In the novel, the racial identities of these characters are important to their interactions with each other.

12. Carey, *The Girl with All the Gifts*, p. 30.
13. Catherine Robson, *Men in Wonderland: The Lost Girlhood of the Victorian Gentleman* (Oxford: Princeton University Press, 2001), p. 7.
14. Oyeyemi, *The Icarus Girl*, p. 72.
15. Natalya Din-Kariuki, '"Nobody ever warned me about mirrors": Doubling, Mimesis and Narrative form in Helen Oyeyemi's Fiction', in Chloe Buckley and Sarah Ilott (eds), *Telling it Slant: Critical Approaches to Helen Oyeyemi* (Brighton: Sussex Academic Press, 2017), p. 62.
16. Oyeyemi, *The Icarus Girl*, p. 178.
17. Frantz Fanon, *Black Skin, White Masks*, trans. by Charles Lam Markmann (London: Pluto Books, 2008 [1952]), p. 86.
18. Oyeyemi, *The Icarus Girl*, p. 174.
19. Carey, *The Girl with All the Gifts*, p. 27.
20. John Harding, *Florence and Giles* (London: Blue Door, 2010), p. 7.
21. Sarah Ilott, '"The genesis of woman goes through the mouth": Consumption, Oral Pleasure, and Voice in The Opposite House and White is for Witching', in Buckley and Ilott (eds), *Telling it Slant: Critical Approaches to Helen Oyeyemi*, pp. 137–8.
22. Oyeyemi, *The Icarus Girl*, p. 289.
23. Giorgio Agamben, *State of Exception*, trans. by Kevin Attell (Chicago IL: University of Chicago Press, 2005), p. 49.
24. J. A. Mbembe, 'Necropolitics', trans. by Libby Meintjes, *Public Culture*, 15/1 (2003), 16–17.
25. Judith Butler, *Precarious Life: The Powers of Mourning and Violence* (London: Verso, 2004), p. 20.
26. Mbembe, 'Necropolitics', p. 12.
27. Jasbir K. Puar, *Terrorist Assemblages: Homonationalism in Queer Times* (Durham NC: Duke University Press, 2017), p. 33.
28. Challenging the assumptive refrain heard throughout transnational feminist discourse of recent decades that the nation state is heteronormative, Puar's project in *Terrorist Assemblages* is to call attention to something that she calls 'homonationalism'. An over-simplified and incorrect definition of this term might identify homonationalism as racism within queer communities, but Puar qualifies that its meaning is more in-keeping with Lisa Duggan's notion of homonormativity, in that it is a conceptual framework designed to enable critiques of the domesticisation and privatisation of queer bodies and queer culture. Puar's analysis of global politics and how they intersect with queer projects of equal rights was written in reaction to the United States's imperialist interest in the Middle East and post-9/11 masculinist

rhetoric. Puar describes the complicity foisted on queer communities by far-right political parties (globally) to show active interest in supporting the vilification of Iraq and Afghanistan, using fearmongering suggestions of Islamic homophobia. An example of one such party gaining traction with white, middle-class gay voters is the French Front National led by Marine le Pen using strategies that work to co-opt LGBTQ liberation politics for xenophobic party agendas.

29 Carey, *The Girl with All the Gifts*, p. 275.
30 Giorgio Agamben, *State of Exception*, trans. by Kevin Attell (Chicago IL: University of Chicago Press, 2005), p. 2.
31 Christopher Ouma, 'Reading the Diasporic Abiku in Helen Oyeyemi's *The Icarus Girl*', *Research in African Literatures*, 45/3 (2014), 190.
32 Oyeyemi, *The Icarus Girl*, p. 86.
33 Jordan Stouck, 'Abjecting Hybridity in Helen Oyeyemi's *The Icarus Girl*', *Ariel: A Review of International English Literature*, 41/2 (2011), 93.
34 Carey, *The Girl with All the Gifts*, p. 456.

Conclusion

1 The term 'queer' was rejected by other relevant auteur directors such as Bruce La Bruce who preferred the 'gay' moniker and denied being a part of New Queer Cinema.
2 Heather O. Petrocelli, *Queer for Fear: Horror Film and the Queer Spectator* (Chicago IL: University of Wales Press, 2023), p. 27.
3 Williams won the Critics' Choice Super Award for Best Supporting Actor in a Drama Series in 2021 for his role in *Lovecraft Country*, just four months before his death.
4 Maisha L. Wester, *African American Gothic: Screams from Shadowed Placed* (New York: Palgrave Macmillan, 2012), p. 102.
5 See Patricia Hill Collins, *Black Feminist Thought: Knowledge, Consciousness, and the Politics of Empowerment* (London: Routledge, 2000).
6 Robin R. Means Coleman, *Horror Noire: Blacks in American Horror Films from the 1890s to Present* (New York: Routledge, 2011), p. 41.
7 See W. E. B. Du Bois, *The Souls of Black Folk* (Chicago IL: A. C. McClurg and Co., 1903).
8 M. R. Carey, *The Girl with All the Gifts* (London: Orbit, 2014), p. 143.
9 Heather Love, 'Truth and Consequences: On Paranoid Reading and Reparative Reading', *Criticism: A Quarterly for Literature and the Arts*, 52/2 (2010), 239.

Bibliography

Primary Sources

Carey, M. R., *The Girl with All the Gifts* (London: Orbit, 2014).
Carter, Angela, *Fireworks: Collected Short Stories* (London: Vintage, [1974] 1996).
Carter, Angela, *Nights at the Circus* (London: Penguin, [1984] 1994).
Carter, Angela, *The Infernal Desire Machines of Doctor Hoffman* (London: Penguin, ([1972] 2011).
Carter, Angela, 'The Lady of the House of Love', in Angela Carter, *The Bloody Chamber, and Other Stories* (London: Vintage, ([1979] 2006), pp. 107–25.
Carter, Angela, *The Magic Toyshop* (London: Virago, [1967] 2008).
Carter, Angela, *The Passion of New Eve* (London: Virago, 1982).
Carter, Angela, *The Sadeian Woman: An Exercise in Cultural History* (London: Virago, 1979).
Carter, Angela, *Wise Children* (London: Vintage, [1991] 1992).
Collins, Wilkie, *The Woman in White* (London: Macmillan, [1859] 2018).
Condé, Maryse, *Moi, Tituba, Sorcière . . . Noire de Salem* (Charlottesville VA: University of Virginia Press, 1992 [1986]).
Dickens, Charles, *Bleak House* (London: Wordsworth Editions, [1853] 1993).

Bibliography

Dostoevsky, Fyodor, *The Double* (London: Dover Thrift, [1846] 1997).

Gomez, Jewelle, *The Gilda Stories* (San Francisco CA: City Lights, 2016 [1991]).

Harding, John, *Florence and Giles* (London: Blue Door, 2010).

Hoffmann, E. T. A., *The Sandman*, trans. by Peter Wortsman (London: Penguin, [1816] 2016).

Jackson, Shirley, 'The Lottery', in *The Lottery and Other Stories* (London: Penguin, [1948] 2009).

Jackson, Shirley, *Life Among the Savages* (London: Penguin, [1957] 1997).

Jackson, Shirley, *Raising Demons* (Chicago IL: Academy Chicago, [1957] 1994).

Jackson, Shirley, *The Haunting of Hill House* (London: Penguin, 1959).

Jackson, Shirley, *We Have Always Lived in the Castle* (London: Penguin, [1962] 2009).

James, Henry, *The Pupil* (Philadelphia PA: Chelsea House, [1891] 1991).

James, Henry, *The Turn of the Screw* (London: Penguin, [1898] 2017).

James, Henry, *What Maisie Knew* (Hertfordshire: Wordsworth, [1897] 2000).

Oyeyemi, Helen, *The Icarus Girl* (London: Bloomsbury, 2005).

Oyeyemi, Helen, *The Opposite House* (London: Bloomsbury, 2007).

Oyeyemi, Helen, *White is For Witching* (London: Picador, 2008).

Radcliffe, Ann, *The Italian* (Idaho: Pacific, [1797] 2010).

Radcliffe, Ann, *The Mysteries of Udolpho* (Oxford: Oxford University Press, [1794] 1998).

Rice, Anne, *Interview with the Vampire* (New York: Knopf, 1976).

Rice, Anne, *Memnoch the Devil* (New York: Ballentine, 1995).

Rice, Anne, *The Queen of the Damned* (New York: Knopf, 1988).

Rice, Anne, *The Vampire Lestat* (New York: Knopf, 1985).

Shelley, Mary, *Frankenstein* (London: Penguin, [1818] 1985).

Stevenson, Robert Louis, *Strange Case of Dr Jekyll and Mr Hyde* (London: Wordsworth, [1886] 1993).

Walpole, Horace, *The Castle of Otranto* (London: Dover, [1764] 1966).

Waters, Sarah, *Affinity* (London: Virago, [1999] 2000).
Waters, Sarah, *Fingersmith* (London: Virago, 2002).
Waters, Sarah, *The Little Stranger* (London: Virago, 2009).
Waters, Sarah, *The Night Watch* (London: Virago, 2006).
Waters, Sarah, *Tipping the Velvet* (London: Virago, 1998).
Wilde, Oscar, *The Picture of Dorian Gray*, in *The Complete Works of Oscar Wilde* (Glasgow: HarperCollins, [1891] 2003), pp. 17–159.

Filmography

À l'intérieur, dir. Alexandre Bustillo and Julien Maury, France, 2007.
Bad Girl Boogey, dir. Alice Maio Mackay, Australia, 2022.
Basic Instinct, dir. Paul Verhoeven, United States, 1992.
Black Swan, dir. Darren Aronofsky, United States, 2010.
Boys Don't Cry, dir. Kimberley Pierce, United States, 1999.
Bride of Frankenstein, dir. James Whale, United States, 1935.
Carol, dir. Todd Haynes, United States, 2016.
Carrie, dir. Brian De Palma, United States, 1976.
Crimson Peak, dir. Guillermo Del Toro, United States, 2015.
Dans ma peau, dir. Marina de Van, France, 2004.
Daughters of Darkness, dir. Harry Kümel, United States, 1970.
Dracula, dir. Tod Browning, United States, 1931.
Dracula's Daughter, dir. Lambert Hillyer, United States, 1936.
Far from Heaven, dir. Todd Haynes, United States, 2002.
Frankenstein, dir. James Whale, United States, 1931.
Frisk, dir. Todd Verow, United States, 1995.
Frontière(s) (Frontier(s)), dir. Xavier Gens, France, 2007.
Get Out, dir. Jordan Peele, United States, 2017.
Ginger Snaps, dir. John Fawcett, United States, 2001.
Go Fish, dir. Rose Troche, United States, 1994.
Good Will Hunting, dir. Gus Van Sant, United States, 1997.
Haute Tension, dir. Alexandre Aja, France, 2003.
Ils, dir. David Moreau and Xavier Palud, France, 2006.
Ingagi, dir. William S. Campbell, United States, 1930.
Jack & Diane, dir. Rust Gray, United States, 2012.
Junior, dir. Julia Ducournau, France, 2011.

Bibliography

King Kong, dir. Merian C. Cooper and Ernest B. Schoedsack, United States, 1933.
La mala Educacion, dir. Pedro Almodóvar, Spain, 2004.
LA Zombie, dir. Bruce La Bruce, Germany, 2010.
Lovecraft Country, HBO, USA, 2020.
Mama, dir. Andy Muschietti, United States, 2011.
Martyrs, dir. Pascal Laugier, France, 2008.
Morocco, dir. Josef von Sternberg, United States, 1930.
mother!, dir, Darren Aronofsky, United States, 2017.
Mulholland Drive, dir. David Lynch, United States, 2001.
My Own Private Idaho, dir. Gus Van Sant, United States, 1992.
Nightmare on Elm Street 2: Freddy's Revenge, dir. Jack Shoulder, United States, 1985.
Nosferatu, dir. F. W. Murnau. Germany, 1922.
Oldboy, dir. Chan-wook Park, Korea, 2003.
Orphan, dir. Jaume Collet-Serra, United States, 2009.
Otto; or, Up with Dead People, dir. Bruce La Bruce, Germany, 2008.
Paris Is Burning, dir. Jennie Livingston. United States, 1990.
Parting Glances, dir. Bill Sherwood, United States, 1986.
Peeping Tom, dir. Michael Powell, United Kingdom, 1960.
Poison, dir. Todd Haynes, United States, 1992.
Psycho, dir. Alfred Hitchcock, United States, 1960.
Psycho, dir. Gus Van Sant, United States, 1998.
Queen Christina, dir. Rouben Mamoulian, United States, 1933.
Raw, dir. Julia Ducournau, France, 2016.
Rebecca, dir. Alfred Hitchcock, United States, 1940.
Requiem for a Dream, dir. Darren Aronofsky, United States, 2000.
Rosemary's Baby, dir. Roman Polanski, United States, 1968.
Scary Movie 2, dir. Keenan Ivory Wayans, United States, 2001.
Scream, Queen! My Nightmare on Elm Street, dir. Roman Chimienti and Tyler Jensen, United Kingdom, 2019.
Shaun of the Dead, dir. Edgar Wright, United Kingdom, 2004.
She's All That, dir. Robert Iscove, United States, 1999.
So Vam!, dir. Alice Maio Mackay, Australia, 2021.
Superstar: The Karen Carpenter Story, dir. Todd Haynes, United States, 1988.
Suspiria, dir. Dario Argento, Italy, 1977.
Swoon, dir. Tom Kalin, United States, 1992.

Bibliography

T Blockers, dir. Alice Maio Mackay, Australia, 2023.
The Babadook, dir. Jennifer Kerr, Australia, 2013.
The Cabinet of Dr Caligari, dir. Robert Wiene, Germany, 1920.
The Celluloid Closet, dir. Rob Epstein, Jeffrey Friedman, United States, 1995.
The Chilling Adventures of Sabrina, Netflix, USA, 2018–20.
The Conjuring, dir. James Wan, United States, 2010.
The Handmaiden, dir. Chan-wook Park, Korea, 2016.
The Haunting, dir. Jan De Bont, United States, 1999.
The Haunting, dir. Robert Wise, United States, 1963.
The Hunger, dir. Tony Scott, United Kingdom, 1982.
The Innocents, dir. Jack Clayton, United Kingdom, 1961.
The Living End, dir. Gregg Araki, United States, 1992.
The Neon Demon, dir. Nicolas Winding Refn, United States, 2016.
The Old Dark House, dir. James Whale, United States, 1932.
The Red Shoes, dir. Michael Powell and Emeric Pressburger, United Kingdom, 1948.
The Seventh Victim, dir. Mark Robson, United States, 1943.
The Vampire Lovers, dir. Roy Ward Baker, United States, 1970.
The Watermelon Woman, dir. Cheryl Dunye, United States, 1996.
The Witch, dir. Robert Eggers, United States/Canada, 2015.
The Woman in Black, dir. James Watkins, United Kingdom, 2010.
Them, Amazon Prime, USA, 2021.
Thundercrack!, dir. Curt McDowell, United States, 1975.
Us, dir. Jordan Peele, United States, 2019.

Secondary Sources

Aaron, Michele (ed.), *New Queer Cinema: A Critical Reader* (Edinburgh: Edinburgh University Press, 2004).
Abbott Zimmerman, Gail, 'The World of the Vampire: Rice's Contribution', in Katherine Ramsland (ed.), *The Anne Rice Reader* (New York: Ballentine Books, 1997).
Agamben, Giorgio, *State of Exception*, trans. by Kevin Attell (Chicago IL: University of Chicago Press, 2005).

Aldana Reyes, Xavier, 'Beyond psychoanalysis: Post-millennial horror film and affect theory', *Horror Studies*, 3/2 (2012), 243–61.

Aldana Reyes, Xavier, *Body Gothic: Corporeal Transgression in Contemporary Literature and Horror Film* (Cardiff: University of Wales Press, 2014).

Aldana Reyes, Xavier, *Horror: A Literary History* (London: The British Library, 2016).

Aldana Reyes, Xavier, *Horror Film and Affect: Towards a Corporeal Model of Viewership* (London: Routledge, 2016).

Andeweg, Agnes, and Zlosnik, Sue, *Gothic Kinship* (Manchester: Manchester University Press: 2013).

Anwell, Maggie, 'Lolita Meets the Werewolf: The Company of Wolves', in Lorraine Gamman and Margaret Marshment (eds), *The Female Gaze: Women as Viewers of Popular Culture* (London: The Women's Press, 1988).

Armitt, Lucie, 'The Gothic Girl Child', in Avril Horner and Sue Zlosnik (eds), *Women and the Gothic* (Edinburgh: Edinburgh University Press, 2017).

Atwood, Margaret, 'Running with the Tigers', in Lorna Sage (ed.), *Flesh and the Mirror, Essays of the Art of Angela Carter* (London: Virago, 1994), pp. 133–51.

Barton-Fumo, Margaret, 'Pleasures of the Flesh', *Film Comment*, 53/2 (2017), 42–6.

Beaumont, Matthew (ed.), *Adventures in Realism* (Carlton VIC: Blackwell, 2007).

Becker, Susanne, *Gothic Forms of Feminine Fictions* (Manchester: Manchester University Press, 1999).

Benshoff, Harry M., *Monsters in the Closet: Homosexuality and the Horror Film* (Manchester: Manchester University Press, 1997).

Benshoff, Harry M., and Sean Griffin, *Queer Images: A History of Gay and Lesbian Film in America* (Lanham MD: Rowman and Littlefield, 2006).

Benefiel, Candace R., 'Blood Relations: The Gothic Perversions of the Nuclear Family in Anne Rice's *Interview with the Vampire*', *Journal of Popular Culture*, 38/2 (2004), 261–73.

Bersani, Leo, 'Is the Rectum a Grave?', *AIDS: Cultural Analysis/Cultural Activism*, 43 (1987).

Bhabha, Homi K., *The Location of Culture* (London: Routledge, 1994).

Blake, Linnie, 'Neoliberal Gothic', in Maisha Wester and Xavier Aldana Reyes (eds), *Twenty-First-Century Gothic: An Edinburgh Companion* (Edinburgh: Edinburgh University Press, 2019).

Botting, Fred, 'Aftergothic: Consumption, Machines and Black Holes', in Jerrold E. Hogle (ed.), *The Cambridge Companion to Gothic Fiction* (Cambridge: Cambridge University Press, 2002).

Botting, Fred, *Gothic* (London: Routledge, 2014).

Bourcier, Hélène, *Queer Zones*, trans. by Lisa Downing (Paris: Balland, 2001).

Boyle, Claire, 'Post-Queer: (Un)made in France', *Paragraph: Queer Theory's Return to France*, 35/2 (2012).

Bray, Abigail, 'Governing the Gaze: Child Sexual Abuse Moral Panics and the Post-Feminist Blindspot', *Feminist Media Studies*, 9/2 (2009).

Blum, Virginia, *Hide and Seek: The Child Between Literature and Psychoanalysis* (Chicago IL: University of Illinois Press, 1995)

Braidotti, Rosi, 'Writing as a Nomadic Subject', *Comparative Critical Studies*, 11/2–3 (2014).

Bradbury-Rance, Clara, *Lesbian Cinema after Queer Theory* (Edinburgh: Edinburgh University Press, 2019).

Bristow, Joseph, and Trev Lynn Broughton (eds), *The Infernal Desires of Angela Carter: Fiction, Femininity, Feminism* (London: Longman, 1997).

Brown, Jennifer, *Cannibalism in Literature and Film* (New York: Palgrave Macmillan, 2013).

Brown, Steven T., 'Ambient Horror: From Sonic Palimpsests to Haptic Sonority in the cinema of Kurosawa Kiyoshi', *Horror Studies*, 7/2 (2016).

Bruhm, Steven, 'Contemporary Gothic: why we need it', in Jerrold E. Hogle (ed.), *The Cambridge Companion to Gothic Fiction* (Cambridge: Cambridge University Press, 2002).

Bruhm, Steven, 'Gothic Sexualities', in Andrew Smith and Anna Powell (eds), *Teaching the Gothic* (Basingstoke: Palgrave, 2006).

Bruhm, Steven, 'Nightmare on Sesame Street: Or, The Self-Possessed Child', *Gothic Studies* 8/2 (2006).

Bruhm, Steven, 'The Counterfeit Child', *English Studies in Canada*, 38/3 (2012).

Bruhm, Steven, 'Work in Progress: The Gothic Child', http://faculty.msvu.ca/sbruhm/gothchild.htm (accessed 7 October 2019).

Bruhm, Steven, and Natasha Hurley (eds), *Curiouser: On the Queerness of Children* (Minneapolis MN: University of Minnesota Press, 2004).

Buckley, Chloé Germaine, *Twenty-First-Century Children's Gothic* (Edinburgh: Edinburgh University Press, 2018).

Butler, Judith, 'Against Proper Objects', *Differences: A Journal of Feminist Cultural Studies*, 6/2–3 (1994).

Butler, Judith, *Bodies that Matter: On the Discursive Limits of 'Sex'* (New York: Routledge, 1993).

Butler, Judith, 'Performativity, Precarity and Sexual Politics', *AIBR: Revista de Antropología Iberoamericana*, 4/3 (2009).

Butler, Judith, *Precarious Life: The Powers of Mourning and Violence* (London: Verso, 2004).

Carroll, Noël, 'Paradoxes of the Heart: The Philosophy of Horror Twenty-Five Years Later: An Interview by Caetlin Benson-Allott', *Journal of Visual Culture*, 14/3 (2015).

Carroll, Rachel, *Rereading Heterosexuality: Queer Theory and Contemporary Fiction* (Edinburgh: Edinburgh University Press, 2012).

Carroll, Rachel, 'Rethinking Generational History: Queer Histories of Sexuality in Neo-Victorian Feminist Fiction', *Studies in the Literary Imagination*, 39/2 (2006).

Castle, Terry, *The Apparitional Lesbian: Female Homosexuality and Modern Culture* (New York: Columbia University Press, 1993).

Chaplin, Sue, *Gothic Literature: Texts, Contexts, Connections* (York: York Press, 2011).

Chaplin, Sue, 'Female Gothic and the Law', in Avril Horner and Sue Zlosnik (eds), *Women and the Gothic* (Edinburgh: Edinburgh University Press, 2017).

Chaudhuri, Shohini, *Feminist Film Theorists: Laura Mulvey, Kaja Silverman, Teresa de Lauretis, Barbara Creed* (London: Routledge, 2006).

Cohen, Jeffrey J., and Todd R. Ramlow, 'Pink Vectors of Deleuze: Queer Theory and Inhumanism', *Rhizomes*, 11/12 (2005–6).

Ciocia, Stefania, '"Queer and Verdant": The Textual Politics of Sarah Waters's Neo-Victorian Novels', *Literary London: Interdisciplinary Studies in the Representation of London*, 5/2 (2007), unpaginated.

Contreras, Daniel T., 'New Queer Cinema: Spectacle, Race, Utopia', in Michele Aaron (ed.), *New Queer Cinema: A Critical Reader* (Edinburgh: Edinburgh University Press, 2004).

Creed, Barbara, 'Horror and The Monstrous-Feminine: An Imaginary Abjection', in Barry Keith Grant (ed.), *Dread of Difference: Gender and the Horror Film* (Austin TX: University of Texas Press, 2015), pp. 32–68.

Creed, Barbara, 'Horror and the Monstrous-Feminine: An Imaginary Abjection', *Screen*, 1 (1986), 44–70.

Creed, Barbara, *The Monstrous-Feminine: Film, Feminism, Psychoanalysis* (London: Routledge, 2003).

Davidson, Alex, '10 great gay and lesbian horror films', *BFI* (7 November 2013), www.bfi.org.uk/news-opinion/news-bfi/lists/10-great-gay-horror-films (accessed 1 November 2023).

Davies, Helen, *Gender and Ventriloquism in Victorian and Neo-Victorian fiction: Passionate Puppets* (London: Palgrave Macmillan, 2012).

Davis, Oliver and Kollias, Hector 'Editor's Introduction', *Paragraph: Queer Theory's Return to France*, 35/2 (2012).

Deneuve, Catherine, 'Open Letter', www.liberation.fr/debats/2018/01/15/metoo-controversy-read-catherine-deneuve-s-letter-published-in-liberation_1622561/ (accessed 7 November 2023).

Din-Kariuki, Natalya, 'Nobody ever warned me about mirrors: Doubling, Mimesis and Narrative form in Helen Oyeyemi's Fiction', in Chloe Buckley and Sarah Ilott (eds), *Telling it Slant: Critical Approaches to Helen Oyeyemi* (Brighton: Sussex Academic Press, 2017).

Doane, Mary Ann, *The Desire to Desire: The Woman's Films of the 1940s* (London: Macmillan, 1988).

Dogra, Sakshi, 'Lacan, "The Mirror Stage" and Subjectivity: A Psychoanalytic Reading of *Black Swan*', *New Man International Journal of Multidisciplinary Studies*, 2/6 (2015), 62–8.

Donovan, Sean, 'Becoming Unknown: Hannibal and Queer Epistemology', *Gender Forum: Queer Film and Television*, 59 (2016).

Douglas, Mary, *Purity and Danger: An Analysis of the Concepts of Pollution and Taboo* (London: Routledge, 1966).

Downing, Lisa, 'Interdisciplinarity, Cultural Studies, Queer: Historical Contexts and Contemporary Contentions in France', *Paragraph: Queer Theory's Return to France*, 35/2 (2012).

Driver, Susan, *Queer Girls and Popular Culture: Reading, Resisting, and Creating Media* (New York: Peter Lang, 2007).

Du Bois, W. E. B., *The Souls of Black Folk* (Chicago IL: A. C. McClurg and Co., 1903).

Dyer, Richard, *Pastiche* (London: Routledge, 2006).

Dyer, Richard, *White* (London: Routledge, 1997).

Edelman, Lee, 'An Ethics of Desubjectivation?', *Differences*, 27/3 (2016), 106.

Edelman, Lee, 'Learning Nothing: *Bad Education*', *Differences*, 28/1 (2017).

Edelman, Lee, *No Future: Queer Theory and the Death Drive* (Durham NC: Duke University Press, 2004).

Edelman, Lee, 'Unnamed: Eve's Epistemology', *Criticism*, 52/2 (2010), 186–7.

Edwards, Justin D., and Agnieszka Soltysik Monnet, *The Gothic in Contemporary Literature and Popular Culture* (London: Routledge, 2012).

Elliott-Smith, Darren, *Queer Horror Film and Television: Sexuality and Masculinity at the Margins* (London: I. B. Tauris, 2016).

Fanon, Frantz, *Black Skin, White Masks*, trans. by Charles Lam Markmann (London: Pluto Books, 2008 [1952]).

Felman, Shoshana, 'Turning the Screw of Interpretation', *Yale French Studies (Literature and Psychoanalysis. The Question of Reading: Otherwise)*, 55/56 (1977), 94–207.

Firestone, Shulamith, *The Dialectic of Sex: The Case for Feminist Revolution* (New York: William Marrow, 1970).

Fisher, Mark, and Amber Jacobs, 'Debating *Black Swan*: Gender and Horror – Mark Fisher and Amber Jacobs disagree about Darren Aronofsky's film', *Film Quarterly*, 65/1 (2011), 58–62.

Foucault, Michel, *The History of Sexuality, vol. 1*, trans. by Robert Hurley (New York: Pantheon Books, 1978).

Foucault, Michel, *The History of Sexuality 1: The Will to Knowledge* (London: Penguin, 1998 [1976]).

Foucault, Michel, 'A Preface to Transgression', in *Language, Counter-memory, Practice: Selected Essays and Interviews*, ed. and trans. by Donald F. Bouchard (Ithaca NY: Cornell University Press, 1997).

Freeman, Elizabeth, 'Queer Temporalities', *GLQ: A Journal of Lesbian and Gay Studies*, 13/2–3 (2007), 162.

Freud, Sigmund, *The Uncanny* (London: Penguin, 2003 [1919]).

Friedan, Betty, *The Feminine Mystique* (London: Penguin, 1963).

Fuss, Diane, *Identification Papers* (London: Routledge, 1995).

Gamble, Sarah, *Angela Carter: Writing from the Front Line* (Edinburgh: Edinburgh University Press, 1997).

Gamman, Lorraine, and Margaret Marshment (eds), *The Female Gaze: Women as Viewers of Popular Culture* (London: The Women's Press, 1988).

Garland, Kathy, and Rodesiler, Luke, 'Supremacy with a Smile: White Saviour Complex in The Blind Side', *Screen Education*, 3 (2019).

Glick, Megan H., 'Of Sodomy and Cannibalism: Dehumanisation, Embodiment and the Rhetorics of Same-Sex and Cross-Species Contagion', *Gender and History*, 23/3 (2011).

Gordon, Joan, and Veronica Hollinger (eds), *Blood Read: The Vampire as Metaphor in Contemporary Culture* (Philadelphia PA: University of Pennsylvania Press, 1997).

Grant, Barry Keith (ed.), *Dread of Difference: Gender and the Horror Film* (Austin TX: University of Texas Press, 2015).

Greenhill, Pauline, and Sidney Eve Matrix (eds), *Fairy Tale Films: Visions of Ambiguity* (Logan UT: Utah University Press, 2010).

Groom, Nick, *The Gothic: A Very Short Introduction* (Oxford: Oxford University Press, 2012).

Gunew, Sneja, 'Feminist Cultural Literacy: Transferring Difference, Cannibal Options', *Ilha do Desterro*, 45/4 (2003).

Gutierrez Albilla, Julian Daniel, 'Reframing *My Dearest Señorita* (1971): Queer Embodiment and Subjectivity through the poetics of cinema', *Studies in Spanish and Latin American Cinema*, 12/1 (2015).

Guzik, Elizabeth, 'The Queer Sort of Fandom or Heavenly Creatures: The Closeted Indigene, Lesbian Islands, and New Zealand National Cinema', in John C. Hawley (ed.), *Postcolonial*

Queer Theories: Intersections and Essays (London: Greenwood Press, 2001).

Haggerty, George E., *Queer Gothic* (Chicago IL: University of Illinois Press, 2006).

Hague, Angela, '"A Faithful Anatomy of our Times": Reassessing Shirley Jackson', *Frontiers*, 26/2 (2005).

Halberstam, Jack, *In a Queer Time and Place* (New York: New York University Press, 2005).

Halberstam, Jack, *Skin Shows: Gothic Horror and the Technology of Monsters* (Durham NC: Duke University Press, 1995).

Halberstam, Jack, 'The Anti-Social Turn in Queer Studies', *Graduate Journal of Social Sciences*, 5/2 (2008).

Hanson, Ellis, 'Queer Gothic', in Catherine Spooner and Emma McEvoy (eds), *The Routledge Companion to the Gothic* (London: Routledge, 2007).

Hanson, Ellis, 'Screwing with Children in Henry James', *GLQ: A Journal of Lesbian and Gay Studies*, 9/3 (2003).

Harvey, Benjamin, 'Contemporary Horror Cinema', in Catherine Spooner and Emma McEvoy (eds), *The Routledge Companion to the Gothic* (London: Routledge, 2007).

Hattenhauer, Darryl, *Shirley Jackson's American Gothic* (New York: State University of New York Press, 2003).

Hawley, John C. (ed.), *Postcolonial Queer Theories: Intersections and Essays* (London: Greenwood Press, 2001).

Heilmann, Ann, and Llewellyn, Mark, *Neo-Victorianism: The Victorians in the Twenty-First Century, 1999–2009* (Basingstoke: Palgrave Macmillan, 2010).

Hill Collins, Patricia, *Black Feminist Thought: Knowledge, Consciousness, and the Politics of Empowerment* (London: Routledge, 2000).

Hird, Myra, and Noreen Giffney, *Queering the Non/Human* (Aldershot: Ashgate, 2008).

Holmgren Troy, Maria, Elizabeth Kella and Helena Wahlström, *Making Home: Orphanhood, Kinship, and Cultural Memory in Contemporary American Novels* (Manchester: Manchester University Press, 2014).

hooks, bell, *Black Looks: Race and Representation* (New York: Routledge, 2015).

Horner, Avril, and Sue Zlosnik (eds), *Women and the Gothic* (Edinburgh: Edinburgh University Press, 2017).

Howard, Cerise, 'Raw (2017): Horror in the Eyes of Women', *Diabolique*, https://diaboliquemagazine.com/raw-2017-horror-eyes-women/ (accessed 3 January 2019).

Huffer, Lynne, *Are the Lips the Grave? A Queer Feminist on the Ethics of Sex* (New York: Columbia University Press, 2013).

Hughes, William, and Smith, Andrew, *Queering the Gothic* (Manchester: Manchester University Press, 2009).

Hutcheon, Linda, *The Theory of Adaptation* (London: Routledge, 2006).

Hutchings, Peter, 'Tearing your soul apart: Horror's New Monsters', in Victor Sage and Allan Lloyd Smith (eds), *Modern Gothic: A Reader* (Manchester: Manchester University Press, 1996).

Kent, Sarah, '"The Bloody Transaction": Black Vampires and the Afterlives of Slavery in *Blacula* and *The Gilda Stories*', *The Journal of Popular Culture*, 53/3 (2020).

Ilott, Sarah, 'Postcolonial Gothic', in Maisha Wester and Xavier Aldana Reyes (eds), *Twenty-First-Century Gothic: An Edinburgh Companion* (Edinburgh: Edinburgh University Press, 2019).

Sarah Ilott, '"The genesis of woman goes through the mouth": Consumption, Oral Pleasure, and Voice in The Opposite House and White is for Witching', in Chloe Buckley and Sarah Ilott (eds), *Telling it Slant: Critical Approaches to Helen Oyeyemi* (Brighton: Sussex Academic Press, 2017).

Ilott, Sarah, and Chloé Buckley, '"Fragmenting and becoming double": Supplementary twins and abject bodies in Helen Oyeyemi's *The Icarus Girl*', *Journal of Commonwealth Literature*, 41/3 (2016).

Irigaray, Luce, *This Sex which is not One*, trans. by Catherine Porter (Ithaca NY: Cornell University Press, [1977] 1985).

Jagose, Annamarie, *Inconsequence: Lesbian Representation and the Logic of Sexual Sequence* (New York: Cornell University Press, 2002).

Jagose, Annamarie, 'Queer Theory', *Australian Humanities Review*, 4 (1996), unpaginated, http://australianhumanitiesreview.org/1996/12/01/queer-theory/ (accessed 18 September 2019).

Jagose, Annamarie, 'Feminism's Queer Theory', *Feminism and Psychology*, 19/2 (2009).

Jeffreys, Sheila, *Unpacking Queer Politics* (Malden: Blackwell, 2003).

Joy, Eileen, 'Improbable Manner of Being', *GLQ: A Journal of Lesbian and Gay Studies*, 23/2–3 (2015).

Kahane, Claire, 'The Gothic Mirror', in Shirley Nelson Gardener, Claire Kahane and Madelon Sprengnether (eds), *The (M)other Tongue* (Ithaca NY: Cornell University Press, 1985).

Kaplan, Cora, *Victoriana: Histories, Fictions, Criticism* (Edinburgh: Edinburgh University Press, 2007).

Kavka, Misha, 'The Gothic On screen', in Jerrold E. Hogle (ed.), *The Cambridge Companion to Gothic Fiction* (Cambridge: Cambridge University Press, 2002) pp. 209–28.

Keenan, Sally, 'Angela Carter's *The Sadeian Woman*: Feminism as Treason', in Joseph Bristow and Trev Lynn Broughton (eds), *The Infernal Desires of Angela Carter: Fiction, Femininity, Feminism* (London: Longman, 1997), pp. 132–48.

Keith Grant, Barry, 'Genre Film: A Classic Experience', in B. K. Grant (ed.), *Film Genre Reader III* (Austin TX: University of Texas Press, 2003).

Kemp, Sandra, and Judith Squires, *Feminisms* (Oxford: Oxford University Press, 1997).

Kincaid, James, *Child-Loving: The Erotic Child and Victorian Culture* (London: Routledge, 1992).

Kincaid, James, *Erotic Innocence: The Culture of Child Molesting* (Durham NC: Duke University Press, 1998).

King, Richard C., 'The (Mis)Uses of Cannibalism in Contemporary Cultural Critique', *Diacritics*, 30/1 (2000), 106–23.

Kohlke, Marie-Luise, 'Into history through the back door: The "past historic" in *Nights at the Circus* and *Affinity*', *Women: A Cultural Review*, 15/2 (2004), 153–66.

Kohlke, Marie-Luise, and Christian Gutleben (eds), *Neo-Victorian Families: Gender, Sexual and Cultural Politics* (Amsterdam: Rodopi, 2011).

Kollias, Hector, 'Queering it Right, Getting it Wrong', *Paragraph: Queer Theory's Return to France*, 35/2 (2012), 144–63.

Koresky, Michael, 'Queer & Now & Then: 1963', *Film Comment*, www.filmcomment.com/blog/queer-now-1963/ (last accessed 28 February 2019).

Kristeva, Julia, *The Powers of Horror: An Essay on Abjection* (New York: Columbia University Press, 1982).
Kristeva, Julia, *Strangers to Ourselves* (New York: Columbia University Press, 1988).
Lacan, Jacques, *Écrits: A Selection*, trans. by Alan Sheridan (London: Routledge, 1977).
Lane, Anthony, 'Women's Work: The Handmaiden and Christine', *The New Yorker*, 92/34 (2016).
Lee, Eunah, 'Trauma, Excess, and the Aesthetics of Effect: The Extreme Cinemas of Chan-wook Park', *Postscript: Essays in Film and the Humanities*, 34/2 (2014), non-paginated.
Ledger, Sally, *The New Woman: Fiction and Feminism at the* Fin de Siècle (Manchester: Manchester University Press, 1997).
Lewis, Christopher S., 'Queering Personhood in the Neo-Slave Narrative: Jewelle Gomez's *The Gilda Stories*', *African American Review*, 47/4 (2014), 447–59.
Lindenbaum, Shirley, 'Thinking About Cannibalism', *Annual Review of Anthropology*, 33 (2004).
Lindner, Katharina, *Film Bodies: Queer Feminist Encounters with Gender and Sexuality in Cinema* (London: I. B. Tauris, 2018).
Love, Heather, 'Truth and Consequences: On Paranoid Reading and Reparative Reading', *Criticism: A Quarterly for Literature and the Arts*, 52/2 (2010).
Löwy, Michael, 'The Current of Critical Irrealism: "A moonlit enchanted night"', in Matthew Beaumont (ed.), *Adventures in Realism* (Carlton VIC: Blackwell, 2007).
Mafe, Diana Adesola, 'Ghostly Girls in the "Eerie Bush": Helen Oyeyemi's *The Icarus Girl* as Postcolonial Female Gothic Fiction', *Research in African Literatures*, 43/3 (2012).
Makinen, Merja, 'Sexual and textual aggression in *The Sadeian Woman* and *The Passion of New Eve*', in Joseph Bristow and Trev Lynn Broughton (eds), *The Infernal Desires of Angela Carter: Fiction, Femininity, Feminism* (London: Longman, 1997), pp. 149–66.
Manlove, Clifford T., 'Visual "Drive" and Cinematic Narrative: Reading Gaze in Lacan, Hitchcock and Mulvey', *Cinema Journal*, 46/3 (2007), 88.
Marinucci, Mimi, *Feminism is Queer: The Intimate Connection between Queer and Feminist Theory* (London: Zed Books, 2010).

Marouan, Maha, *Witches, Goddesses, and Angry Spirits: The Politics of Spiritual Liberation in African Diaspora Women's Fiction* (Columbus OH: Ohio State University Press, 2003).

Massé, Michelle, 'Gothic Repetition: Husbands, Horror and Things that go Bump in the Night', *Signs*, 15/4 (1990), 679–709.

Mavor, Carol, *Becoming: The Photography of Clementina, Viscountess Hawarden* (Durham NC: Duke University Press, 1999).

Mbembe, J. A., 'Necropolitics', trans. by Libby Meintjes, *Public Culture*, 15/1 (2003), 11–40.

McAfee, Noelle, *Julia Kristeva* (London: Routledge, 2004).

Means Coleman, Robin R., *Horror Noire: Blacks in American Horror Films from the 1890s to Present* (New York: Routledge, 2011),

Merck, Mandy, *Perversions: Deviant Readings* (New York: Routledge, 1993).

Merck, Mandy, 'Savage Nights', in Mandy Merck, Naomi Segal and Elizabeth Wright (eds), *Coming Out of Feminism?* (Oxford: Blackwell, 1998).

Meyers, Helene, *Femicidal Fears: Narratives of the Female Gothic Experience* (Albany NY: State University of New York Press, 2001).

Mezzadra, Sandra, Julian Reid and Ranabir Samaddar, *The Biopolitics of Development: Reading Michel Foucault in the Postcolonial Present* (New Delhi: Springer, 2013).

Minsky, Rosalind, *Psychoanalysis and Gender: An Introductory Reader* (London: Routledge, 1996).

Modleski, Tania, *The Women Who Knew Too Much* (London: Routledge, 1988).

Morton, Stephen, *States of Emergency: Colonial, Literature and Law* (Liverpool: Liverpool University Press, 2013).

Moers, Ellen, *Literary Women* (London: The Women's Press Ltd., 1986).

Mulvey Roberts, Marie, 'The Female Gothic Body', in Avril Horner and Sue Zlosnik (eds), *Women and the Gothic* (Edinburgh: Edinburgh University Press, 2017).

Mulvey, Laura, 'Cinema Magic and Old Monsters', in Lorna Sage (ed.), *Flesh and the Mirror, Essays of the Art of Angela Carter* (London: Virago, 1994), pp. 241–53.

Mulvey, Laura, 'Visual Pleasure and Narrative Cinema', *Screen* 16/3 (1975), 6–18.

Munford, Rebecca, *Decadent Daughters and Monstrous Mothers: Angela Carter and European Gothic* (Manchester: Manchester University Press, 2013).

Munford, Rebecca, 'Spectral Femininity', in Avril Horner and Sue Zlosnik (eds), *Women and the Gothic* (Edinburgh: Edinburgh University Press, 2017).

Nelson Gardener, Shirley, Claire Kahane and Madelon Sprengnether (eds), *The (M)other Tongue* (Ithaca NY: Cornell University Press, 1985).

Newman, Saul, and John Lechte, *Agamben and the Politics of Human Rights* (Edinburgh: Edinburgh University Press, 2013).

Ouma Christopher, 'Reading the Diasporic Abiku in Helen Oyeyemi's *The Icarus Girl*', *Research in African Literatures*, 45/3 (2014).

Owens, Andrew J., 'Queer Gothic', in Maisha Wester and Xavier Aldana Reyes (eds), *Twenty-First-Century Gothic: An Edinburgh Companion* (Edinburgh: Edinburgh University Press, 2019).

Parker, Sarah, '"The Darkness is the Closer in which Your Lover Roosts Her Heart": Lesbians, Desire, and the Gothic Genre', *Journal of International Women's Studies*, 9/2 (2008), 4–19.

Palmer, Paulina, *Lesbian Gothic: Transgressive Fictions* (London: Cassell, 1999).

Palmer, Paulina, *Queering Contemporary Gothic Narrative 1970–2012* (London: Palgrave Macmillan, 2016).

Palmer, Paulina, *The Queer Uncanny, New Perspectives on the Gothic* (Cardiff: University of Wales Press, 2012).

Paravisini-Gebert, Lizabeth, *Literature of the Caribbean* (Westport CT: Greenwood, 2008).

Patterson, Orlando, *Slavery and Social Death: A Comparative Study* (Cambridge MA: Harvard University Press, 1982).

Petrocelli, Heather O., *Queer for Fear: Horror Film and the Queer Spectator* (Chicago IL: University of Wales Press, 2023).

Pinkerton, Nick, '*Raw* Review', *Sight and Sound*, 27/5 (May 2017), 88.

Power, Nina 'Motherhood in France: Towards a Queer Maternity', *Paragraph: Queer Theory's Return to France*, 35/2 (2012), 254–64.

Puar, Jasbir K., *Terrorist Assemblages: Homonationalism in Queer Times* (Durham NC: Duke University Press, 2017).

Punter, David, *A Companion to the Gothic* (Oxford: Blackwell, 2000).

Punter, David, *The Literature of Terror: A History of Gothic Fictions from 1765 to the Present Day*, vol. 2: *The Modern Gothic* (Harlow: Pearson Education, 1996).

Ramsland, Katherine (ed.), *The Anne Rice Reader* (New York: Ballentine Books, 1997).

Rank, Otto, *The Double: A Psychoanalytic Study*, trans. by Harry Tucker Jr (Chapel Hill NC: North Carolina Press, 1971 [1914]).

Resmini, Mauro, 'Reframing the New French Extremity: Cinema, Theory, Mediation', *Camera Obscura*, 90 (2015).

Rich, B. Ruby, 'New Queer Cinema', in Michele Aaron (ed.), *New Queer Cinema: A Critical Reader* (Edinburgh: Edinburgh University Press, 2004).

Rifkin, Adrian, 'Does Gay Sex Need Queer Theory?', *Paragraph: Queer Theory's Return to France*, 35/2 (2012), 197–214.

Rigby, Mair, '"Do you share my madness": Frankenstein's queer Gothic', in William Hughes and Andrew Smith (eds), *Queering the Gothic* (Manchester: Manchester University Press 2009), pp. 36–55.

Rivkin, Julie, and Michael Ryan (eds), *Literary Theory: An Anthology* (Oxford: Blackwell, 1998).

Robbins, Ruth, *Subjectivities* (Basingstoke: Palgrave Macmillan, 2005).

Robson, Catherine, *Men in Wonderland: The Lost Girlhood of the Victorian Gentleman* (Oxford: Princeton University Press, 2001).

Rosky, Clifford T. 'Fear of the Queer Child', *Buffalo Law Review*, 61/3 (2013), 607–97.

Rubin, Gayle, 'The Traffic in Women: Notes on the "Political Economy" of Sex', in Julie Rivkin and Michael Ryan (eds), *Literary Theory: An Anthology* (Oxford: Blackwell, 1998), pp. 901–25.

Russo, Vito, *The Celluloid Closet: Homosexuality in the Movies* (New York: Harper and Row, 1985).

Sage, Lorna, *Flesh and the Mirror, Essays of the Art of Angela Carter* (London: Virago, 1994), pp. 20–43.

Sage, Victor, and Allan Lloyd Smith (eds), *Modern Gothic: A Reader* (Manchester: Manchester University Press, 1996).

Savoy, Eric, 'Between as if and is: On Shirley Jackson', *Women's Studies*, 46/8 (2017).

Savoy, Eric, 'Theory *a Tergo* in *The Turn of the Screw*', in Steven Bruhm and Natasha Hurley (eds), *Curiouser: On the Queerness of Children* (Minneapolis MN: University of Minnesota Press, 2004), pp. 245–77.

Schaefer, Jerome, *An Edgy Realism: Film Theoretical Encounters with Dogma* (Cambridge: Cambridge Scholars publishing, 2015).

Sedgwick, Eve Kosofsky, *Between Men: English Literature and Male Homosocial Desire* (New York: Columbia University Press, 1985).

Sedgwick, Eve Kosofsky, *Epistemology of the Closet* (Berkeley CA: University of California Press, 1990).

Sedgwick, Eve Kosofsky, 'How to Bring Your Kids Up Gay', in Michael Warner (ed.), *Fear of a Queer Planet: Queer Politics and Social Theory* (Minneapolis MN: Minnesota University Press, 1993).

Sedgwick, Eve Kosofsky, 'Paranoid Reading and Reparative Reading, or, You're so Paranoid, You Probably Think This Essay is About You', in Eve Kosofsky Sedgwick, *Touching Feeling: Affect, Pedagogy, Performativity* (Durham NC: Duke University Press, 2003).

Sedgwick, Eve Kosofsky, *Tendencies* (Durham, NC: Duke University Press, 1993).

Sedgwick, Eve Kosofsky, *The Coherence of Gothic Conventions* (London: Methuen, [1980] 1986).

Sedgwick, Eve Kosofsky, *Touching Feeling: Affect, Pedagogy, Performativity* (Durham NC: Duke University Press, 2003).

Shaviro, Steven, *The Cinematic Body* (London: Minneapolis University Press, 1993).

Shaviro, Steven, 'The Cinematic Body REDUX', *Parallax*, 14/1 (2008), 48–54.

Shelley, Mary, *Frankenstein* (Cambridge: Wilson and Son, 1869 [1818]).

Sélavy, Virginie, 'Fresh Meat', in *Sight and Sound*, 27/5 (May 2017), 53.

Smelik, Anneke, 'Art Cinema and Murderous Lesbians', in Michele Aaron (ed.) *New Queer Cinema: A Critical Reader* (Edinburgh: Edinburgh University Press, 2004).

Smith, Andrew, and Anna Powell (eds), *Teaching the Gothic* (Basingstoke: Palgrave, 2006).

Smith, Joan, *Hungry for You: From Cannibalism to Seduction – A Book of Food* (London: Vintage, 1997).

Smith, Patricia, *Lesbian Panic: Homoeroticism in Modern British Women's Fiction* (New York: Columbia University Press, 1997).

Snowden, Kim, 'Fairy Tale, Film and the Classroom: Feminist Cultural Pedagogy, Angela Carter and Neil Jordan's *The Company of Wolves*', in Pauline Greenhill and Sidney Eve Matrix (eds), *Fairy Tale Films: Visions of Ambiguity* (Logan UT: Utah University Press, 2010).

Sonchack, Thomas, 'Genre Film: A Classic Experience', in B. K. Grant (ed.) *Film Genre Reader III* (Austin TX: University of Texas Press, 2003).

Spooner, Catherine, *Contemporary Gothic* (London: Reaktion, 2006).

Spooner, Catherine, *Fashioning Gothic Bodies* (Manchester: Manchester University Press, 2004).

Spooner, Catherine, and Emma McEvoy (eds), *The Routledge Companion to the Gothic* (London: Routledge, 2007).

Stallybrass, Peter, and Allon White, *The Politics and Poetics of Transgression* (Ithaca NY: Cornell University Press, 1986).

Stouck, Jordan, 'Abjecting Hybridity in Helen Oyeyemi's *The Icarus Girl*', *Ariel: A Review of International English Literature*, 41/2 (2011).

Stockton, Kathryn Bond, *The Queer Child, or Growing Up Sideways in the Twentieth Century* (Durham NC: Duke University Press. 2009).

Sullivan, Nikki, *A Critical Introduction to Queer Theory* (Edinburgh: Edinburgh University Press, 2003).

Tate, Alison, 'Christine Vachon on Queer Cinema and the Legacy of *Carol*', *Advocate* (18 May 2017), www.advocate.com/arts-entertainment/2017/5/18/christine-vachon-queer-cinema-and-legacy-carol (last accessed 31 October 2023).

Tuhkanen, Mikko, *Leo Bersani: Queer Theory and Beyond* (New York: State University of New York Press, 2014).

Tomc, Sandra, 'Dieting and Damnation: Anne Rice's *Interview with the Vampire*', in Joan Gordon and Veronica Hollinger (eds), *Blood Read: The Vampire as Metaphor in Contemporary Culture* (Philadelphia PA: University of Pennsylvania Press, 1997), pp. 95–115.

Townshend, Dale, 'Love in a Convent: Or, Gothic and the Perverse Father of Queer Enjoyment', in William Hughes and Andrew Smith (eds), *Queering the Gothic* (Manchester: Manchester University Press, 2009), pp. 11–34.

Walsh, Sue, 'Gothic Children', in Catherine Spooner and Emma McEvoy (eds), *The Routledge Companion to the Gothic* (New York: Routledge, 2007), pp. 183–93.

Walton, Priscilla L., *Our Cannibals, Ourselves* (Champaign IL: University of Illinois Press, 2004).

Warner, Marina, *No Go the Bogeyman: Scaring, Lulling and Making Mock* (London: Virago, 2000).

Warner, Michael (ed.), *Fear of a Queer Planet: Queer Politics and Social Theory* (Minneapolis MN: Minnesota University Press, 1993).

Weiss, Gail, *Body Images, Embodiment as Intercorporeality* (London: Routledge, 1999).

Wester, Maisha L., *African American Gothic: Screams from Shadowed Places* (New York: Palgrave Macmillan, 2012)

Wester, Maisha, and Xavier Aldana Reyes (eds), *Twenty-First-Century Gothic: An Edinburgh Companion* (Edinburgh: Edinburgh University Press, 2019).

Wheatley, Helen, *Gothic Television* (Manchester: Manchester University Press, 2007).

Whyte, Jessica, *Catastrophe and Redemption: The Political Thought of Giorgio Agamben* (Albany NY: State University of New York Press, 2013).

White, Patricia, *Uninvited: Classical Hollywood Cinema and Lesbian Representability* (Bloomington IN: Indiana University Press, 1999).

Williams, Anne, 'The Horror, the Horror: Recent Studies in Gothic Fiction', *Modern Fiction Studies*, 46/3 (2000), 793.

Williams, Linda, 'Film: Gender, Genre, and Excess', *Film Quarterly*, 44/4 (1991), 2–13.

Williams, Linda, 'When the Woman Looks', in Barry Keith Grant (ed.) *The Dread of Difference: Gender and the Horror Film* (Austin TX: University of Texas Press, 2015), pp. 17–37.

Wilson, Michael T., '"Absolute Reality" and the Role of the Ineffable in Shirley Jackson's *The Haunting of Hill House*', *Journal of Popular Culture*, 48/1 (2015).

Wolff, Rebecca, 'Maryse Condé', *BOMB*, 68 (1999), *https://web.archive.org/web/20161101132353/http://bombmagazine.org/article/2248* (accessed 5 February 2020).

WReC, Sharae Deckard, Nicholas Lawrence, Neil Lazarus, Graeme Macdonald, Upamanyu Pablo Mukherjee, Benita Parry and Stephen Shapiro, *Combined and Uneven Development Towards a New Theory of World-Literature* (Liverpool: Liverpool University Press, 2015).

Yates, Louisa, 'The Figure of the Child in Neo-Victorian Queer Families', in Marie-Luise Kohlke and Christian Gutleben (eds), *Neo-Victorian Families: Gender, Sexual and Cultural Politics* (Amsterdam: Rodopi, 2011), pp. 93–119.

Young, Iris Marion, 'Gender as Seriality: Thinking about Women as a Social Collective', *Signs*, 19/3 (1994), 737.

Index

A
Abjection 12–13, 40, 54, 99, 119, 133, 135–6, 145, 148, 152, 158, 162, 165–6, 178, 189, 199, 215
AIDS/HIV 9–10, 13, 16–17, 113, 132, 187–8
Aldana Reyes, Xavier 17–18, 173, 182–4

B
Bersani, Leo 19, 31, 40, 90, 112, 113–14, 139, 194, 196
Bildungsroman 204–5
Biopolitics 30, 41, 171, 186, 199–200, 218–19
Black Gothic 229–30
Black Swan 40, 119–42, 178
Body Horror 17, 121–2, 126–8, 136, 177–8, 180, 183
Butler, Judith 12, 23, 30, 47, 75, 77, 78, 130, 141, 158, 194, 218

C
Cannibalism 41, 62, 88, 94, 106, 108, 120, 122, 162, 171–97, 200, 220
Carter, Angela 40, 45–6, 58–66, 81, 85–6
Creed, Barbara 111, 122, 132, 166, 182

E
Edelman, Lee 19, 26, 31, 34–40, 90–1, 112, 114, 139, 174
Elliott-Smith, Darren 18–19, 33, 189

F
'Female Gothic' 1–2, 5, 20–3, 48, 57, 92, 112–13, 150, 205, 213, 225
Femininity 22, 51–2, 60, 63, 84–5, 109, 121, 124, 129, 133, 136, 172–3, 176, 188, 190, 231
Feminism and the Gothic 2, 19–41
Florence and Giles 40, 87–116, 200

Index

G

Gothic Child 3, 28, 40, 51, 70, 85, 87–95, 98, 174, 199, 200–2, 209, 231
Gothic Film 2, 9, 11, 14–17, 26, 31, 41, 119–20, 127, 136, 139, 141, 143–4, 178
Gothic Space(s) 126, 149, 151, 199, 213

H

Haggerty, George 4–8, 53–6, 73–4
The Handmaiden 40–1, 83, 86, 143–6, 148, 150–9, 162–3, 165–7
Hays Code *see* Production Code
Huffer, Lynne 40, 89–91, 111–15
Hybridity 29–30, 41, 150–2, 158–60, 172, 198–215, 219, 221–3, 227

J

Jack and Diane 40, 119–33, 137, 140, 142, 178, 191
Jackson, Shirley 5–6, 21, 40, 46, 48–54, 56–7, 61, 84–5, 215
Jagose, Annamaria 23–4, 35, 141, 148

K

Killer Queer 11, 16, 123
Kosofsky Sedgwick, Eve 3, 9, 31–7, 40, 47, 71, 85, 137–8, 141–3, 194, 233
Kristeva, Julia 122–3, 133, 140, 166, 178, 196

L

Lacanian Psychoanalysis 13, 32, 36, 50, 128, 156, 160, 182, 194, 196, 215

Lindner, Katharina 120, 133, 139, 141

M

Marquis de Sade 60–3, 85, 171–3, 179
Metamorphosis 64, 71, 119, 126, 135, 175
#MeToo movement 175–6
Mirroring 40, 94, 98, 110–11, 119, 121, 123, 125, 128, 130–6, 139, 145, 152, 155–7, 159, 177, 199, 211
Monstrosity 14, 28, 75, 77, 111, 119, 123–4, 136, 147, 171, 180, 185, 190, 197, 202, 207, 209, 228
Monstrous Feminine 111, 123, 132, 142, 199

N

Necropolitics/Necropower 218, 223
New French Extremity (NFE) 178–82
New Queer Cinema 2, 9–16, 23, 226

P

Palmer, Paulina 24–5, 83, 124, 189
Paranoia 7, 16, 31, 34, 37, 40–1, 53, 58, 87–8, 94–5, 101, 107, 109, 113, 121, 123, 126, 128, 131–2, 134–43, 146, 148–50, 152, 154–5, 157–9, 162, 166–7, 172, 210, 213, 226, 232–3
Paranoid Reparative 19, 29, 31, 40–1, 68, 83–4, 121–2, 126, 130, 132, 134, 137–43, 146–49, 166, 205, 210, 233

Index

Paris is Burning 11–12, 16
Pornography 32, 60–3, 82–4, 86, 125, 131, 141, 158, 162, 164–6, 190–1
Postcolonial 29–30, 41, 66–8, 75, 86, 145, 152, 159, 163, 166, 171, 197, 199–200, 204–5, 207, 211, 218–19
Production Code 14, 33, 57, 120

Q

Queer Child 51, 88, 91–2, 99, 101, 115, 186, 202
Queer Feminism 5, 12, 32, 35, 40–1, 60–1, 80, 89–91, 111–14, 120, 141, 148, 175, 223
Queer Girlhood 1–2, 25, 116, 186, 200, 223, 226, 233
Queer Gothic 1–9, 11–12, 15–17, 19, 22–4, 27–33, 36–7, 39–42, 48, 50–1, 57–8, 60, 64, 70, 72, 76–8, 80–1, 85, 88, 91, 93–4, 99, 102, 112, 115, 119–20, 122, 127, 132, 136–7, 139, 141, 143–4, 148, 150, 158, 166, 171, 173, 178, 186, 198–201, 208, 211, 213–14, 218–19, 225–7, 230–3
Queer Horror 15, 18–19, 189, 227

Queer Subjectivity 23–4, 26, 38, 61, 82, 86, 119, 123, 133, 137, 140, 146, 148, 160, 171

S

Sade *see* Marquis de Sade
Shelley, Mary 5, 8, 20, 92, 121, 206
Sinthhome/Sinthhomosexual 37

T

The Turn of the Screw 39–40, 51, 53, 87–8, 92, 95–6, 100–1, 105–6, 111, 113, 115, 215

U

Uncanny 24, 51–3, 98, 107, 110–11, 124–5, 131, 133, 140, 149–50, 153–4, 163, 173–4, 200, 232

V

Vachon, Christine 13
Vegetarian feminism 185, 197

W

The Watermelon Woman 11–12, 16
Waters, Sarah 5, 40–1, 46, 64, 77–86, 143, 149
White, Patricia 33, 55, 120, 145
Wilde, Oscar 7, 154